A 16 78

FOUR CROWDED YEARS.

FOUR CROWDED YEARS
The Diaries of Auberon Waugh 1972-1976

EDITED BY N.R. GALLI

Nicolas Bentley Drew the Pictures

PRIVATE EYE/ANDRÉ DEUTSCH.

Published in Great Britain 1976 by Private Eye Productions Limited,
34 Greek Street, London W1.
In association with André Deutsch Limited, 105 Great Russell Street,
London WC1.

© 1976 Pressdram Limited.

SBN 233 96825 3

Designed by Peter Windett.
Printed by Morrison & Gibb, Edinburgh.
Cover Photo: Eric Hands.

INTRODUCTION

The germ of this book originated in the contemporary political studies department of the American university to which I was attached in the fall of 1974. With the approval of the Head of my Department I had requested the transfer of all files of the British satirical magazine *Private Eye* from the section in the English Department's Library dealing with ephemeral and 'underground' publications to my own department — largely, it must be admitted, for my own entertainment. The request met with greater opposition even than was usual from English departments, and the Chief Librarian, who was and remains a wise and valued friend, requested me to write a memorandum explaining why the magazine was relevant to the courses being followed in my department.

This memorandum advanced the argument, which I later came to believe, that the proper study of society and especially political society, lies in the study of contemporary attitudes. In other words, the student of British or even American history is wasting his time if, in concentrating on the weighty political arguments and economic events of the period, he ignores what people were saying and thinking in London or Washington at the time when decisions were being taken and history, of a sort, being made. It is not a particularly original argument nor, in any examination of the uses to which it has been put, does it emerge as a particularly reputable one.

The ploy worked, and *Private Eye* was moved to the current affairs reference library where, I believe, it is still to be found. However, my memorandum achieved a wider circulation than was intended and resulted in a request for an edition of annotations and explanatory footnotes for the benefit of future research students; it appeared that many (if not most) of the references were incomprehensible to an American readership, and such as might have been comprehensible were rapidly fading from the memory. With the help of two researchers I embarked on this work under the auspices of the Chief Librarian, but in the event it proved impossible — explanatory footnotes alone would have required several times as many pages as the original material, much of which was trivial, ephemeral or inaccurate, and the enterprise simply did not lend itself to the methodology of academic research. It was in the course of this preparatory work that I chanced on Auberon Waugh's Diary as offering exactly what I had hoped to achieve in the whole annotated *Private Eye*.

The four years under review were not without significance either in world affairs or in British domestic politics. They marked the defeat of America in Vietnam, the American retreat from Indo-China, efforts toward settlement in the Middle East (not mentioned in these Diaries), the oil crisis and the first manifestations of Soviet-American *detente.* At home, they marked the collapse of Heath's Conservative government, accession to the European Economic Community, the return of Harold Wilson and rise of the trade unions to a position of greater authority than Parliament or Courts of Law. This last phenomenon was scarcely mentioned in 'responsible' quarters, and not at all, of course, in official documents. Even if in Waugh's Diary it is chiefly discussed in terms of unnecessary secrecy surrounding the question of a Trade Union wife's underwear, we learn at least that this development was at the fore-front of people's minds and considered sufficiently important to joke about.

Apart from their relevance to the political atmosphere of the time, we find much of rare sociological interest in the author's outspoken comments on the arrival of 'Women's Lib', the rise in lesbianism, the sexual insecurity and ambiguity of London males. If Waugh's Diaries are to be seen as the sum and substance of the age they describe, then people may reasonably decide that these years were characterised by flippancy, irresponsibility, intellectual capitulation and moral collapse. It is not my intention to urge either the truth or the false-hood of that proposition, merely to examine an alternative approach to the Diaries, that they represent no more than the idle diversions of a small, unrepresentative clique at the eccentric and sometimes distressing antics of a licensed jester.

Prima facie there is something to be said for this approach. Waugh's views on current affairs are certainly not typical of those being advanced either in public or in private at the time under consideration, but the fact remains that they were read avidly not only by the students and young people who have always made up a substantial proportion of *Private Eye*'s readership, but also by politicians, captains of industry and even, in a few instances, trade union leaders. The sale of *Private Eye* when Waugh joined it as political correspondent in February 1970 was 54,000 and even at the end of the four year period under scrutiny it was only 115,000. To claim that it exercised a profound influence on the history of its times would plainly be absurd, or, indeed, that it exercised any influence at all. My case rests on the proposition that it illustrates more accurately than anything else a certain reaction among educated Englishmen to the historical pressures of the time — one could call it anarchistic fatalism or even nihilism — without which no understanding of the period is complete.

It remains only to add, as a matter of common prudence, the warning with which Waugh introduced his Diary — that the material in it is entirely jocular; it contains no serious allegations whatever and everything in it is untrue.

N.R. GALLI
School of American Studies, Singapore

For Ms Maria Dawson, of Durham University,
without whose assistance these pages would never have been assembled.

Thursday 1st October
Another 14 inch nude woman in my copy of
The Times this morning, advertising something called the Export Credits Guarantee
Department. I see Rees-Mogg[1] still asks his
women to hide their pubic hair, but I wonder
if he is right. Perhaps he is of the opinion
that the less explicit the image the greater
the sexual arousal. But is sexual arousal what
we are looking for at breakfast time, rather
than clarity and truth?

His brother editor, Mr Harold Evans[2] of
the *Sunday Times*, seems to have been rather
more experimental. A young woman accused
of having manufactured petrol bombs in
Kensington explains that she was only following instructions which she read in the *Sunday
Times*. The judge expressed surprise at this,
and I confess I agree with him.

Sexual titillation is one thing. Many people
nowadays argue that masturbation is not
only harmless but even beneficial in certain
circumstances. If Mogg and Evans think they
can increase their sales by helping their
readers to masturbate, that is a matter for
their own judgement. But there is all the
difference in the world between this and
peddling detailed instructions on how to
make petrol bombs and other murderous

devices to readers, many of whom may be
emotionally immature and unstable.

Friday 2nd October
The English Country Cheese Council has
allocated £500,000 to promote British
cheeses against foreign ones from the
Common Market. At a special press reception, the Cheese Council had the amusing idea
of wrapping each piece of cheese in a £5 note.
Journalists were given whisky, and encouraged
to keep the wrappings as a souvenir.

We were also given an off-the-record briefing by Mr Pinkerton[3] from the Foreign and
Commonwealth Office, who told us that
many foreign cheeses like Camembert and
certain Alpine goat cheeses, are suspected of
causing cancer, syphilis, St Vitus' Dance and
other diseases of the brain, skin and central
nervous system. Foreign Office analysts
suspect that the unconventional behaviour
of Uganda's General Idi Amin may be due in
part to immoderate eating of foreign cheeses.

I must say, I'd quite forgotten how good
English cheese can be. You can keep your
Camembert and your goat cheeses from the
Alps. Give me scrumptious, mumptious,
cheesy Cheddar every day! I sometimes
imagine that Wensleydale is not a cheese at

1. William Rees-Mogg, b. 14 July 1928. Became Editor of The Times in 1968. Noted for support of
   remonetizing gold.

2. Harold Evans, b. 28 June 1928. Became Editor of Sunday Times in 1967. Noted for anxiety about
   reimbursement of Thalidomide victims.

3. I can trace no-one of that name in the Foreign Office lists.

all, it is a poem, an intricate symphony of diverging yet mutually dependent clusters. It is a song, a celebration of life's ultimate source. It is the sperm which runs through the veins of our primitive post-bourgeois tribal taboos like a needle through a haystack. I have never eaten so much cheese before.

Monday 5th October
Early call at 5.30 followed by a busy morning at the office. In the afternoon I went to see *Young Winston* at the Leicester Square Theatre. I only met Sir Winston once, when I was with Randolph — I think it must have been in White's Club. Randolph introduced me as "this boring little creep who keeps following me around" — pure vintage Randolph, of course. Sir Winston eyed me up and down, and I'll always remember his words: "Get out of here you guttersnipe," he said, "and leave my son alone."

There can be no doubt that there was a certain grandeur about the old man although we were always on opposite sides of the fence politically. On the other hand I can't see any reason for all this fuss about young Winston, who seems to have settled down as a perfectly ordinary run-of-the-mill Conservative back-bencher — scarcely the sort of thing you want to make a 2½ hour film epic about. I really must draw the line at Robert Shaw's impersonation of my old friend Randolph, in his efforts to promote the young member for Stretford. Shaw could not have caught Randolph's strange, almost elfin charm, but to portray him as bearded and syphilitic goes too far. What a shame Randolph is not here to issue writs[1].

Tuesday 6th October
I see the BBC decided to celebrate the Pope's 75th birthday by allowing Frank Longford on television's Ludicrous Kennedy Show. But what on earth would the Pope have thought of Miss Jackie Gillot[2]? Longford was on top form, but this terrible woman had to spoil a most delightful occasion by intruding her silly, second-rate opinions at every opportunity. Is this, perhaps, the new role of women in our society?

Wednesday 7th October
Lunch with Frances Hope, the *Spectator*'s brilliant new columnist, at the Gay Hussar, Greek Street. She was looking most attract-

ive, I thought. We discussed American war crimes in Vietnam over very good Hungarian Goulash, and were both delighted to discover how very progressive we were in our views. Frances has a most attractive giggle.

"Tee, hee," she said. "I sometimes think I am almost a racialist, I hate the Americans so much."

How I yearned for her then! But the goulash was between us and I could only squeeze her hand tenderly, and, I hope, sympathetically[3].

Friday 9th October
A very grand luncheon given by the Friends of Roy Jenkins at the Imperial. We were all there — David Marquand, George Thomson, John Mackintosh, Bill Rodgers, Michael Barnes, myself, Roy — all that is brightest and most civilised in the Labour Party. Roy told me that the reason he decided not to speak at the Conference debate on the Common Market was because he could not bear the thought that William Rees-Mogg's damp, adoring eyes would be on him.

There was much laughter over the brandy and cigars when Mackintosh revealed how he had put up little Willie Hamilton to speak in favour of the Market at the debate. Willie would get all the boos and cat-calls being prepared for Roy which was funny, you see, because Willie is a left-winger and not really a Friend of Roy Jenkins at all. Rodgers said he didn't think that Hamilton had even been to university, and we all agreed that he must be incredibly stupid.

I said, "Smoothiechops and all his little Smoothiechickens." but nobody seemed to find this very funny[4].

Monday 12th October
To get into the Women of the Year lunch at the Savoy Hotel I was forced to dress up in drag and give my name as Miss Glenda Slag, first lady of Greek Street. I disliked doing this, as it seems to cheapen everything the Women's Freedom Movement stands for. I also thought my beard might excite ribald comment, but in this I underestimated the sisterhood.

As Jill Tweedie of the *Grauniad*[5] (who happened to be with me) points out, it is time people recognised that women have the fundamental right to grow beards if they want to. Men have taken it for granted for too long that theirs is the only sex capable

---

1. Waugh appears to have misunderstood the film, which is not about Winston Churchill Jr. (b. 10 October 1940, elected MP [Cons] for Stretford 1970, noted for interest in sporting and outdoor activities) but about the early life of his grandfather, the Prime Minister.

2. A female novelist.

3. Francis Hope (d. 1973) wrote for the New Statesman. Waugh persistently mistook him for a woman.

4. It is hard to disagree. This entry refers to a number of Labour MPs at the Party Conference in Blackpool and is of no interest to the general reader.

5. Ms Tweedie is elsewhere referred to as 'travelling companion'. b. 1906, she was noted for her bodily measurements, believed to be 36-22-36, and later married the feminist writer Alan Brien, sometimes referred to as 'my rival' by Waugh.

of an act which is, fundamentally, as natural as going to the lavatory.

I found myself hypnotised by the shimmering patterns on Princess Anne's dress. Although I stared at her throughout the whole meal and although she must have been aware of the effect she was having on me, she refused to meet my eye, or indeed, have anything to do with me. Normally, of course, I don't give a fig for the Royal Family, having spent my childhood in the reeking slums of Jericho[1] but there was something about the lift of her young bosoms, the haughty aristocratic neck and the deep, horsey voice which really tickled my fancy for the moment. It is a pity she would not take advantage, as I feel I could have given her a much better time than any of the double-barrelled chinless wonders she is used to.

Tuesday 20th October
A rather touching letter from someone called Chris Dunkley who apparently works for *The Times*. "Dear Auberon, I have been a communications reporter for this newspaper for two years now and I still don't find *Private Eye* funny, which some of my friends say I should of. Is this because I did not go to a public school, or is it because of my pimples?"

Dear Chris, I don't think it is because of your pimples, or even because you are working-class, although I am sending a cream which should help you with both these troubles. The real reason is that you haven't a sense of humour. When you laugh with your friends in the office, this isn't because you are amused. If you are completely honest with yourself, you will realise you only laugh because you are frightened of Charlie Vass, your gifted young Features Editor. Remember, Vass is much smaller than you, even if he did go to public school. I am sending you the collected jokes of William Davis, which you will probably not find very funny as they are in a foreign tongue. Try practising a natural, unaffected laugh as you read them, and nobody will ever guess your secret.

Wednesday 21st October
Back to Blackpool for the Tories. The news of John Betjeman's appointment as Poet Laureate came as a burst of sunshine on the melancholy scene. Ever since Day-Lewis died one has scarcely dared breathe on the subject for fear of putting Grocer's[2] back up, but for once he has disregarded all the vain pretentious hacks of the poetic establishment and appointed the only poet who writes with passion and sincerity about the times we live in, the only one with any discernible talent at all. God Bless Sir John Betjeman and well done, Grocer.

Musing thus at one o'clock in the morning in the corridors of the Imperial Hotel, Blackpool, I was pleased to meet my old friend Grey Gowrie[3], the dusky, foreign-looking poet who was the Conservative Government's most exciting choice of junior Minister since his immediate predecessor in the job, Lord Bethell[4]. As it happened, I had just written an encouraging review of some rather mediocre poems by Lord Gowrie and expected a pat on the back. But the swarthy poet's Afro hair-style was quivering like a peacock's tail: "You can say what you like about me but don't insult my wife," he hissed. I replied I had never mentioned his dear wife and was not even sure he had one but he strode away, muttering tribal curses.

Are the strains of office proving too much for this young man, and if so, should one tell Grocer of one's suspicions? It is very worrying. With Grocer's hatred of being told anything, he might easily appoint Gowrie Foreign Secretary on the spot. God help England, these are terrible times we are living through.

Wednesday 28th October
Lunch with the Douglas-Homes at Hampton Court Palace for the German President and Frau Heinemann, a most formidable lady. When I asked her how much she had liked visiting John Piper's studio at Fowley Bottom near Henley, she told me she had much preferred visiting the grave of the Unknown Warrior in Westminster Abbey the day before. Does the Queen lay wreaths on the grave of the Unknown Nazi Soldier whenever she visits Germany? It is amazing how much simple and inexpensive pleasure one can give by a little thoughtfulness.

The Baillie[5] was absurdly excited about his visit to China — anybody would think he had never been abroad before. When I said how sad I was to hear that he was getting the sack on his return, he said he wished I could learn to behave myself like a Prime Minister for once. Plainly he had mistaken

---

1. This is only the first of various accounts which Waugh gives for his childhood.

2. Edward Heath, b. in humble circumstances 9 July 1916, was Prime Minister 1970-1974. It is Waugh's view that this appointment redeems Heath's otherwise disastrous period of office.

3. Earl of Gowrie, b. 26 November 1939. A Junior Whip in Heath's government, he was also a very bad poet, noted for his unconventional appearance.

4. Little is known about this man, a journalist and translator.

5. Sir Alec Douglas-Home, b. 2 July 1903, a contemporary of Cyril Connolly at Eton.

me for Mr Roy Smoothiechops[1] who was also present, although he has never, of course, been Prime Minister.

Thursday 29th October

I went to the *Sunday Times* exhibition in the National Portrait Gallery — a hideous and depressing display which traces the decline of this once great newspaper to the sad bum-and-tit affair we know today. In the middle of admiring an excellent waxwork of Lord Thomson I found to my dismay that it was the old gentleman himself. I congratulated him on the nipples of the Colour Section's young lady last week (fabulous Fiona Lewis, 35-18-33) and he beamed with delight, offering me a Thomson holiday to Moscow for the incredibly cheap price of £29.

When he told me that Harold Evans had been offered Hugh Cudlipp's job on the *Daily Mirror*, I told him I had always thought that Harry was more of a *Mirror* man than anything else. He should be able to recover some of the ground they have lost to the *Sun*, especially if he takes fabulous Fiona with him. Harry and his young proteges — Ron "Badger" Hall and "left-wing" Bruce Page etc. — always seemed a little out of their depths on a newspaper which is still seen by a fair proportion of AB readers from educated backgrounds in the south of England[2].

A more worrying aspect is that if public buildings like the National Portrait Gallery are to involve themselves in commercial promotions of this sort, it will not be long before the *Observer* demands a show, then *Boy's Own Paper*, *Titbits* and everybody else. Roy Strong may like to be in Lord Thomson's good books, but I can't help feeling that the public ought to have a say in the matter.

Friday 30th October

Saw Alan Brien coming out of a small door in Greek Street, looking rather furtive. He tells me he has been trying to write a column like this one for some time in the *Sunday Telegraph*, but nobody ever reads it, and now he has run out of ideas. There must surely, in the whole of London, be plenty of things for keen, politically committed columnists to write about without making furtive visits to Greek Street, an area of most unsavoury reputation. I suggested he should write about how pretty women look on bicycles, but he disagreed, saying he never saw anything of interest on these occasions.

Poor Alan, this is how we shall all end up.

Monday 3rd November

Spent the day in court[3]. My eye was caught by one of plaintiff's junior counsel, a most delightful creature with her little barrister wig perched demurely over what looked like a pony tail. There was a sweet frown of concentration on her face as she listened to all the sonorous denunciations and pregnant pauses of judge and senior counsel. This was altogether lovelier than anything my solicitors had chosen and I felt a pang of sorrow that circumstances had put her on the other side.

For one delicious moment our eyes met and I gave her a friendly wink. It seemed to make her at the same time happy and confused. She blushed and lowered her beautiful eyes with perhaps the faintest hint of a smile on her generous lips. I thought of following up my initiative with a Peace sign, but judged it imprudent under the circumstances.

Yet in that moment it seemed to me we had brought a touch of beauty into the four grey walls of the courtroom, accustomed as they are to tales of heartbreak and distress: reputations unjustly besmirched, fathers of families reduced to penury; tales of pomposity, spite, avarice and iniquity in every form. For one brief moment the light shone in that dingy corner of our capital city. If the young lady concerned would like to get in touch with me, I am to be found here on many mornings of the week.

Tuesday 4th November

One middle-class prejudice from which I will never be shaken is my profound belief in the law. Timothy Evans, James Hanratty, the Man in the Iron Mask — all these must have been guilty of something or they would never have got into trouble. I can't accept the view that our judges are no better than bandits and hooligans who listen to nothing except their own unpleasant ideas. Of course, there will always be a few bad eggs in every nest, but these are not typical of the generally very high standard, and in any case we always have our Court of Appeal.

The acquittal of Sir Gerald Nabarro[4] is a triumph for British justice. Now this blameless man can resume his normal legislative duties without a stain on his character after all the disgraceful and reckless allegations

1. Mr Roy Jenkins, b. 11 November 1920. A Labour politician of literary pretensions. He features throughout the Diary as a social climber to be avoided.

2. These people are all journalists. 'Badger' 's nickname probably arose from the smell which is, in fact, characteristic of many Thomson House journalists. Waugh attributes it to their humble origins, but it seems more likely to arise from a different cause — possibly desire to please their Editor (Cf. Note for 6th October 1972, under Evans).

3. A libel action was brought against Waugh by Ms Norah Beloff, a spinster, of London. He lost it. The young barrister whom Waugh admired later turned out (26th January 1973) to be Mary Claire Hogg, daughter of the Lord Chancellor, Lord Hailsham, whom Waugh describes as 'that slippery old lunatic'.

4. Nabarro (1913-1974), a flamboyant Conservative backbencher, had plainly had a narrow escape in the same week that Waugh lost his libel case.

made against him in court by Sir Joseph
Moloney QC, counsel for the prosecution.
We may ask ourselves whether on this
occasion Sir Joseph did not go beyond the
bounds of duty but in the event he has
damaged nobody but himself while Sir Gerald
has earned a name in the legal history books
of our island story.

Monday 10th November

When I was at school a favourite lark of the
English Sixth Form was to send off a letter
every month to poor Ezra Pound in his
Washington mad house, asking him some
earnest question about his ridiculous *Cantos*.
Sometimes he would answer with a brief
obscenity — always typed, unsigned and un-
dated — sometimes with a long, passionate
screed of gibberish. These were read aloud
in various satirical voices to great laughter
and applause.

We always threw them away afterwards,
but there are others who have not been so
considerate, and I fear the literary world will
be bored by volume after volume of them in
the next few years. Connolly[1], not surprisingly, reveals that he has a hoard: "It is tempting
to go on quoting from letters and telegrams
from him whom I have described as my *sola
et sera voluptas*", drooled the Greatest Living
Englishman in last week's *Sunday Times*.
Sola voluptas indeed. Alas, there is no reason
to suppose he will be able to resist the
temptation very much longer.

Perhaps Pound could have written decent
poetry if he had tried, and if he had not been
surrounded by half-witted sycophants
encouraging him to turn out this solemn
drivel. There may not be any particular
reason to suppose he had a talent for poetry,
but we have no means of being sure.

Pound was indeed one of the luminaries
of what is laughingly called the Modern
Movement which has encouraged poets,
writers and artists to get away with preposterous rubbish for the last 50 years.
Thank heaven that at last we have got the
great and good Sir John Betjeman for our
Laureate. Soon there will be nobody left in
the Modern Movement but a handful of ageing critics — Connolly, Alvarez, Lambert,
Arthur Crook — tunelessly singing *O sole mio*
into the sunset.

Tuesday 11th November

All the newspapers today are full of photographs of our beloved Royal Family to
celebrate the silver wedding of Prince Philip
and Her Majesty. My wife was reminded of
a play she had seen on television called
Coronation Street, but to me they were an
irresistible reminder of the wedding scene in
Goodbye Columbus.

In this special study for *Private Eye* by my
friend Patric Leischfeld[2] — a second cousin,
once removed, as it happens, of the Queen's
last corgi—I had hoped to provide a *Times*
index chart with numbers to identify which
are the Greek Glucksburgs from Schleswig-
Holstein and which are the original Saxe-
Coburgs from Gotha, but to tell the truth
I am a little confused myself. Where, for
instance, is my old friend Harry Gloucester[3]
whom we all call "Bonkers"? I hope nothing
has happened to him, and he is safely asleep
under one of the chairs.

Or he may just be lost in the crowd. It all
goes to show the risk of letting a few of these
people in on a work permit.

Wednesday 19th November

Lunch at Buckingham Palace. I always enjoy
these "meet the people" luncheons but I am
afraid the Queen must find them very trying.
Wives are not invited which is obviously a
good idea, but on this occasion we had
Princess Anne to think about. Anne often
seems to look her best at lunch time.

Among the guests were Frank Chapple,
of the Electricians' Union; Bob Edwards,
who used to edit a newspaper called the
Sunday People but has now settled down
and edits the *Sunday Mirror*; Archbishop
Beck of Liverpool, who was not asked to say
Grace and Harold Pinter, the well-known bore.
Another guest was Professor Peter Bauer
from the LSE, a delightful man with most
unusual opinions about overseas aid.

I asked Bob if he was going to kiss hands
on his appointment as Hugh Cudlipp's successor in the *Mirror* Group, but nobody
thought it very funny[4]. They probably knew
that good old Harry Evans of the *Sunday
Times* has already been offered the job, and
if he turns it down it will go to someone
called Roger Wood, who once had an
accident on the carpet of the *Daily Express*'s
Manchester office.

---

1. Connolly (1903-1975) was chief book reviewer of the Sunday Times.

2. Earl of Lichfield, b. 25 April 1939. He could not have known Waugh at Eton, as Lichfield went to
Harrow. Nor could they have met at Oxford or in the Army. It seems unlikely that they were great
friends.

3. The Duke of Gloucester had been incurably insane for some years.

4. Once again, it is hard to disagree with the general sentiment. Cudlipp is presumably a journalist.

After the Queen had retired we had a most amusing half hour while Professor Bauer explained to the lovely young Princess how aid to developing countries actually prevents them from developing. But the happy atmosphere was spoilt when Frank Chapple stood up and said he wanted to wash his hands. He disappeared down a long corridor and came back three quarters of an hour later looking very red in the face. We were all too delicate to ask what had happened.

Thursday 20th November

Now I am on a lightning six-hour tour of the Soviet Union, organised for the unbelievably cheap price of £29 by Gnomitours Ltd., the philanthropic foundation. Our plane was diverted to Archangel in one of those unbelievably beautiful snowstorms you only see in Russia, somehow, and with unbelievable efficiency we were put straight into charabancs for a six-hour drive round the historic airport.

The bars were all closed, as it turned out, owing to military exercises. Our group leader was young Bruce Page, supplied by Intourist, who asked us to call him Colonel while we were in the USSR. He advised us not to look out of the windows, but in fact there would have been very little to see as we were soon thrillingly stuck in one of those snowdrifts you only see in Russia and which seem somehow to express the great warm soul of a continent.

Two of our party were taken off to the Lubiayanka discussion centre in Moscow after making ill-advised and anti-Soviet comments on the perfectly adequate toilet facilities — everybody in Russia uses the windows. For the rest of us, it was quite simply the trip of a lifetime.

Thursday 27th November

My telephone at *Private Eye* has been ringing all day as anxious readers draw my attention to pictures of Joanna, the baby black rhinoceros born in London Zoo. They point out that although her mother, June, has two magnificent horns on her nose, Joanna has none.

One woman, in tears, asked if it was true that the Foreign Office had them cut off so that ghastly old Baillie Vass[1] could present them to the Prime Minister of China. Others assumed that Joanna was not a baby rhinoceros at all, but some sort of dog or bear which had wandered into the photograph. It would be typical of the nation's drunken and incompetent corps of zoological reporters to make such a mistake.

1. Sir Alec Douglas-Home (q.v.). His 'ghastliness' may have been due to ill-health, as well as extreme old age. Rhinoceros horns are much prized in China as an aphrodisiac.

But by far the greatest number of callers made allowance for the rhinoceros's longer period of gestation and decided that poor Joanna was a victim of Thalidomide poisoning. This would also explain why no Fleet Street editor has dared to draw attention to her missing noses, for fear of Distillers' Company advertising and a long prison sentence.

In fact I was able to reassure my callers that rhinoceroi are always born without horns, as are cows and most other animals. But this incident shows the sort of misunderstanding that the Distillers' Company must expect if they insist on paying their money to lawyers and judges instead of to the victims of their revolting substance.

Friday 28th November

Today is my 23rd[1] birthday, a time for careful self-questioning. Thank God my looks are improving, but am I getting more radical? In what ways throughout the year have I grown less like myself and more like wonderful old Cyril Connolly, our Greatest Living Englishman?

Today we learn that Connolly has awarded Booker McConnell's £5,000 prize for the best English novel to Mr John Berger. Would I ever have the guts, the manliness, the plain bloody spunk to play a practical joke like

[1]. This seems most unlikely.

that on the British public?

Just think of all the earnest people, bent on self-improvement, who will now go out and buy this extraordinary collection of pompous, boring rubbish because of its "humanity and intellectual distinction, its grasp of modern history and sympathy with the oppressed".

Here are a few of Mr Berger's very wonderful observations for them to ponder:

On eating a cherry: "The eating of a cherry in no way prepares you for its stone. The stone feels like a precipitate of your mouth, mysteriously created through the act of eating a cherry. You spit out the result of your own eating."

On sugar: "This is a taste whose effects are not confined to the mouth. Sweetness is like Eurydice's thread: it leads from the tongue down to the throat and then, mysteriously, through the stomach to the sexual centre, to the tiny region (distinct in a male from the sexual organs themselves) where sexual pleasure accumulates before extending outwards in waves."

On death: "The taste of milk is the cloud of unknowing."

On sex: "The experience = 1 + life."

Monday 3rd December
Tea-time walk-around talk-around in Soho to
give ordinary people a chance of meeting me.
I must admit I find the friendliness and in-
formality of ordinary people quite delightful,
even though some of them, I believe, are
terribly poor.

A coloured lady kindly asks me into her
house. It is not furnished in my sort of taste,
but I suppose she likes it. She absolutely
insists we have a drink before she can show
me upstairs. I suppose this is some native
custom, and sip watery beer while she drinks
four tiny glasses of fruit juice, mysteriously
thanking me each time. Suddenly she says
I must pay £6 for the drink and if I want to
go upstairs I must pay £25 more. Giving her
all the money I have, I hastily make my
excuses and leave. I wonder how Their
Majesties avoid this sort of embarrassment
on their walk-arounds among ordinary
people.

Tuesday 4th December
To the Savoy for the *Daily Express* Sportsman
of the Year banquet. I had hoped from the
fact of being asked that my own contribution
in this field was going to be recognised at
last, but the award went to bloody old
Gordon Banks, the C.P. Snow of football.
Imagine my confusion on arriving, to discover
Princess Anne in the place of honour. It seems
one can't go anywhere nowadays without
bumping into this pushy, opinionated young
woman. It astounds me that anybody, let
alone myself, ever found her attractive.

She was not looking her best, in a pale two-
piece outfit and paisley scarf. The highlight
of this gruesome event came when she
presented an award and shook hands with
Richard Meade, the repulsive looking young
man who is often described as her "sporting
companion". From the hysterical applause
you would think they had rubbed noses.
It was a most boring and depressing occasion
and I certainly shan't go there again.

Wednesday 5th December
The traditional *Private Eye* lunch. After Grace
has been said by Blessed Arnold we have to
listen to poor old Max Aitken moaning on
about all the Australians, New Zealanders and
Indonesians who laid down their lives in
seven World Wars. He really is becoming the
most dreadful bore and his tip-offs about
Vere Harmsworth are becoming less and less

reliable. Soon, I fear, we will have to stop
asking him.

On the other hand, the food is so filthy at
these lunches I can never ask any of my smart
friends like Roy Jenkins or Kenneth Rose[1].
We have to make do with what we can, week
after week: Eldon Griffiths, Ron "Badger"
Hall, Lady Hartwell, Andrew Sinclair, Lord
Snowbum, the late Dame Edith Sitwell,
Sir Joseph Godber, Clive James — how on
earth is one supposed to get a lively magazine
out of that lot?

Thursday 6th December
We shall probably never know exactly how
many contestants for the Miss World title in
any given year are actually female impersonators. Unlike the organisers of
Olympic and other sporting events which
involve women, nobody in the Albert Hall
demands on-the-spot inspection or sex tests.
Yet it is a curious and undeniable fact that
wherever women compete publicly together,
a few men are tempted to join in the fun.

This may explain the outcry from
contestants whenever anybody suggests
they should parade in the nude. Certainly it is
much more fun trying to spot the female
impersonators. I thought I recognised the
Features Editor of a well known Printing
House Square newspaper in the saucy tilt
of one young bottom[2], and I could have
sworn I spotted the familiar foxy countenance of my old friend John "Sniffer" Wells[3]
behind the heavy eyelashes of Miss
Nicaragua.

Friday 7th December
Judge Ungoed-Thomas has collapsed and died
in the Strand. The Bench can ill afford to

1. Kenneth Rose, author of The Later Cecils and Curzon's biography. Griffiths was a Conservative MP,
   so was Godber; Sinclair a very bad novelist; Snowdon is the diminutive Royal photographer, Dame
   Edith a poet of the 1930s. The rest are journalists. Plainly, this was a very dull lunch.

2. This must refer to The Times whose Features Editor at that time was Charles Douglas-Home (alias
   Vass), b. 1 September 1937, noted for his unconventional dress.

3. A journalist.

lose his intelligence and kindly wisdom.
I watched him at work recently in a complicated case involving the law of copyright.
The matter did not concern me at all, but it
was such a pleasure to follow his razor sharp
brain at work that I turned up day after day.

I only wish I could think that high
intelligence, sophistication and wit were
universal among our High Court Judges.
Alas, as everybody learns who takes the fool-
hardy course of litigation, it is the luck of
the draw whether one is allotted a man of
intelligence and humanity like Judge Ungoed-
Thomas or whether one gets some oaf of
impenetrable stupidity, too bemused by his
own unpleasant and perverted ideas to take
in a word that is said to him[1].

Saturday 8th December
Old Lady Lloyd-George has also died at 84.
Few of us could understand what she saw in
the appalling little man, yet she was Lloyd-
George's mistress for 30 years — six of them
in Downing Street — before their marriage in
1943 when Lloyd-George, at 80, was
presumably past it.

The astounding thing is that as recently as
1916 a British Prime Minister could be living
in a sinful *menage a trois* at Number 10
Downing Street while the obsequious hacks
of the press never breathed a word. Thank
God our own beloved Grocer is unlikely to
inflict this sort of embarrassment on us.

Sunday 9th December
Whatever the knockers may say, it isn't all
beer and skittles being a member of the
Royal Family. Today's photographs by Lord
Snowbum[2] of the *Sunday Times* show just
how far they sometimes have to go to stay
in the public eye.

Snowbum's grand tour of hospital wards
provides some deeply compassionate photographs of all the seamier sights which others
try to ignore. In one of them, a man has
actually died while pretty nurses make an
unsuccessful attempt to resuscitate him.
The poor man never could have guessed how
photogenic it all was.

Another patient, who has had the misfortune to lose both his legs, seems to view
the small Royal photographer with less than
friendly eyes while nurses change the
dressings on his stumps.

Never mind, Tony. I always say everybody should have a hobby, and this is far
healthier than chasing foxes. When my time
comes, nothing will make me happier than
the thought that a small Royal photographer
is there to catch the scene.

Monday 10th December
Nobody should be surprised at the result of
the Uxbridge by-election. The great Mr
Bernard Levin urged those like himself who
support Labour to vote Liberal because the
Labour Party stands with the unions to the
"country's greatest single obstacle to progress,
modernisation and increasing national prosperity for everybody."

This, of course, might have persuaded all
those like oneself who have reservations about
progress, modernisation and general prosperity to vote Labour — except for another
bizarre development. Reading Levin's words
the former Paul Johnson[3] wrote to *The Times*
saying that Levin had persuaded him and his
wife to go and canvass full time for Labour
in Uxbridge. Bernard Levin's letter was
"counterproductive", harrumphed this
controversial, red-headed Old Stonyhurst
Boy.

But not nearly as counterproductive as
this last-minute intervention by the Johnson
family. Poor Uxbridge voters who opened
their doors to find the terrible, twitching face
of the *New Statesman*'s last editor but one
promptly deserted the Labour Party in
droves.

Tuesday 11th December
At the *Spectator* Christmas party Mr Enoch
Powell accosted a colleague of mine with
these pregnant words: "There are frequently
black men to be found sitting around in my
house. Make what you like of that."
My colleague has handed this problem to me.

One's first thought is that poor Enoch
may be suffering from hallucinations.
These are quite common with people who
worry too much about things, I had a great-
uncle, a clergyman, with the same feeling
about mice in his church. But this is probably
what Enoch wants us to think, and it is
certainly what I would have thought if I had
not read John Arden's brilliant analysis of
the Royal Shakespeare Company's political
complexion.

According to Arden, the Company works
in an "imperialistic atmosphere, supported
by the Tory Government in order to cultivate
bourgeois society on a consumer level."

---

1. Ungoed-Thomas tried a case against Private Eye in the Chancery Division by Ms Norah Beloff, a
   spinster, of London, alleging breach of copyright. He found for the defendants, leaving Beloff with an
   enormous bill for expenses.
2. Snowdon, although small, was employed by Thomson Newspapers to take these photographs.
3. A former editor of New Statesman.

How true! Mr Arden and his attractive wife, curvaceous yum-yum 52-year-old Miss Margaretta D'Arcy[1], have obviously hit upon the answer to the mystery of black men in Mr Powell's house. They are not black men at all but painted actors from the hot-bed of imperialism which is the Aldwych Theatre. These men sit up with Powell night after night discussing plans for the reconquest of India when Enoch will ride a white charger in front of his army of prancing blackamoor actors, receiving the plaudits of the multitude.

It is a pity that Mr Arden did not include this brilliant analysis in his play. Everything else is there in this enthralling 14-hour expose of revisionism in the time of King Arthur which denounces imperialism, anti-communism and racism while championing Women's Lib and the working class struggle in 18 hours of never-to-be-forgotten sincerity and genuine social commitment.

Wednesday 12th December
George Best[2] is up for sale, I see, priced at £200,000. By an odd coincidence I happen to have this sum available at the moment as the result of a small legacy. It occurred to me as possibly quite an agreeable idea to buy the young man for a companion on my occasional visits to the night club scene of our metropolis.

On the other hand I believe he is rather off-hand with his employers, and I might have a certain amount of difficulty in understanding his conversation. Perhaps I shall buy a little Filipino servant instead.

Thursday 20th December
I went to the House of Commons to hear Baillie Vass announce that the lamps are lighting up again all over Europe. He's a pretty one to talk, although while we are on the subject, one wonders if it isn't time Lord Lambton[3] trimmed his wick a little.

Baillie obviously meant this to be as dramatic a statement as when Sir Edward Grey suggested that the lamps were all going out in August 1914, but in the event, nobody paid the slightest bit of attention to Vass's idiotic remarks. How long will it take for politicians to realise that people are not in the slightest bit interested in anything they may have to say?

Friday 28th December
The vehemence of Foreign Office denials that Russia could possibly have supplied weapons to the IRA must be explained with reference to the Yalta Agreement of 1944 between the arch-criminals Churchill and Stalin. They decided that the Russians would be allowed to tyrannise and murder Eastern Europeans to their hearts' content so long as they left the Western sphere of influence alone.

If Russia is indeed supplying the IRA with weapons, this is in plain breach of the Yalta Agreement, by which we never lift a finger to help Hungarians, Czechs or anyone else in their occasional pathetic uprisings. It would probably not disturb the braying, Communist-infiltrated ranks of the Foreign Office very much. What really upsets the Frank Giles[4] generation is the thought that they may be expected to supply weapons to the poor defenceless Poles, Hungarians or Czechs next time there is an uprising in the Soviet empire.

Saturday 29th December
The death of L.P. Hartley closes a strange chapter in the blood-stained annals of our libel laws. Some years ago Hartley wrote a very bad novel called *Poor Claire*. This was savagely reviewed in the *Evening Standard* by Cuthbert Worsley, the distinguished and perceptive critic who writes under the name of Richard Lister.

His review, when it appeared, wounded Hartley deeply. Instead of licking his wounds and writing a better novel next time or composing a dignified rebuttal of Worsley's criticisms, Hartley consulted his lawyers and instituted libel proceedings against the *Standard* on the curious grounds that the review was of such an offensive nature as to subject him to ridicule.

For once in the craven history of British journalism, the *Standard*'s editor, Sir Charles-um-Wintour, decided to fight the case. Two years later, Hartley dropped out, paying his own and the *Standard*'s expenses, running into four figures. However, approved expenses do not cover the ludicrous fees charged by fancy lawyers, so the *Standard* had to cough up a little. Once again, only the lawyers profited.

Of course, writers of all people should know better than to take their drivelling literary disputes to court, but these tragedies will recur for as long as our insane libel laws tempt poor boobies into the greasy clutches of lawyers.

---

1. This reference may be intended ironically. Ms D'Arcy would not normally be described as 'curvaceous' although Waugh's taste in women is undoubtedly idiosyncratic.

2. A footballer.

3. Lambton, b. 10 July 1922, resigned as Minister for the Air Force in May 1973 after disclosures of sexual irregularity in his private life. He was noted for his enjoyment of life.

4. Giles, b. 1919, m. Lady Kitty Sackville, daughter of Earl de la Warr. A journalist, noted for his elegant wife.

1973

Throughout this year Mr Edward Heath remained Prime Minister, although by the end of it, with the miners' go-slow and the imposition of a three-day working week, we see his position as untenable. Waugh was among the first to foresee the result of the February 1974 election and appealed to the American Central Intelligence Agency to step in and save his country from a fate which otherwise seemed inescapable.

At the beginning, we see Heath at the height of his ill-fated self-confidence with his Policy Review Staff (the 'Wank-Tank'), his policy of 'detente' with Russia (on which Waugh was the first to sound a warning note) and his plans for supersonic aeroplanes, new London airports and even a tunnel under the Channel. Again, Waugh notices the Prime Minister's growing obesity and sounds a cautionary note. It was a year of contrasts, with an ageing, discredited Foreign Secretary, Sir Alec Douglas-Home ('Baillie Vass') yet able to show the world his young nephew ('Charlie Vass') who could come within a stone's throw of winning the Miss World contest as Miss Costa Rican Pygmy. It was the year of Sunday football, heralding the Lambton and Jellicoe scandals which implicated two senior ministers with prostitutes. Most humiliating of all for Waugh and his friends, it was the year of Princess Anne's wedding to the horseman, Mark Phillips, whose likeness appeared on the postage stamps.

Sunday 2nd January

Today I counted 83½ bare nipples on the cover of the *Sunday Times* Colour Supplement and wonder if this is a record for Dame Harold Evans, the newspaper's handsome, brilliant, crusading editor. Much less prominently displayed, on an inside page, is the information that Sir Alec Douglas-Home, our venerable Foreign Secretary, owns 20,000 shares in Distillers' Company.

Why, we ask ourselves, was Dame Harold (who is about to be named winner of the Granada Press Award for his fearless Thalidomide campaign) so coy about this fascinating piece of information? Could it be that the British public would instinctively realise that good old Baillie Vass would never be associated with anything shoddy or underhand?

Vass it was who stood up to be counted at Munich; who patiently got on with his needlework throughout the resulting World War when a bad back laid him low; who refused to be cowed by the tyrant Nasser at Suez; whose unswerving support for Michael Stewart emboldened that timid little man to see his peculiar Nigerian policy through; who keeps trying to sell black Rhodesians down the river, despite repeated discouragement. Sir Baillie Vass, at 89, is widely regarded as the most honourable man in British politics.

I must admit, the news that he owns part of the Distillers' Company made one have second thoughts about the whole Thalidomide campaign. Many will feel it wrong that comparative upstarts like Dame Harold Evans should parade their self-righteousness — and be commended for it — at the expense of established national figures like old Baillie Vass. Chuck it, Evans, and stick to your titties.

Tuesday 4th January

All the newspapers are full of diet sheets and after-Christmas slimming advice, but the person I am worried about is Teddy Heath. Wislon put on weight as Prime Minister, but Grocer seems to think he is entered for the County Pig Show, and we all know how competitive he is. It would be a terrible thing if the first Conservative working-class Prime Minister also became the first British Prime Minister to burst from over-eating.

Last week, newspapers showed a picture of our beloved Grocer receiving a gold medal from a German gentleman called Herr Stresemann. They obsequiously suggested this was yet another bribe for getting us into the Common Market against our wishes, but I would like to think that in fact it was the Stresemann Society's annual award for the fattest European Prime Minister.

If so, Grocer can relax now. If he likes, I will recommend a sauna establishment in Soho where the young masseuses are truly most delightful.

Wednesday 5th January

The great Lusitania controversy has taken another turn. Readers will remember that the BBC accused Winston Churchill of conniving to have the Lusitania sunk in order to bring America into the war; some doubt was cast upon this by the great Nicholas Tomalin, of William Hickey fame, and also by Mr Winston Churchill Jr. MP, a relative of the accused. Today Mr Martin Gilbert, Churchill's biographer, weighs in with a list of war crimes advocated or committed by Churchill during the Great War.

I have always maintained that Churchill should have been hanged at the end of the last war — whether for specific war crimes, like the introduction of civilian bombing, or for Yalta, or merely to herald a return to the civilised standards of peace. Churchill's unsuitability for peace time conditions had been shown well enough by his persecution of P.G. Wodehouse, and this gesture would have spared Englishmen who wanted to hero-worship the old brute from the sad spectacle of his senile degeneration.

It now appears that there was a good case for hanging him at the end of the Great War. This would have saved us the baleful influence he continues to exert on British politics. Whenever a British politician — Wislon, Thorpe, Powell and ever-so-lovely Michael Foot are the worst offenders — starts talking in Churchillian accents, you can be sure they are going to say something particularly mean, fatuous and nasty.

Thursday 6th January

We are none of us getting any younger, and I suppose it is time I penned my memoir of Anthony Powell[1]. A good friend and the best of companions, Toni combined the rare qualities of a love of cats, an appreciation of fine wine and considerable skill (some would put it higher) in the art of knitting.

I saw him most in those halcyon days

---

1. Powell, the fashionable novelist, had recently published a memoir of Constance Lambert in similar terms.

between the wars when I was living in a public lavatory under Cambridge Circus[1].
Toni was always rather surprised to find me in what I suppose he may have considered my somewhat *outre* place of abode. I have reason to believe that his comments on this, reported to a friend, inspired the lines in E.J. Thribb's *Polynesian Pantomime:*

> I once heard of a man
> Who lived in an underground public
> > lavatory
>
> In Regent's Park —

although the exact location has, of course, been changed.

Often, of an evening, we would sit stroking our cats and discussing the rival advantages of purl and plain. It may have seemed trivial at the time — we were young and our talk was probably not distinguished by either the gravity or sense of responsibility which our elders would have deemed suitable — but I like to think that these conversations may have contributed in some way to the long series of jumpers and woolly cardigans Toni was later to knit for his family and close friends when he retired to live in north Somerset on the large private income left to him by his father.

In later years, as is well known, he took to drinking a glass of wine with his luncheon with the result that he usually slept heavily after lunch until breakfast next morning. Some suggested that this was harmful to his knitting, but I was never able to spot that it had had any noticeable effect.

Friday 12th January
To lunch with my old friend Howard Hughes[2] at the Inn on the Park. He was looking much better than when I last saw him in Las Vegas. I think the Nicaraguan earthquake must have done wonders for his bowel movement — always a problem if one lives a more or less sedentary life. He ate the nut cutlets particularly well, despite his eight-inch fingernails.

The conversation inevitably turned on how people like ourselves of a certain wealth and position in the world could avoid the envious attentions of hacks from *The Times* and other newspapers. I told him I kept a savage gander on a lake near the drive, which usually succeeded in putting the hacks to flight.

Mormons are certainly a novel variation of this. One of them stood over us as we ate, ready to swat any germs or newspaper

reporters which came near us. Most hospitable, I must say, and it nearly converted me to the idea of purchasing some Mormons. I forgot to ask whether one had to castrate them first — I am hopelessly vague about all these American religions[3].

Monday 15th January
In the House of Lords today I caught a second glimpse of the delightful young barristerette who appeared as junior counsel for the plaintiff in her libel action some weeks ago. Readers will remember how this fair creature illuminated the dismal scene with her presence. Although she blushed most prettily when I winked at her across the crowded courtroom, she never took up my invitation to get in touch.

She is now appearing for some vending machine merchants who are appealling against a tax assessment by the Customs and Excise. I hope the judges reach the right decision on this occasion. It transpires that she is called Mary Claire Hogg, eldest daughter of Big Breadwinner Hogg, our satirical Lord Chancellor. Ah well, one can't win every time. But who would have thought the old brute could have such a delightful daughter[4]?

Tuesday 16th January
A most disturbing article in *The Times* today by Anne Scott-James entitled "When a Change is as good as a Nightmare". It describes the various hallucinations to which ladies of her age are apparently prone: "Go out to the greengrocer and it has become a boutique. Take a road you could have driven blindfold a year ago and it has become a lunar landscape. Take out your purse and it is full of

---

1. Waugh may be mistaken about the exact location of this public lavatory.

2. An American multi-millionaire recluse, d. 1976 of kidney ailment, weighing six stone.

3. Mormons are not castrated. Waugh was probably confusing them with his own confusion about Roman Catholic priests, which appears elsewhere.

4. Cf. 3rd November 1972.

strange coins. . . Black faces everywhere and foreign voices. Half the streets you knew torn down. Couples copulating on the cinema screen, in colour."

No doubt he intends it kindly, but I am not sure that Sir William Rees-Mogg is really acting for the best when he publishes ladies' anxieties in this way. Perhaps he hopes it will be a form of therapy. For my own part, I always advise them to take a couple of aspirins and if that does not work, to try a wine glass of Doctor Collis Browne's Compound.

Wednesday 17th January

I was slightly annoyed that Harold Wislon should use the Granada Press Awards last night to launch one of his cowardly attacks on myself, comparing me, among other things, to the Aberfan disaster and the massacre of Israeli athletes in Munich.

At least the newspapers had enough good taste not to publish this tiresome diatribe. The *Daily Telegraph* did not even mention the Granada Awards at all, although it gave extensive coverage to other parts of Wislon's speech.

This seems odd, because I thought I saw my old friend Maurice Green, editor of the *Telegraph*, at the party. Perhaps he was hoping to be awarded a prize, but he must be accustomed to these disappointments. By my reckoning, 1974 will be the 135th year in succession in which the *Daily Telegraph* has failed to be nominated Newspaper of the Year. Perhaps Mr Green should institute a special award for the least changed newspaper and present it to himself every year at a huge luncheon party for one in Boulestin's.

Thursday 25th January

Of all the trumpets blown to celebrate the 10th anniversary of Gaitskell's death, the strangest comes from Anthony Howard in the *New Statesman*. Howard has few kind things to say of the dead man but he gives this account from a brigadier who was at school with Gaitskell: "We knew he was a filthy bugger then: used to be at it under the blankets every night".

Howard maintains that this is the sort of reputation "that any middle-class leader of the Labour Party should be proud to earn." I am not sure what Tony is getting at here. Does he mean that nobody is fit to lead the Labour Party who hasn't been seen "at it"

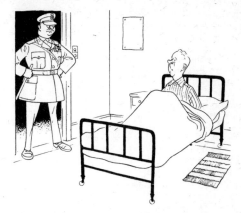

under the blankets every night? The effect which such a ruling might have on impressionable, ambitious young men like Peter Shore and Tony Benn is too horrible to contemplate.

Friday 26th January

When I called on her at her cottage in St Ives, Cornwall, to wish her many happy returns on her 70th birthday, Dame Barbara Hepworth, who is the world's greatest sculptor since the early Donatello, reminded me irresistibly of one of her own statues.

She stood in the garden on this cold January morning quite still and, so far as I could see, completely unclothed. Her stomach, far from showing the expected middle-age spread, was, in fact, a highly polished cavity, spatially related to the idea of a stomach contained within its void. Her breasts, which grew from her shoulder blades at the back, were surprisingly firm and quintessentially feminine.

She answered none of my questions except for one slight moan. I thought I recognised it as middle D in the Vox Humana range with Diapason backing. On the other hand, it might have been caused by the wind blowing through her stomach cavity. In either case, it was a most moving and memorable experience.

Saturday 27th January

Sir Keith Bovis[1], our enterprising Secretary of State for Health and Social Services, made a noble Declaration of Interest during the Thalidomide debate on November 29th: "Through re-insurance effected in the early 1960s by a (Lloyd's) syndicate of which I was

---

1. Sir Keith Joseph, Tory politician, b. 17 January 1918, noted for his advocacy of greater contraceptive facilities for the poor.

then a member, I might be liable for a small percentage of a small share of the cost of any claim arising through legal action against Distillers' ", he said (*Hansard* Col. 438). Adding the suggestion that the amount was "most unlikely to exceed several hundred pounds".

Sir Keith presumably takes the view that liability is restricted to £250,000 "in any one event", rather than the £22 million which Distillers' threaten to claim to cover all the events. If things go very badly wrong, I imagine his personal liability may be nearer £30,000 than the "several hundred pounds" he mentions.

This would be a shocking business indeed and, together with Douglas-Homes' 20,000 shares in Distillers', only serves to underline the need for prompt government action.

Monday 29th January

Index, the distinguished quarterly magazine, has an article in its winter number listing those subjects that are not allowed to be mentioned in the Soviet press. They include: information about earthquakes, fires, floods, explosions, rail disasters or any other disaster in the USSR; figures about the earnings of government or Party workers; comparisons between the budget of Soviet citizens and the price of goods; any mention of food shortages or price increases in the USSR or improved living standards outside the socialist camp.

I hope it has not escaped the attention of fellow progressives that I never mention any of these dismal things in the Diary. If only all journalists of progressive leanings — Frank Giles and Bruce Page on the *Sunday Times*, Iverach Macdonald on *The Times* etc. etc. — could exercise the same voluntary restraint we might at last have a Press I would not be ashamed to show my Soviet friends when they call with their quaint little gifts.

Thursday 30th January

Alas, one seldom seems to find the opportunity to praise a QC in this diary. Most of them appear as unintelligent as they are conceited, as idle and incompetent as they are unscrupulous and grasping. So it was with very real pleasure that one watched Mr Muir Hunter Davies QC[1] conduct the Poulson[2] bankruptcy enquiry with a thoroughness and a passion which one supposed had disappeared from the Bar.

Now we learn that Hunter Davies has been reported to the Bar Council for suspected integrity and one trembles to think of his fate if found guilty. Of course ministers are concerned. We only know about Poulson's generosity because he happened to go bankrupt. Who knows what Aladdin's caves of coffee pots are waiting to be revealed by mute, inglorious Poulsons who have so far managed to remain solvent?

Ministers and MPs are worried in case the average voter is confirmed in his suspicion that politicians are only in it for the money. We who have studied the matter know that they are in it for the feeling of importance — that the leadership urge is no more than unhealthy compensation for a deprived childhood. But they will never get their personality problems sorted out until they can learn to refuse expensive presents from total strangers.

It was mildly disgraceful that Crosland should accept such a gift. What is totally disgraceful is how the *Daily Express* and other British newspapers have joined the politicians in demanding further restraints on the flow of information. As things stand, we have to wait until someone's bankruptcy to hear of these matters. If the *Daily Express* has its way we will not even learn of them then, and not even read the politicians' denials which a sycophantic press is eager to publish quite uncritically and without the tiresome business of cross-examination.

Friday 31st January

Before the much more important matter of the coffee pot distracted public attention, Mr Crosland was making another of his bids for the intellectual leadership of the Labour Party, with a call for the revival of class warfare as a means of winning the general election.

Class warfare is one of the few interesting or worthwhile areas of politics, of course, keeping the rich on their toes and giving the poor something to think about. It also provides employment for gifted journalists like Peregrine Worsthorne and Paul Foot. But how the Parliamentary Labour Party whose backbenchers now receive £6,250 in salary and expenses can hope to be accepted on a soak-the-rich programme remains to be seen. The idea that Captain Anthony Raven Crosland, of the Royal Welch Fusiliers, with his plummy, donnish voice and mandarin life-style, can spearhead such a movement is laughable.

1. Hunter Davies is a bad novelist; Muir Hunter the good QC.

2. Poulson, an architect, was revealed to have bribed important sections of the Northern Labour Party as well as having employed Mr Maudling, the Conservative politician, as director of one of his companies, and presented Anthony Crosland, the Labour politician, with a silver coffee pot.

Perhaps he can afford to throw away perfectly good coffee pots worth £80, but £80 is more than many of his Grimsby constituents take home for a month's work. He must be daft.

Saturday 1st February

Those of us who love and worry about the Grocer will be delighted that he took my advice and went to see his doctor about overeating. If he goes on eating like this he will be dead before he is 57.

We were also relieved to learn in the *Sunday Times* that he built huge underground tunnel systems where he can go in the event of a world war. They are well protected against any civilian survivors who might wish to argue about government policy, being almost impossible to find.

But how, in the general secrecy, can we be sure that these *Grocerbunkers* are properly stocked? Are there plentiful tins of peaches and asparagus tips, *pate de foie gras*, grouse in aspic and the other things Grocer likes? Is there a reasonable wine cellar and a gymnasium where Grocer can do his callisthenic exercises? What measures have been taken for paying Grocer's salary and the salaries of his close friends while they are underground? The public can have no confidence in the arrangements for a nuclear holocaust until assurance has been given on all these points.

Sunday 2nd February

Alan Brien reveals his "sovereign remedy" for a hangover in today's fun-packed *Sunday Times*: "Sex and/or work, preferably first one then the other."

It is most distressing to think of the horror

1. See Note 2, 27th January 1973.

2. A businessman.

3. An aged journalist.

one may have inflicted on some poor woman by giving this wretched man another drink. I hope everyone will take the hint and keep their drinks to themselves while O'Brien is around.

Monday 3rd February

Now that Dr A.L. Rowse has cleared up the problem of Shakespeare's Dark Lady, I hope people will turn to the much greater mystery which surrounds the identity of E.J. Thribb's "my mate Keith".

I have just solved this mystery, using the same rigorous methods as Dr Rowse. A few candidates can be mentioned only to be dismissed: Sir Keith Bovis[1] and Sir Kenneth Keith[2] are out because "Keith" does not enjoy classical music and disapproves of the Royal Family. Again, Keith Waterhouse[3] is far too old. People who support these candidates are under a misapprehension, barking up the wrong tree, simply so much rubbish — popinjays, charlatans, people of no consequence.

The answer came to me one day when I was asleep in the Soda Fountain at Fortnum's: quite plainly, Keith was a person of lower or working class origin. That being so, what more likely than he should occasionally sniff, most especially when suffering from a cold. Only one name suggests itself in this context — John (or Jawn) Wells. References to Wells's habit of sniffing abound throughout the literature of the period.

I still needed an essential clue to link "Sniffer" Wells with Thribb's mysterious "Keith". It came to me when I was being massaged by a young Filipino for some reason at the Turkish Baths in Jermyn Street. Many people of Thribb's generation were devotees of the drug marijuana — in Arabic, *Khif*. What more likely, if Thribb had a friend known as "Sniff", than that this should become, in cockney rhyming slang, the drug *Khif*? From *Khif* to "Keith" is not even a step, if one allows for the cockney's traditional difficulty with his labiodental aspirates.

All of which, when it appears in my foreword to *The Poetical Works of E.J. Thribb* (Snipcock, £1.00) next year, should confuse the pipsqueaks of the literary establishment and open a glorious vista of peace, progress and prosperity for us all.

©A.L. Rowse 1973

Tuesday 11th February

My rival on *The Times* Diary today advises those who can no longer afford meat to try eating cows' feet raw with vinegar at a shilling a pound. This is an extremely cruel trick to play on the poor, who should be the object of our compassion in these hard times, not the butt of tasteless practical jokes.

Wednesday 12th February

Counsel for Lord Rothermere and others in their action against the great Bernard Levin have announced that they will have to produce ten thousand documents in order to establish what they seek to establish, that Lord Rothermere is a philanthropist of spotless reputation, humanity and wisdom, whose management of his newspapers has been completely brilliant and guided by the best possible motives from start to finish.

It is a sad fact of modern life, I suppose, that the richer a man is the more complicated becomes the task of defending his reputation. But congratulations to my old friend David Hirst, the eminent libel barrister, who seems to have landed a most lucrative brief.

Thursday 16th February

The Queen is back from holiday, hurrah! I have been missing our little get-togethers. Photographs show her with two of the Royal Corgis at Liverpool Street Station, all looking very well and much younger. I could scarcely recognise *Buzz*, my favourite and the only male among the five Royal Pets.

Many members of the public must be in the same difficulty. There is something almost racist in the way Court Circulars never mention which Corgis have accompanied the Royal Pair. To assist in identification, I am permitted to give the following particulars:

Buzz is the only male dog — you look between the hind legs for identification; this is made easier by the fact that *Buzz* has no tail.

Heather and *Brush* are both bitches, both tailless and can only be distinguished by the look in their eyes.

Pickles is half-Corgi and half-Dachshund, and the same is true of *Tinker*, but they can be distinguished by the fact that *Pickles* is short-haired and *Tinker* is long-haired.

So there we are. But I still think it would be kinder to name them in the Court Circulars. And if the Duchess of Windsor is going to be allowed to call herself Royal Highness, why shouldn't the same privilege be extended to the Royal Corgis? Incidentally, if anyone is worried about how *Buzz, Heather* and *Brush* came to lose their tails, the *Daily Mirror* Pets Information Service tells me that Corgis are often born without tails, like guinea pigs, so probably it was not necessary for the Queen to cut them off, like the Three Blind Mice!

Friday 17th February
Servan-Schreiber, the French politician, is the only person who talks any sense about the Concorde apart from our own home-grown Richard Crossbum[1]. Schreiber points out that the initial mistake was to suppose that future progress in air travel must necessarily involve greater speed.

In fact, progress is much more likely to be represented by anything which will carry a greater number of people more cheaply. Jumbo jets and charter flights are a step forward, while Concorde, in this respect, is a mammoth jump backwards.

It is a fatal flaw in the Grocer mentality — and one which is obviously shared by Pompidou — to equate progress with anything which makes life easier for high-powered business executives. So far, Grocer's madness and obstinacy have cost us £1,200,000,000. One would not grudge it him so much if he were not so obviously such an unpleasant person.

Saturday 18th February
People have already started saying that President Nixon is mad, just because he shuts himself up in his room at Camp David and won't see anybody. They used to say the same about poor, dear President Johnson, because he used to pull out his male organ and show it to visitors.

When will people realise that it is one of the most unpleasant parts of any American President's job that he has got to pretend to be mad, or the nuclear deterrent would lose all credibility. Only a madman is prepared to blow up the other half of the world as a natural response to the fact that his own half is about to be blown up.

Lyndon Johnson, I happen to know, was a profoundly modest man, and it upset him very much to expose himself in this way.

But he did it, nevertheless, from a sense of duty, so that we would all have a secure and prosperous future.

Monday 19th February
Before very long we will know the result of the thrilling Lincoln by-election, between likeable, handsome ("You haven't lived until you've had a Guinness") Chairman of the Monday Club, Jonathan Guinness, and hideous, balding Dick Taverne, QC[2].

Taverne is not representing the Labour Party, of course, but announces that he is standing for Honesty in Politics and other satirical notions. The Liberals have tried this one before, but they have never won so much as a single vote with their hopelessly idealistic proposal for a Public Register of MPs' Bribes. They are now waiting in the wings to join the big laugh when Lincoln's results are announced.

Tuesday 20th February
I hope someone in authority will look into the current unscrupulous campaign to raise £2,500,000 for LSE's Library of Political and Economic Science. The existing library contains more rubbish than any other single building on earth, and not a word which any sane person would wish to believe. The library's only serious function is to provide a little extra income for LSE students who steal books from it and sell them second-hand.

Almost anybody you name seems to be in the plot — Grocer, Wislon, somebody called Jeremy Thorpe[3], Huw Wellbred[4], the absurd Lord Drogheda[5], Pierre "Trendy" Trudeau, the disgusting Canadian. . . if this continues we must launch a rival appeal, to pay for the legal defence of anyone who will burn it down again.

Wednesday 28th February
A heart-rending advertisement in *The Times* agony column. Peregrine Worsthorne[6], the celebrated Belgian thinker, is being turned out of his home by avaricious landlords and appeals for someone to take him in — "to restore my faith in the capitalist system". All he wants is a six-room apartment somewhere — anywhere (within reason) — where he and his family can huddle together in the cold.

What sort of employer is Lord Hartwell who will let one of his oldest employees starve

---

1. Richard Crossman (1907-1974) was a Labour politician and journalist, noted for fraudulently suing the Spectator for libel and winning £5,000.

2. Taverne, formerly the official Labour candidate, had been dropped by his Constituency Committee in punishment for supporting the Common Market and other right-wing causes.

3. Jeremy Thorpe, b. 29 April 1929, a Liberal politician noted for gifted impersonations.

4. Huw Weldon, a BBC employee.

5. 11th Earl of Drogheda, b. 23 April 1910, Chairman of Financial Times and Governor of the Royal Ballet, noted for handsome profile.

6. A journalist, born Koch de Goreynd, noted for elegant apparel.

to death on the pavement? Why is there no mention of his plight in *The Times* Diary?

What sort of society are we building in this country which can stand by and watch it happen? It is no good blaming Lord Hartwell or his beautiful wife or even *The Times* Diary for the fate of poor "Cathy" Worsthorne. We are all guilty. Articles of clothing, Chippendale commodes etc. should be sent to the Peregrine-Come-Home Appeal, the *Sunday Telegraph*, Fleet Street, EC4.

Sunday 4th March

One of the few consolations of literary life nowadays is the knowledge that as soon as you die, Cyril Connolly will hail you as a best friend. Connolly's obituary of Elizabeth Bowen also clears up the great mystery of how last year's £5,000 Booker Prize for novels came to be awarded to something which was not a novel at all, but something far, far more exciting.

John Berger's *G*, which won the prize, was a serious attempt to explore new frontiers of experience by means of apparently unconnected epigrams and seemingly inane pronouncements on life, politics, sex, etc. It was a gallant attempt, and in the opinion of the few discerning people who were able to read it, the final result was suitably devoid of any intelligent meaning.

The judges were Elizabeth Bowen, hitherto considered a gifted and intelligent novelist; Connolly himself — probably the most fashionable Sunday book reviewer of the 1950s, who was once described by Alisdayre Clayre[1] as "the Greatest Living Englishman"; and Dr George Steiner, a pseud.

In announcing the winner, Connolly revealed that his own first choice had been an almost equally fatuous book by Aidan Higgins about expatriates in Southern Spain: "A large, untidy, self-indulgent book, but for one who also wears a Malaga tie — it rang a bell," said Connolly. But Dr Steiner convinced him that *G* was even more important. Both books, of course, represent the sort of rubbish that was considered smart in the 1950s, and might easily have rung a bell in Connolly's poor, 69-year-old brain. But how a gifted and intelligent lady like Miss Bowen was persuaded to concur — that was the mystery.

The gruesome truth now emerges in Connolly's obituary. By the time of the Booker award, he reveals, Miss Bowen "had already become seriously ill and had lost her voice almost completely". The poor lady was able to communicate only in whispers.

With a certain blandness, Connolly concludes that she suffered a "deep regret at not being well enough to provide greater moral support for the other judges".

Monday 5th March

In the present meat crisis, I have decided to throw the column open to anyone with original ideas for survival. Lord Gowrie[2], Grocer's ebony-skinned Junior Whip in the House of Lords, suggests removing goldfish from other people's drawing-rooms in a handkerchief. He says it is amazing how seldom they are missed, and hints that they have an aphrodisiac effect when well washed and baked in clay.

Caroline Wedgwood-Benn[3] has sent her husband digging for worms. She claims they taste much the same as old gym-shoe-laces if boiled for three hours.

Lady Magnesia Freelove[4] suggests a water-ice made from selected sweet papers, while Lady Kaldor and Balogh is delighting her Oxford guests with a goulash of used cigarette packets and old copies of *The Listener*.

If you adopt another fun-idea from Allan Hall, of Atticus, invite a poet to read during dinner; these things can also be used for pelting him with before the plates are cleared away.

Mrs Walter Annenberg has contrived a very dainty *fricassee* of nasturtium leaves, served in a sauce of brandy, cream, Grand Marnier, *foie gras truffe*, caviare and crushed nightingales' tongues; but Lady (Pamela) Fartwell, whose guest list has included such glittering names as Maurice Green, Kenneth Rose, Gordon Broeck-Shepherd and Brian Roberts[5], seems to have given up the struggle and is serving Kit-e-Kat *pur et simple.*

In Kensington, I hear the situation is so bad that many people in desperation have taken to eating their Filipino servants — - with appalling results in at least one case.

Tuesday 12th March

I hear that Marion Harewood[6] is to remarry — to someone called Jeremy Thorpe. He is a politician but not, apparently, one with any prospect of success. George Harewood is, of course, still alive, and the announcement prompted a furious argument between myself and my travelling companion about the sanctity of the marriage bond.

---

1. I have been unable to discover anything about this person and doubt whether he exists.

2. Cf. Note 5, 20 November 1972.

3. Born Caroline Middleton de Camp, of Cincinnatti, Ohio, she married the Labour politician in 1949. Noted for great wealth.

4. Lady Antonia Fraser, b. 27 August 1932, eldest daughter of Lord Longford (q.v.), a Society beauty.

5. All these people are Telegraph journalists.

6. Born Marion Stein, she married 7th Earl of Harewood in 1949.

For my part, I cannot see why these people bother to contract a marriage at all if they do not see it as something binding and indissoluble until death. Why don't they just live together? Thorpe can't imagine that his marriage to a divorced woman will do him much good with the non-Conformist Liberal voters of North Devon, and if anybody accused them of living in sin they could always deny it, sue for libel, and almost certainly win handsome damages.

Wednesday 13th March
I asked Lord Gnome if he would buy my ticket for a private dinner party to be given at Apothecaries' Hall on April 2nd by the friends of Sir John Betjeman, to honour his appointment as Poet Laureate. The tickets were £10 each, but I thought the *Eye* should be represented. Unfortunately, the mean old sod refused to pay, saying £10 was far too much.

So I spent the evening at a Tupperware Party given by the Charles Vasses[1] at their rather touching home in Mortimer Crescent, NW6. After drinking two cups of coffee, I bought a receptacle for babies' nappies. Vass asked me if I thought he was the sort of young man the Conservative Party was looking for at the present time. I said I didn't know.

Thursday 14th March
Delighted to see they have burnt down the British Council Library in Rawalpindi again — this time in protest against the shooting of two Pakistani youths in London. The last time they burnt down this particular library was in February 1970, in protest against an article I had written in *The Times*, telling a joke about Allah which I had heard in the Army. This burning remains the only public recognition my little jokes have ever received.

Wednesday 20th March
It is seldom one needs to use emotive words like "genocide" in political commentary, but I think that Tony Barber's Budget comes close to meriting such a charge where it deliberately reduces the price of sweets. Charitable left-wingers like the late Paul Foot[2] insist that Barber's only motive is loyalty to the family confectionery business in Doncaster, where Barber's Barley-Sugar Balls have long been a by-word for their sweetness and scarcely less famed for their long-suck possibilities. But I see something altogether more sinister behind it.

In Somerset, where I happen to be a Schools Health Visitor as well as a County Councillor and "lay" magistrate, it is noticeable that although incidence of obesity and dental collapse is increasing among all sections of the school population, it is disproportionately high — in fact almost total — among children of unskilled and lower paid workers. Very few children from this background leave secondary school without a complete set of dentures and a serious weight problem.

Mr Barber's measure means that such child-

1. Charles Douglas-Home (q.v.).

2. Radical journalist. Educ. Shrewsbury & University College, Oxford. Editor Socialist Worker. m. Rosanne Harvey. Had recently left Private Eye, to Waugh's great sorrow.

ren will be able to buy even more sweets for their money. This, of course, is what he intends — so that in a few years' time, when Paul Foot and other idealists call on the lower classes to arise and throw off their chains, their cry will fall on an otiose collection of flabby, apathetic human footballs without a tooth between them.

Thursday 21st March

The first time I was taken to tea with Ivy Compton Burnett must have been in 1945 or 1946 when I was about six. She had expressed a desire to meet me, but at that age I had a particular taste for jam tarts, and Miss Burnett neglected to serve them — whether from incompetence or deliberate malice I was never able to discover.

To make matters worse she placed me on a high chair like a two-year-old and proceeded to feed me by hand with scones dipped in milk, much to the amusement of Sir Max Beerbohm and Bernard Shaw.

Understandably annoyed by this, I bit her finger and proceeded to be violently sick all over the tablecloth and into the lap of H.G. Wells, to whom I had also taken a dislike.

Wells died soon after, and Miss Burnett never asked me to tea again, which I can't help thinking a pity, as I am sure we could have got along quite well and had some good fun together once she learned the simple rules of hospitality.

Friday 22nd March

All Englishmen will have been stirred by the Lord Chancellor's call to "sound once more the organ notes of patriotism". The only problem is what to do once our patriotism has been stirred and our organs sounded. We don't actually seem to be at war with anyone at present.

Lord Hailsham, as the Big Breadwinner Hogg now prefers to be known, suggests we could usefully employ it by showing deeper admiration for our politicians and giving them even greater power over our daily lives. To encourage us to trust him still further, the slippery old lunatic reveals that he has recently had a change of wind, whatever that may involve. Not even this, I fear, will convince reasonable citizens.

Once again, it is to the much loved 86-year-old Foreign Secretary that the nation turns in its moment of bewilderment. Unnoticed by most of us, Sir Baillie Vass has been conducting a little war of his own for some time now — against Iceland. The purpose of this war is to enforce what is apparently the legal right of British trawlermen to deprive Iceland of its codfish and therefore of its only source of livelihood.

Here at last is a call to arms. Recently the Baillie announced that his patience was nearly at an end. Hurrah — it may not be long before these frigid midgets get a taste of the British deterrent up their Arctic Passage. Personally, I think Vass would be well advised to go further and declare war on Sweden, with its moronic inhabitants and hideous, fish-like Prime Minister, Olaf Palm Sundae. But I suppose we ought to leave the timing of this to our wonderful politicians.

Saturday 23rd March
Last Sunday there was a mendacious article
by someone called Alan Brien in the *Sunday
Times*, implying that I had sent a telegram of
congratulation to Jonathan Guinness, chairman of the Monday Club, supporting his
immoral suggestion that prisoners should be
encouraged to commit suicide.

I do not suppose many people read it,
or believed it if they did, but thinking it my
duty to correct this sort of slipshod reporting,
I wrote a letter to the Editor, Dame Harold
Evans, pointing out that I had not sent the
telegram and naming the person who did.

Later, I received a terrified call from the
Sunday Times saying they could not possibly
publish the letter in its present form for fear
of a libel writ from Alan Brien — "he is so
sensitive". Could they not make some alter-
ations? Certainly not, I said.

Monday 25th March
Barbara Castle has come down to Taunton
and Tiverton, Devon, as part of her campaign
against Roy Jenkins. "I have always been a
left-wing rebel," announced this absurd lady
to the gaping rustics. "Mr Roy Jenkins should
say whether he was in favour of Mr Harold
Wilson and myself reaching an agreement
with the TUC and so withdrawing *In Place
Of Strife*[1]."

Not many people down here have much
time for Smoothiechops, it is true — but then
few of them have any very clear idea who
Mrs Castle is, or why she has to come down
here proclaiming these half-witted boring lies
about her own ignominious role in the Labour
Government to people who have not the
faintest idea of what she is talking about.

Tuesday 26th March
Mr Robin Day has a letter in *The Times* describing an incident at the Labour Party
Conference a few years ago when the then
Prime Minister, Mr Harold Wislon, had to send
a message from his suite at the Imperial Hotel,
Blackpool, to request that Day should stop
singing in the bar below, in view of the late
hour. Day quotes this murky tale as evidence
that he can sing.

As one who was present at the time, I must
testify that the noise Day made was in fact
something between that of a rat drowning,
a lavatory flushing and a hyena devouring its
after-birth in the Appalachian Mountains
under a full moon. It was this incident which
is now thought to have driven Wislon mad.

Wednesday 27th March
Today I am off to New Zealand where I hope
to start a new and more wholesome life as a
sheep farmer. Friends may reach me at PO
Box 132, Wankitanki, New Zealand 10045,
Southern Hemisphere[2].

Monday 1st April
So gang-bangs are legal, at any rate until our
lawyers can think of some way to make them
illegal: conspiracy to commit indecent
exposure, perhaps. Many people will be
tempted to take advantage of the present
state of the law, but I have never been able
to understand the particular advantages and
pleasures of a gang-bang, especially from the
male point of view. Some women may find
it satisfactory, I suppose.

The six Hell's Angels acquitted of raping
a WRAC girl look very pleased with themselves, announcing that the Court's verdict
and attendant publicity will do wonders for
their organisation. Well, we shall see which
has the greater rise in recruitment figures —
Hell's Angels or the Women's Royal Army
Corps.

Wednesday 3rd April
Writing obituaries and such like is a ticklish
business as I know to my cost, but I don't
see how anyone could improve on this
memoir of Sir William (Bill) Ramsay, the
elder statesman of English rugby football
and one-time fellow member of the East
India and Sports Club. Consequently I will
not try, but give it in full as it appeared in
The Times under the heading: "A Friend
Writes:-"

"You could always get a straight answer
out of Bill Ramsay, for he never passed the
buck. He would look you square in the eye,
and usually answer without the book, for his
administrative experience covered almost
every aspect of Rugby football. He also had
the capacity of listening to contrary opinions,
and if necessary agreeing to differ, without
rancour, which it takes a big man to do on
important subjects. Being reared on Old Boy
football, he was an amateur to his marrow
bones, and regarded amateurism as an attitude
of mind, although another part of his mind
shrewdly nursed the purely business side of
the RFU, as hon treasurer for 20 years, to
a state of great prosperity. It needs unusual
flair to make a front row forward understand
a balance sheet, but Bill could do it.

1. In Place Of Strife, Labour Government White Paper (1969) proposing exactly the same remedies as the
   Tory Industrial Relations Bill (1971). Wilson withdrew it when faced with the certainty of defeat at the
   hands of his own party.

2. It is not certain that Waugh ever left.

"He was a kindly, generous elder statesman, as many youngsters discovered, a genial companion who believed that the game should be played for pleasure and for the lifelong friendships that it created both on and off the field. If ever anybody put back into the game, with interest, what he had taken out of it, that man was Bill Ramsay, for he loved it genuinely, and will be missed wherever it is played."

How many of the present generation of young people will have earned a tribute of this sort when their time comes?

Thursday 4th April

My attention has been drawn, as they say, to a most extraordinary series appearing in the *Observer* Colour Section[1]. This is the naughty knickers magazine with which David Astor tries to prop up the ailing circulation of his weekly political comic, the pompous and absurd *Observer* newspaper. The series purports to be the intimate diaries of a celebrated English novelist, but in fact seems to be little more than a collection of reckless allegations about drunkenness, drug addiction, sodomy, flagellation and other unnatural sexual practices among some of the most respected people in the land.

Obviously, Astor must try to sell his newspaper somehow, but I am amazed that he should think there is such widespread popular interest in unnatural sex. When his own half brother, the late Bobbie Shaw, was imprisoned for sexual deviations, the *Observer* did not feel the matter was worth mentioning, nor did any other English newspaper.

Soon, no doubt, he will be offering large sums of money to reproduce my own Diary, especially where I describe my experiences in Treblinka extermination camp during the war. Unfortunately, I will have to refuse, as I fear nobody would believe my account if they read it in the *Observer*.

What worries me most is the effect all this will have on impressionable young people. I never allow the *Observer* Colour Magazine into the house myself, for fear it should fall into the hands of the children or servants. But anybody might find himself affected by this sort of thing. Can Astor honestly say that his conscience is clear?

Friday 5th April

More rain. "Lunchie" O'Brien[2] wanted to go whoring, but I decided to stay at home and sodomise with Charlie V***[3]. Afterwards, we prayed together in front of the shrine to St Philibert in my bedroom. A most enjoyable day. I think I may be going to become a monk[4].

---

1. Astor was serialising the Diaries of Evelyn Waugh.

2. A notorious sodomite of the time was protected by the pseudonym 'Hot Lunch' in Evelyn Waugh's diaries. 'Lunchtime' O'Brien would probably be Alan Brien (q.v.).

3. Charles V*** is inscrutable.

4. This appears to be another unfulfilled ambition.

Sunday 7th April

Kenneth Allsopp[1]'s memoirs, now appearing in the *Sunday Times* under the titillating heading of 'Look!' reveal how easy it is at 53 to make the transition from teenage freshness to piteous senility without any intermediate stage. Long hailed as the oldest teenager in show business, he now tries to recall an occasion, thirteen years ago, when he was once allowed into my house as a "Grub Street lackey. . . to record (Waugh's) reflections upon literature for the instruction of the common people".

To the eternal shame of my house, this is quite true. Allsopp describes himself as being given Stilton and claret, whereas in fact he was given Farmhouse Cheddar and burgundy, but one never supposed he would be able to tell the difference. The strongest impression he left behind was of an unpleasant habit of clearing his throat in conversation, but this was attributed to nervousness.

"Old men forget: But he'll remember with advantages what feats he did that day". Allsopp rounds off his story with an account of how he returned to dinner that evening; drove my poor mother and an unnamed brother out of the dining-room — whether with his boring conversation or unpleasant throat-clearing habit is not revealed — and then proceeded to bore my poor father quite literally into a stupor:

"I realised that Waugh had fallen silent. He had slumped down in the chair, chin on scrumpled shirt. . . I turned and uncertainly prodded the sleeping form, now looking frail and vulnerable, but he didn't stir. Feeling treacherous, I trod softly across the hall and down the steps and drove away through the night. . . "

The only interesting thing about Allsopp's extraordinary behaviour on this occasion is that as far as I am able to discover it is a complete fabrication. Allsopp wrote a tolerably accurate account of his visit in the *Daily Mail* thirteen years ago. If Dame Harold Evans must look for scoops among 13-year-old *Daily Mail* clippings, he should at least bother to check the file rather than rely on the memory of gaga old men on the staff.

Monday 8th April

No need to think of any jokes on the day Picasso's death is announced. That genial old rogue spent the best part of 91 years taunting the pseuds who have now taken over art criticism more or less completely. Today he has what may prove his last great field day, while the intelligent and civilised world rolls around in appreciation of his joke.

Here is a small selection of finalists, with the judges' verdict:

Henry Moore, the sculptor: "Picasso was

1. Kenneth Allsop (1920-1974), a journalist, noted for interest in wild life.

probably one of the most naturally gifted artists since Raphael."

Judges' verdict: Very high marks. Note particularly the use of "probably", "one of", and choice of "Raphael" to give judicious scholarly tone to this facetious pronouncement.

Dame Barbara Hepworth, the sculptress: "We think of it as a light going out, but taken as a matter of light years, it's not, it's an eternal light."

Judges' verdict: Confused. Try again.

M. Maurice Drouon, French Minister of Culture: "He will have filled his century with his colours, his forms, his searchings, his audacity and his vital personality."

Judges' verdict: Very good indeed. Second prize.

First prize goes to Sir Roland Penrose[1], who said he was too upset to comment. This means, when interpreted, that if you give him £50 and three days to write it he will churn out some standard drivel about "an underlying continuity that runs through Picasso's work and gives it finally, in spite of its vast dimensions, a monolithic structure" — otherwise, **** off.

Tuesday 16th April

The Greater London Census Report, published today, throws shocking light on the housing scandal. It reveals that there are 100,000 empty homes, as well as 53,000 households with no one present.

Exactly how to distinguish between an empty home and a household with no one present will probably remain one of the mysteries of government. Of course, one can quite understand why people don't wish to live in London. Apart from the expense and the dirt, it is now full of unpleasant, hysterical people, with their Filipino servants and silly, affected ideas.

But if there are really 153,000 empty houses already, it seems mad of Grocer to go distributing free contraceptives among those who remain. Soon London will be completely empty and there will be nobody left to sell one an evening paper or take one's coat on one's occasional visits to the capital.

Wednesday 17th April

My friends in Conservative Central Office are seriously worried at the Harris Poll finding that women are withholding their traditional support from the Conservative Party because Grocer lacks sex appeal. At a hastily summoned conference in Smith Square on the eve of the local elections, I was asked to give my advice to the meeting of Party chiefs, leaders of industry and PR advisers.

My opinion was that we should forget about women and concentrate on the 15% of male homosexuals in this country. If all male homosexuals voted one way, they could swing any general election. A Party Political Broadcast which showed Grocer and some of his younger MPs in blue nylon swimwear playing with a beach ball to the accompaniment of abandoned laughter might do the trick.

Thursday 18th April

New Statesman parties only come once every ten years, but it was nice to see so many old people still game for a bit of fun.

Stationer's Hall looked quite like the old days of the Evelyn Waugh Diaries, with old codgers ogling each other and thinking wistfully about Uganda. Veteran bore Kenneth Tynan[2], 72, was heard to remark: "I was at the 50th anniversary party. That was really left wing," with a dirty gleam in his hideous, yellowing eyes.

All these people should read Barbara Cartland in the *TV Times*, where she says: "My recipe against sexual fatigue is to take honey in large quantities, two Gev-E-Tabs, ten vitamin E pills, four wheat-germ oil tablets, four vitamin A pills, four bonemeal tablets, six Liverplus tablets, two dessert spoonfuls of Bio-Strath Elixir twice a day."

If only the nation's ageing lefties would follow this sensible advice, the next *New Statesman* party, celebrating the paper's 70th anniversary in ten years time, should be quite a lively affair.

Sunday 21st April

Sometimes I worry about our children. They sit watching odious, patronising rubbish like *Blue Peter* week after week, and when a chance comes to get their own back they do nothing about it.

The *Blue Peter* Old Folks Appeal for treasures from the attic was a golden opportunity for the nation's kiddies to show their satirical mettle. My own attics are a treasury of rotting mattresses, fossilised dog shit, old sets of false teeth, dead bats, broken light bulbs and old plastic potties.

If only I had heard of the Appeal in time,

1. Sir Roland Penrose, b. 14 October 1900. A pseud.
2. K. Tynan, a journalist, b. 2 April 1927, noted for voracious sexual appetite.

it would have been the work of a moment to send the entire contents round to *Blue Peter*. If enough people had done the same we might have put a stop to this sentimental filth which is perverting the moral awareness of an entire generation.

Monday 22nd April
Mr Cord Meyer, the CIA's gifted and agreeable new station chief in London, should take a long hard look at these repeated attempts by Iron Curtain countries to secure Harold Wislon's re-election. The Czech's recent stunt with a Methodist minister is only the latest in a series which includes Wilson's Soviet invitation to visit Russia as Prime Minister after the last election.

I am not, of course, suggesting that Wislon may be a Russian agent[1], which would be completely absurd, or that there could be any connection between these events and his close relations with various Russian leaders after Mr Wilson's numerous visits to Moscow as "economic consultant" to Montague Meyer (no relation), the timber merchant.

There are Labour men who say that Wislon is "best forgotten", or that "whatever happened in 1964-1970 is now past and over" The point is not that Wislon sent his troops into Anguilla, or even that for 2½ years he helped to starve millions of civilians to death in Nigeria so that the military dictator there could have a tribal reapportionment of land.

The point is not that Anguilla has now been reabsorbed into the British Empire, or even that the two million Biafrans whom Wislon helped to starve are still dead.

The point is that Wislon is only waiting in the wings to do it all again. Still surrounded by sycophants and placemen, still convinced he was right in everything he ever did, he is almost certain to be the next Prime Minister[2]. It is high time the CIA took an interest in this curious man, if only to counter the efforts being made on his behalf from the other side of the Iron Curtain.

Tuesday 23rd April
Dinner at Downing Street for Australia's exciting new Prime Minister, Gough "breast-stroker" Whitlam and his interesting wife, Margaret[3]. A bevy of choirboys had been invited to the Grocery for this occasion — or perhaps they live there — but we were not allowed to chat them up after the meal.

I asked Mrs Whitlam if it was true that

ladies in Australia, called "Sheilahs", could really bang like shithouse doors in a gale. How do they do it? If she heard such a door banging in the night, for instance, how would she know whether her husband had merely gone to choke a darkie, or whether he might not be dipping the old wick and rooting like a rattlesnake with some other Sheilah in a far corner of the official residence?

She replied that she always watched her man closely. Three minutes are allowed for pointing Percy, eight minutes for straining the potatoes. "After that," she said, "I start rattling my boomerangs."

This is a very sensible attitude, I feel. It is never a good idea for men in public life to spend too long on the lavatory. This was always A.J. Balfour's great problem and one which he never really overcame[4].

---

1. This is confusing. At a later stage, Waugh claims that he has never disguised his belief that Harold Wilson was a Russian agent.
2. Wilson was re-elected in February 1974.
3. Mrs Whitlam had revealed that her husband always swam breast-stroke.
4. This suggestion appears to be completely baseless.

Wednesday 1st May
A telephone call today from Pauline Peters
of the *Sunday Times,* asking if she could
interview me for a profile in the Colour Mag.
Someone obviously wants a knocking job
done, which might be quite fun. But then
I think of Mr Eldon Griffiths' sensible speech
at Margate over the weekend on the subject
of knockers:

"There is too great a readiness to knock
and snipe and smear," he said, "particularly
among opinion formers in the communications industry."

Of course, I knew nothing about this
Pauline Peters, but I didn't particularly like
the sound of her voice which seemed a little
highly strung for my taste, so I decided to
take Eldon's advice. If only they had sent
around the delightful Susan Barnes —
preferably without her deplorable husband,
the boorish and conceited Anthony Crosland.
It would be a real privilege and pleasure to be
knocked by her.

Thursday 2nd May
There was an unusually festive atmosphere at
the Tupperware evening which the Charles
Vasses now hold every week in their really
very sweet little home in Mortimer Crescent,
NW6. We all got two spoonfuls of sugar in our
coffee without asking!

It seems that Charlie has got his promotion
in *The Times*! In a long encyclical to the staff,
the great Sir William Rees-Mogg explains that
Charlie will be in charge of home news, at any
rate by day. In the evening, Mr Hamlyn will
put it all together, and by day there is Mr
Grant, an older and more experienced man,
to look after the practical side and see that
nothing goes wrong.

We all crowded round to congratulate him.
Some of us were nearly in tears, but he just
gave a modest grin. He's such an attractive
little chap, one honestly feels that promotion
could not have come to a more deserving
person or one who has tried harder.

He may be young, but at least people in
The Times can feel that they are being led by
someone whose birth and Eton education
have helped him understand about leadership. All too many jumped-up grammar
school types are being put in charge nowadays, and quite frankly it only causes bad
blood. It was a great pity when the Tory
Party turned its back on his uncle, the
wonderful Baillie. Now we have a chance to
make amends.

Tuesday 7th May
Not enough attention in the Lonrho crisis
has been paid to the role of the Wankel
engine. This ingenious and pleasing device
is almost certainly the brainchild of the
Downing Street think-tank headed by Lord
Rothschild[1], Grocer's foul-mannered but
rich adviser on birth control and Rolls
Royces.

When Mr Teeny-Weeny "Rollsy" Row-
land (né Fuhrop) bought Wankel, his first
thought was of a possible use for it.
What could be more delightful than to have
such a machine installed in the back of every
Rolls Royce motor car? British businessmen
could avail themselves of it between important business engagements and amaze their
friends by arriving fresh and relaxed.

By a happy coincidence, Rolls Royce was
being offered for sale at that moment by
Lord Rothschild's unattractive but hard
working son, Jakob. Under normal circumstances, it would have been the work of a
moment for Teeny-Weeny to snap up Rolls
Royce for £38 million, but the Lonrho board
was otherwise occupied — reading each
others' letters, circulating the juicier bits to
African heads of state, expressing doubt
about each other's mental stability and
arranging for vast golden handshakes in the
sun-kissed islands of the Caribbean.

Wednesday 8th May
A very dull "working dinner party" for
Henry Kissinger at the Grocery — just myself,
Denis Greenhill, Burke Trend, Rennie[2],
Grocer and a handful of lesser mandarins.
No choirboys were offered for our entertain-
ment, and Grocer, much too delicate to ask
about Watergate, was pretending to be
interested in this ridiculous "detente" with
Russia.

Hoping to liven things up, I asked why
Baillie Vass had not been invited — he is
supposed to be Foreign Secretary, after all.

There was an embarrassed silence and then
everybody spoke at once. Greenhill said the
Secretary of State had to go to dinner with
some boring Spaniards who were visiting
London; Trend said he thought the Foreign
Office was tied down by its Cod War; Grocer
said Baillie wasn't really interested in this
sort of thing; and Kissinger said he often had
difficulty in making Vass understand what
was said.

Carrington came in after dinner, but said

1. Lord Rothschild, b. 31 October 1910, an expert on spermatazoa. When he was appointed Head of
   Mr Heath's Central Policy Review Staff, or Think-Tank, it became known as the Wank Tank. This
   family connection with the Wankel engine was spotted only by Waugh.

2. Greenhill, Trend and Rennie were Civil Servants — permanent head of the Foreign Office, Cabinet
   Office and Intelligence Services respectively. Rennie later resigned when his son was convicted for
   trafficking in Chinese heroin.

nothing of interest that I can remember.
I told him that two nights earlier I had dined
with the Vasses in Carlton Gardens for some
Dago whose name I never caught. When I asked Vass why he didn't retire at 89 (the Baillie
will be 90 on July 2nd), the old fool replied
that there was "nobody in the government of
sufficient calibre" to take his place. Grocer
looked thoughtful at this.

Thursday 16th May
Three candidates now emerge for the Oxford
Professorship of Poetry:

Stephen Spender, 64, who has the surprise
backing of wrinkled American bachelor
W.H. Auden, 66. It is thought that Mr Christopher Isherwood, 68, might also support
this candidate if he were available for
comment and had a vote.

John Wain, 48, who although a third rate
poet (and fourth rate novelist) hopes to
attract support from workers and progressive
intellectuals in their late 40s who have reached a position of rejecting neo-fascism, etc. etc.

Mr George Pringle McAllister, 56, who has
no support at all from anyone and has been
the victim of concerted abuse from all sides
on grounds of his humble origins and lack of
academic qualifications. It is true that he has
never been a lecturer in English at the
University of Reading like the abysmal John
Wain, or Professor of English at University
College, London, like the miserable Sock
Suspenders. But Pringle is the only one to
have written any worthwhile poetry.

Here are some lines on a visit to Scotland
by Prince Charles.

Bonny Prince Charlie Returns

Sad today the Scottish Highlands
Sad, indeed, myself, am I;
Sadder still the Western Islands
And most of all the Isle of Skye.
"Will ye no come back?" they chanted
For years they waited, still undaunted
And now he's back — as Prince of Wales!
Yet, let us not forget our manners
A Scottish welcome never fails.
So let us all, with Pipes and Banners
Say — "Welcome Charlie, Prince of Wales!"

I hope every Oxford M.A. who values
purity, integrity and benevolence will vote for
George McAllister against the clapped-out
charlatans and pseuds who are ranged against
him[1].

Friday 17th May
Today I received my first Value Added Tax
Return, asking questions about my input and
output such as I would not normally reveal
even to my doctor, except in extreme
emergency.

However, the Customs and Excise Inspector
in Taunton is very soothing and agreeable.
After half an hour I think I understand what
must be done.

By way of assessing total input, I ask the
price of a leg of lamb which my dear wife has
served for dinner. Two pounds and twenty-
seven New Pee!

Who will free me from this turbulent
Grocer!

1. Wain was elected

Saturday 18th May

"The rest of the world needs to have a strong and effective President of the United States to deal with," I read in my newspaper. Who does Rees-Mogg think he is speaking for? Most of us don't even meet the wretched President more than once every three years or so on our rare visits to Washington.

For my own part, I would prefer to deal with a weak and giggly President — the sort of man who isn't too much involved in it all, who intervenes only to rattle his hydrogen bombs at the Russians once in a while when he is drunk or to hang some State Governor or other politician who grows too obviously corrupt and conceited.

Sunday 19th May

Sandy Gordon Lennox, Grocer's mad Serjeant-at-Arms[1] in the House of Commons has struck again, refusing to give a Member of Parliament details of the Parliamentary Press Lobby on the grounds that this list of drunks, hacks and wobbling jellyfish is "too confidential".

Mr George Cunningham, Labour MP for Islington North, should have applied to me. I have a list which gives not only their names but also details of their ridiculous wives, sexual failures and disappointments, business interests, regrettable personal habits and price for various services. All of this is freely available to bona fide seekers after truth.

Tuesday 21st May

I fear I may have done poor Mr Heath an injustice. When I saw the photographs of him and President Pompidou with sycophantic captions describing the horrible thing which appears to have happened to his face as a "splendid nautical suntan", I wrote a curt note saying I could not possibly accept any further invitations to Downing Street until he had had it removed.

People will accuse me of lacking compassion. I know that Grocer has his emotional problems, and that he lost his Mummy when he was still at the tender age of 35. Nevertheless, this so-called "suntan" seemed to represent the unpleasant and unacceptable face of modern Toryism. I also had my own reputation to consider, if anybody saw me with him in that state.

Now it appears almost certain that the disfigurement was not a "suntan" at all. It was the deep blush of a man who has just read all the wild rumours about his government colleagues sent in a despatch box from London by Robert Carr, our boring and dirty-minded Home Secretary[2].

Wednesday 22nd May

Poor Tony[3]. He has never treated me with anything except the greatest kindness and generosity, and I think it reasonable to accede to his request that criticism should be instantaneous and not prolonged. So here goes.

Our sympathy for this unhappy man would be much greater if only he had not decided to become a politician. It is quite right that politicians should be hounded, reviled and photographed in embarrassing positions, because their only reason for wanting to be politicians is to exert power and boss other people around. When politicians start hounding each other, it is even funnier and righter.

If Lambton had not gone round viciously and bossily confiscating his children's dope, the wretched Carr would have found nothing to pin on him when the bully boys came round. Serve Lambton bloody well right, some will say.

But the real moral of this sordid tale concerns all parents, who must never relax their vigilance. As soon as a child shows any sign of wishing to organise his fellows, or any other symptom of this distressing illness called political ambition or "leadership", the child must be isolated and sent to a special institution where he will spend his days contemplating nature, miming farm animals, eating brown rice and other constructive activities.

Thursday 30th May

So Switzerland has voted to end its ancient ban on Jesuits and there is now no church in Europe where one can be certain of not meeting Father Tom Corbishley SJ[4], the dreaded Farm Street thinker. Refugees from Corbishley in this country have tried joining the Anabaptists, the Plymouth Brethren, even the Church of England, only to be met by his plummy, progressive tones wherever they go.

Jesuits have already infiltrated most levels of London society from their new headquarters in Cavendish Square. Every evening a contingent of the Pope's shock troops — often quite personable young men, and always in plain clothes — is sent out to the cocktail parties and the *thé dansants* of the capital. They are under strict orders to return

1. Rear Admiral Sir Alexander Gordon Lennox, KCVO, CB, DSO, b. 9 April 1911. This distinguished officer had been appointed Serjeant at Arms by Mr Macmillan in 1962 and was noted for hiccuping in the Chamber — the result of an ailment. He refused Waugh accreditation to the Palace of Westminster as Political Correspondent of Private Eye, despite individual pleas from over 50 MPs.

2. This passage refers (as does the next one) to the Lambton Scandal, q.v.

3. Lord Lambton had resigned after photographs of him with various prostitutes had fallen into the hands of a London newspaper.

4. Corbishley, a former Superior of Farm Street and distinguished oecumenical theologian, was b. 30th May 1903. Noted for soft, damp handshake. He died in 1976.

by midnight, causing many broken hearts and much sexual confusion.

One dreads to think what effect the new developments will have on Switzerland's tourist trade. Traditionally, English holiday-makers have left their modesty behind them as they danced in their *Après Ski* outfits in the arms of their ski instructors. Their reckless abandon stemmed from the certainty that there were no Jesuits watching them.

Friday 1st June

The Schools' Council is attempting to end the pass/fail concept in GCE 'O' level exams. This is long overdue. Exams can only be tolerated at all if everyone passes them. Present proposals to replace the concept of "pass" and "fail" with a system of "assessment" will only be acceptable if everybody is assessed equally and at a very high level, or we shall be back again to the outdated notion of second class citizens.

But why should this sensible proposal be restricted to school examinations? One of the least admirable features of our present system of government is that general elections require somebody to lose them. Many people believe that Mr Heath's most extreme emotional problems date from the time when he "lost" the 1966 general election and thought himself relegated to second class status as a result.

1. A further reference to the Lambton scandal.
2. Another Conservative politician.

In future elections, both parties must be declared to have won, and all candidates elected. Those who see themselves as Prime Minister can then proceed to strike the appropriate attitudes, issue statements about their Ministers' sex lives[1] and make far-reaching decisions. Sycophantic political reporters will continue to print exactly what anyone tells them, without fear or favour.

Those who like to think of themselves as Cabinet Ministers can then accept silver coffeepots, enjoy casual affairs with call girls, announce increases in old age pensions, order invasions of Anguilla, plot against the Prime Minister or whatever their fancy suggests.

Saturday 2nd June

In Somerset, people have been taking the moral collapse of the capital quite calmly. None of my country neighbours is implicated in the present round of scandals and at least one — Mr Rees-Mogg — seems to be setting an example of calmness and moderation.

I was particularly pleased to discover that my local MP, Mr Edward du Cann, is quite untouched by this scandal at least; and even the fashionable North Somerset novelist Mr Anthony Powell seems to have kept his nose clean.

Some anxiety was felt for that old Taunton schoolboy Mr Geoffrey Rippon[2], exposed to so many of the cruel temptations of office, and we accepted Grocer's assurance that no further ministerial names will be involved with great relief.

There is even greater relief that Grocer has climbed down from his initial promise to avoid whitewash or protection of his colleagues. It began to look as if we would be left without anybody to govern us.

As it is, the principal of aristocratic government has taken a hard knock, and we can be grateful that Jellicoe[1] leaves at least one young nobleman behind on the Front Bench of the House of Lords to carry the torch of decency and clean living — perhaps his most inspired appointment, the likeable and idealistic Earl of Gowrie, 33.

Tuesday 5th June
Will nobody speak up for my old friend Rupert Murdoch? Only three newspapermen seem to have come badly out of the Lambton-Jellicoe circus so far. The first two are Lord Hartwell and Brian Roberts, proprietor and editor of the *Sunday Telegraph*.

These infamous men chose to humiliate their most distinguished contributor and assistant editor Sir Peregrine Worsthorne publicly for daring even to say "Fuck" — nobody suggests he actually *did* anything.

The third journalist to bring discredit on his profession is someone called Mike Randall, a "senior managing editor" of the *Sunday Times* (why can't Lord Thomson give his understrappers proper Christian names like Michael or Peregrine?). Randall writes a hysterical and ridiculous letter to *The Times* accusing everyone except himself of hypocrisy: "Does *The Times* really believe that every Minister who visits a prostitute must resign if found out?"

Yes, certainly. My personal view is that Ministers should resign if there are reasonable grounds for believing that they have gone to the lavatory. This is a most disgusting habit, quite out of keeping with the sort of behaviour the British public has a right to expect.

This system would allow for a much faster turnover of Ministers. Some might burst with the effort of staying in office a little longer, but this fate would be entirely self-inflicted, and presents an ethical way of removing a very tedious section of the community from our midst.

Wednesday 6th June
Meanwhile I continue my private search for the Third and Fourth men in the case. Grocer has assured us that they are innocent of the slightest impropriety, which makes it all the odder that their identity is being kept secret. One would have thought that any government nowadays would be proud to have such blameless people in it and use them on posters and television advertisements as an example to us all.

I tried contacting all the innocent Third and Fourth men of my acquaintance — all to no avail. It would be a real privilege to shake the hand of the one Government Minister who has never done a dirty or disreputable thing in his life.

Thursday 14th June
Today I had intended to go to the village hall and vote Conservative in the district council elections. This was not only to keep the lower orders in their place and to show support for Grocer's handling of the Lambton affair. It was also because the Conservative candidate for Combe Florey, Lydeard St Lawrence and the villages around is a pleasantly hopeless-looking individual who describes himself as an author.

Although I can't claim to be a close student of the published work of Mr Mervyn Sealy, it seems to me that we should all do our best to give authors an opportunity for making money while the present iniquitous library system robs them of any livelihood from their books. I would do the same for Stephen Spender.

Alas, I could not help seeing the Conservative Party Political Broadcast last night. It brought home the full moral obliquity of voting for Grocer's Britain: motorway boxes, supersonic aeroplanes; vast new airports; more money for all the most stupid, hideous and dull people in the country to spend on their unappetising pleasures — nothing was spared. Central Office had even found something called "Clive Landa", a sort of futuristic human being even more horrible to behold than Peter Walker[2] who was put beside him.

After this gruesome experience I needed considerable refreshment before I could stagger down to register my traditional spoiled vote.

---

1. 2nd Earl of Jellicoe, b. 4th April 1918, a Senior Cabinet Minister who resigned with Lambton when revealed to have been consorting with prostitutes. Father of Rothschild's Wank Tank (q.v.), Patron of Lord Gowrie (q.v.), noted for loud laugh and fun-loving propensities.

2. Conservative politician, noted for having dangerously sick son, Jonathan.

Friday 15th June

As one was going to have to see a lot of young Mark Phillips[1] in the years ahead, I thought I might as well make myself known. So I asked myself down to tea at the Phillips's home in Wiltshire, pointing out that Mark and I were fellow descendants of Edward the Confessor. I also hinted that I might be a big buyer of Walls Ice Cream and all the other disgusting rubbish which "Major" Phillips, the father, apparently has to sell nowadays to make ends meet.

The meal may not have been quite up to the standard of the best. My girl, Mirabel Cecil, said she would have been happier if the pork pies had been served unwrapped, and thought the sausages could have been a trifle more *engagés*. She also noticed that the wooden spoon was missing from the Walls Family Pack, but tea was plentiful and service was prompt.

Anne had just returned from Germany. She did not seem to understand my little joke about Berlin Walls Ice Cream — or indeed anything else I said.

It is harder to be sure about her *fiancé*. I thought I detected a slight look of our mutual ancestor Harthacnut in the way he answered my inquiry about sugar in his tea:

"I suppose it was after Badminton, really."

Mark is apparently under orders from the highest level to say nothing except "I suppose it was after Badminton, really" until they are married. This must add enormously to the strain on an engaged couple. Badminton is a well known game involving shuttlecocks, but I don't see what it can have to do with the Royal Romance. Most people prefer to take a bath after Badminton.

After tea, "Major" Phillips tried to interest me in a consignment of 200 gross choc ices. They were only slightly sub-standard — a few had been found to contain fish heads and other picturesque additions — but he was prepared to let me have them at a very favourable price, having taken such a liking to me. I made my excuses and left.

Saturday 16th June

I forgot to mention yesterday that the famous engagement ring which Princess Anne flaunts bears a striking resemblance to a ring which was stolen from one of my sisters in Blackheath three years ago.

Luckily, the police have full details of the theft on their files, and are no doubt proceeding with their inquiries. I hope we don't have yet another scandal on our hands. Meanwhile, it might be a good idea if Her Royal Highness kept it out of sight for a while.

1. After many denials, the engagement between HRH Princess Anne and Lieutenant Mark Phillips had been announced.

Monday 2nd July

I was sorry to see none of my colleagues of the Press at Sir Alec Douglas-Home's birthday party in Downing Street, although several of them were looking quite decorative on the pavement outside. Grocer was in sparkling form, and we all had a good laugh about food prices in the supermarkets. Butter at twenty-six new pee a pound! I had to hold on to the Archbishop of Canterbury to stop myself falling under the table.

I sat next to Lady Greenhill, who told me a very sad story about her husband Sir Denis, the Permanent Undersecretary in the Foreign Office. Apparently Denis's recent trip to Rhodesia was kept secret because it was meant to be a surprise for Vass's birthday. The Baillie has always said he will never resign until he has arranged a sellout in Rhodesia.

The idea was that after Vass had blown out the last of his 90 candles and was about to be wheeled off to bed, Denis would rush in announcing the sellout with cries of "Peace in our Time!" Baillie would then quietly expire while everyone sang the Eton Boating Song, Eskimo Nell and other topical ditties of a sentimental nature.

The plan came to nothing after a leak to the press from Miles Hudson[1], the Baillie's trusted servant and greatest admirer. So the grand old Baillie is with us yet, lest we forget, lest we forget.

Tuesday 3rd July

Michael Stewart, the elderly and increasingly convivial former Foreign Secretary in the Labour Government, writes movingly about his friend General Gowon, the military dictator of Nigeria, on his visit to London:

"Meanwhile, what, we may wonder, is General Gowon thinking about us? Let us hope his generosity will lead him to notice the nobler features of our imperfect society."

He must have missed, of course, the public executions, the mass political imprisonments, the riots and massacres and ingenious bartering system of public office which make Nigeria such a model for all western democracies. But one of our noblest features is surely the House of Lords, where people of all colours discuss things like free contraception in an informed and expert manner.

Had he attended the House of Lords, Gowon might have heard Grocer's colourful, idealistic Junior Whip, Lord Gowrie —

probably a distant kinsman — discuss the creative urges he gets from pursuing wealth; Lady Summerskill accuse Lord Longford of never having had a baby; he might have thrilled to see Lord Hailsham, Grocer's amazing Lord Chancellor, wriggling mad as a snake on the Woolsack. Let's be thankful we have something left to show visiting black dictators.

Wednesday 11th July

Sometimes I curse my strict Christian upbringing which prevents me from suing fellow hacks for libel. In this month's *Harper's Queen* there is a revolting article by someone called Len Berger-Jones about literary parties. In it, he claims that Auberon Waugh, a "failed novelist", is frequently to be seen at these gatherings which are "not fit for decent people", being noted for lechery and drunkenness. "An owlish figure", this Waugh is easily recognisable by having "straw and animal substances adhering to his tweeds".

In fact, I have only been to one literary party in the last six years — in a dark suit, without straw or animal substances. No impropriety occurred. In the hands of my old friend Geoffrey Hirst QC[2] or eager young Tom Bingham, this vicious libel would certainly be worth a couple of thousand pounds.

The magazine's proprietor is a sanctimonious and dirty-minded clergyman called the Rev. Marcus Morris. His main line of business is in male pin-ups and such like for *Cosmopolitan*. Perhaps Morris won't pay for better reporters than the abject Berger-Jones, who thinks that Andrew Sinclair is "one of the best novelists in the world". In the long run, however, he might save himself a lot of money.

A good example of fair reporting is given by the meticulous C.P. Snow, Lord Snow of Leicester. Writing in the *Financial Times* on some boring subject, his Lordship reveals: "I have been struck by the sensible remarks Mr Auberon Waugh has written on these subjects in the past three or four years"

Only eleven years ago, C.P. Snurd (as he then was) instituted libel proceedings against me on the *Catholic Herald* for some trifling inaccuracy in a profile. Cynics will conjecture that he has a novel coming out soon, but I prefer to believe that he has seen the light. I commend this man to the snivelling vicar.

---

1. A Central Office functionary.

2. Perhaps Waugh is referring to his old friend David Hirst QC, a noted libel barrister. Geoffrey Hirst, a retired businessman, lives in Switzerland, and would be unlikely to help him.

Thursday 12th July

The great Antony Burgess, who really is one of the better novelists in the world, has come in for heavy criticism in court where a 16-year-old pipe lagger is accused of murder under the influence of Burgess's delightful and instructive novel, *A Clockwork Orange*.

The press has joined in gleefully, and one wonders how many other foolish young men will be tempted to their own do-it-yourself clockwork oranges after reading about it in the newspapers.

The long term answer is surely not to ban intelligent novels, or even cretinous newspapers from reporting these unsavoury things. It is to stop teaching these impressionable people how to read, since they're obviously not equipped to cope with so much emotional and intellectual stimulation.

Friday 13th July

Wild Ted Short, the maniac Deputy Leader of the Labour Party, raised some supercilious eyebrows with his forecast of an autumn Love Election, where the Tories will cash in on Princess Anne's wedding and plumb the depths of the nation's secret lusts. But all the indications are that he may have been right.

Considerable alarm has been caused in government circles by the report of an ancient Egyptian princess whose mummy when X-rayed now turns out to be that of a baboon. Sir Peter Rawlinson, the Attorney General, is considering legislation to make it a serious offence to X-ray members of the Royal Family.

But if the worst comes to the worst, it is agreed that Grocer himself will have to marry in the early autumn. Nobody would dare X-ray him in any case, and the only problem is to find a young woman for the sacrifice. Sir Michael Fraser, head of Conservative Central Office, tells me the Tory planners are considering the idea of an advertisement in the personal columns of *Private Eye*.

Friday 20th July *Languedoc, France*

The collapse of the pound in the world's money markets has had a most salutary effect on the behaviour of British holiday makers in Europe. Where once they sat peeling gloomily in the sun and complaining about the food, they have risen to the challenge with typical British phlegm. Never has the British genius for salesmanship been put to a sterner test.

In Toulouse, I was offered a grandmother from Solihull, guaranteed not more than fifty-eight years old, newly permed and blue-rinsed, skin only slightly foxed, for the price of two Tetley tea bags. While we were haggling over the second tea bag, she was snapped up by an Algerian for half a bottle of coca-cola and a pistachio ice cream.

In Marbella I heard of an entire Mothers' Union excursion from Burnley, Lancs., available for a packet of fish-fingers.

Once again, Britishers are showing the sort of spirit which enabled them to defeat the screaming, yellow hordes of the French army at Dunkirk — something which many foreigners would almost certainly prefer to forget.

Saturday 21st July
Urgent appeals reach me from Mr David Wood, sprightly 83-year-old political editor of *The Times*, to use my influence with Mr Wilson in a matter close to the heart of every freedom-loving citizen.

Few people, of course, attend Parliamentary debates, or they might have heard Wislon's deplorable announcement in the debate on MPs' bribes and outside interests:

"Is he aware of our proposals. . . in which we include not only a register of the interests of Members but also a register of the interests of Parliamentary journalists who report and influence our proceedings?"

If members of the Parliamentary lobby, which includes some of the oldest journalists in the country, have to declare all their quits, retainers, salaries, PR advisory consultantships, directorships and other enterprises, this will be the end of freedom as we know it. These time-honoured customs are as English as Roast Quintin Hogg[1] and one may doubt whether parliamentary democracy could survive the collapse of the lobby system.

"The proposal is nonsense, and I am afraid paranoic and malignant nonsense," writes David. How dare Mr Wilson upset my old friend in this way! What is his reason? Nobody can pretend that the Parliamentary lobby has been particularly active in investigating Poulson or any of the seamier aspects of British public life best left in decent obscurity.

Unless Wislon apologises immediately for the fright he has given these amiable, elderly gentlemen I shall release certain photographs which have come into my possession, taken long ago and apparently overseas.

Sunday 22nd July
"I am an old age pensioner aged 84 and live in a bed-sitter. I find my N.H. pension ample for lunch out every day, postages, newspapers, occasional bus fares and 50 pence for the Offertory on Sunday," writes a correspondent in the *Sunday Telegraph.*

With more careful stewardship, he could probably run a string of race horses, too. Congratulations to the *Sunday Telegraph* for finding this courageous man. So many old age pensioners are in fear of their lives if they mention how happy they are, or how embarrassed by the enormous sums of money the Government pours into their pockets.

Stupefied by food and drink, they can just stagger from their restaurants to church where they hope to secure forgiveness for their indolent, luxurious lives on earth by extravagant bribes to the clergy.

Monday 30th July
It is a pity the *Sunday Times* poll on which professions are considered most trustworthy, and which least trustworthy, did not include a placing on Roman Catholic priests. Probably they would have come out highest of all, strengthening Times Newspapers' case against the Portuguese Prime Minister, whose rating as a politician is extremely low. On the other hand, if the findings rated RC priests lower than might be hoped, the *Sunday Times* was quite right to suppress them[2].

Needless to say, journalists were thought least trustworthy by the greatest number, although to read the *Sunday Times* headline and report one might not have gathered as much. What is really alarming in these figures is that four per cent of the people still think Members of Parliament trustworthy.

Have all my efforts in this field been fruitless, or are these four per cent simply the insanely obstinate, the deaf and the dumb, whom one can only hope to reach through prayer?

Tuesday 31st July
The Pope has retired to Castelgandolfo and in the spiritual vacuum of the summer holidays one's thoughts automatically turn to Guru Maharaj Ji, the fifteen-year-old boy saint from India. A disciple explains his gross, epicene appearance and demented greed for money in these terms:

"When Jesus came people were expecting the saviour to come as a King. Now he is expected to come as a pauper, and he comes as a King. People never recognize the Saviour."

I always imagined the Saviour would come looking rather like my old friend Andrew Sinclair, who seems agreeably surprised when

---

1. Quintin Hogg, Baron Hailsham of St Marylebone, was Lord Chancellor. Noted for wriggling on the Woolsack. In fact, his mother was American.

2. This refers to an allegation of massacres by the Portuguese Army in Portuguese East Africa, made by Catholic missionaries. The Prime Minister was Caetano.

I mention it to him. On the other hand, I think Andrew is probably too modest to carry off the part. But if Prince Philip is really looking for a new image, he could step into it without any difficulty.

Although neither a king nor a pauper, but something in between, Prince Philip could certainly use the money. Even if he failed to carry conviction as a Saviour in any global sense, I am sure there are plenty of impressionable young women prepared to give him a try.

Monday 6th August

Maurice Macmillan[1] obviously expects us to congratulate him for revealing in the House of Commons that while prices have gone up by 20% since the Day of the Grocer, wages have gone up by 38%. So inert and wet has that assembly become, that nobody even shouted: "And what about productivity, you Rascal?"

But there are more important considerations. Many of us are quite prepared to put up with higher prices and tighten our belts in the national interest, or to allow Grocer his little fantasies about Concorde, Chunnel and Maplin Sands. The thing which fills us with endless gloom is the thought of more and more money being given to the working classes to spend on their unpleasant enthusiasms, which can only make England an uglier, dirtier, noisier place for everyone else to live in: transistor radios, sweets, caravans, frozen food, plastic flowers, gramophone records, souvenir spoons from dreadful places and fitted nylon sheets.

It begins to make one wonder whether Grocer is the best man for the job. Only under Labour, it seems, can we be sure of a stable decline into sedate and decorous poverty.

Tuesday 7th August

Clement Freud[2]'s election comes as a hideous shock which might persuade many to live abroad if Grocer had not yet destroyed the pound. It revives yet again the spectre of being governed by the small troop of Exhibitionists, failed vaudeville artists, juicy young Boy Scouts and degenerate old voluptuaries which is the Liberal Party.

Many people claim to find Jeremy Thorpe a bundle of fun, but I have never trusted the bugger since he gave me a dud story on the *Mirror* about the then chairman of the Tory Party having hired a posse of private detectives to pursue George Brown during the 1964 Election. I can just see him, if ever he gets a sniff of office, putting on his prematurely elder statesman act to make the sort of law and order noises we normally hear from the hooligan Hailsham.

Meanwhile, I hear that Grocer, in a desperate bid to woo back the housewives' vote, is taking up body culture. He hopes to win the Mister World Contest later this year in leopardskin briefs and vaseline. This may go some way towards compensating for his 14th

1. A Conservative politician.

2. Clement Freud, b. 24 April 1924, journalist and restaurateur, was elected Liberal Member for the Isle of Ely. Noted for offering dinner in the House of Commons for a large fee.

place in the Morecambe to Lytham St Anne's Offshore Margarine Cup, sponsored by Lever Brothers and Sir Max Aitken, but is unlikely to appeal to more thoughtful voters.

Although we would never normally have thought of voting for Labour, or indeed for anyone else, one thing is clear: if Grocer goes to the country this autumn on the simple question of whether or not we approve of the Royal Wedding, the answer must be a resounding "No". They are both far too young and far too stupid to contemplate such a step. The only excuse for Princess Anne's marrying so far beneath her station must be to introduce a little intellectual vitality into the tired strain of Glucksburg-Saxe-Coburg-Gotha. Phillips is plainly not up to the task. It is high time she went back to her Almanach de Gotha and he to his toothpaste or whatever.

Wednesday 8th August

Warm congratulations to good old Harry Evans, the handsome, likeable, fearless, etc. Editor of the *Sunday Times*, for winning at any rate the first round of the libel action brought against him by Colonel Robert Gayre[1]. The Gayre is currently stuck with legal costs of between £25,000 and £40,000, which should give a few people pause for thought.

Anyone who goes to law puts himself in the hands of an unscrupulous ring of bandits and thugs who will milk both parties as hard as they can until one of them has to pay. If one allows for the stupidity and prejudice of our judges, the conceit and idleness of our barristers and the imponderable diffuseness of English law, neither side can ever have a more certain chance of winning a legal action than it has of winning on a tossed coin, which is a much cheaper way of settling things.

Thursday 9th August

There are various reasons why Norman Mailer might have murdered Pope John. It could have been to protect the good name of Gina Lollobrigida, with whom the Pope was having an affair. It might have been out of pique with the Pope's disapproval of his own affair with Monsignor Casarol, the well-rounded diplomat.

But the real reason, I can reveal, is that Mailer was acting under the personal instructions of President Kennedy. John Kennedy wanted a divorce from Jackie — who was already more than half in love with her 106-year-old Aristotle — in order to marry Magnesia Freelove, a luscious 19-year-old mother of eight whom he had met by chance in the White House swimming pool. Pope John stood in the way of this, having half an eye for Magnesia himself.

However, it was only a few months before the little-known "dirty tricks" department of the Vatican, under dreaded Monsignor Arturo Bougainvillea (a brother, as it happens, of the former chef in the British embassy in Paris), avenged the martyred Pope — at Dallas, on November 22nd, 1963.

I received this version of the story from a man very close to the Pope's nose — Monsignor Felix Bellisario, a kinsman of the distinguished Royal photographer. He became drunk at dinner and implored me afterwards to forget everything he had said. Next morning, he was found hanged in his bedroom. But only Norman can tell the full story (advt)[2].

---

1. Col. Robert Gayre of Gayre and Nigg, b. 6 August 1907, genealogist and author of Miscellaneous Racial Studies (2 vols, 1972).

2. An alternative account of Pope John's death is given in the Diary for 7th January 1975.

Friday 10th August

I have been asked to collaborate in a musical version of Nigel Fisher's Life of Iain Macleod[1] The project should appeal to PEST whose chairman, Keith Laffam, will probably be asked to play the title role.

The part of Laffam, who features largely in the new version, will probably go to Eric Morley[2], Laffam's unsuccessful opponent for his South London constituency. Eric Morley's part will be taken by Robert Morley[3], who will be played by Lord Boyle of Handsworth[4], the former Midland tap-dancer. Michael Crawford[5], the public heart-throb, will play Clive Landa[6], Ted Heath's baby.

All in all, it should be a fitting memorial to that very wonderful man whose death has left such a hole.

Monday 13th August   *France*

I was delighted to learn that my old friend Maurice Oldfield has been made head of the Secret Service. One has almost despaired of his finding any use for his particular talents.

Even at school, where we became close friends, he usually wore a nylon stocking over his head. We assumed at the time he was sensitive about his eczema, but he was probably just cultivating a certain air of mystery, so essential in his profession. He was, of course, some years older than I was, and eyebrows may be raised at this difference in our ages, but Maurice had some difficulty with his 'O' levels and became known to generations of Gregorians as he valiantly tried again, year after year, to win the two 'O' level passes then demanded by the Secret Intelligence Services.

He left under a slight cloud at the age of 40 without ever, so far as I know, securing a pass in French and Elementary Mathematics, the two required subjects. The "cloud" was over an alleged break-in to the school sanatorium involving the theft of some cough mixture. I never believed he had anything to do with the murder of the Under-Matron or the burning down of the gymnasium, which were almost certainly outside jobs.

Even if he was implicated, one must remember that his political master, Sir Alec Douglas-Home, was involved in the amazing Eton cricket stump murder[7], There is much to be said for sowing one's wild oats early. I have no doubt that Maurice, who is still a bachelor at 57, will make a much better job of it than his predecessor, the wretched Sir John Rennie, and we will have fewer Communist agents in Downing Street and other Government appointments.

Tuesday 14th August

So many lies appear in the newspapers every day that a few people may be tempted to disbelieve me when I reveal that the mysterious Kensington socialite called Lady Pamela Onslow, who appears to be the brains behind the Carrington/Littlejohn Scandal, is my dearly beloved mother-in-law[8].

I am not in her confidence over the matter, and can only assume that she introduced her young friends to Geoffrey Johnson-Smith[9] in the hope that he would have an improving influence on them. Certainly, she has never invited me to sit on a sofa alone with Mr Johnson-Smith, and I should plainly refuse if she did, having my own reputation to consider. But I chose her, from all the mothers-in-law on offer, for her patriotism, her concern for those in prison and her sense of fun.

It is a sad commentary on our times if these same qualities have now led her to be hounded and insulted by the Press, her front door used as a backdrop for photographs of extraordinary young women hired by the *Daily Express*. No doubt she will have the front door thoroughly disinfected before we next go to tea, but the episode will remain a grim warning to those whose compassionate natures lead them to mix with criminals, politicians and suchlike. On the other hand, everyone should have a hobby. In the autumn of my days, I think I will raise silk-worms.

Wednesday 21st August

A very civil young man called, I think, Edward Vale, with highly-polished black shoes, arrives from the *Daily Mirror* in London — a round trip of some 1,600 miles — to enquire if my dear mother-in-law is staying with us in France. On being told that she is not, he thanks us politely, climbs into his chauffeur-driven car and heads back for London.

1. Two Conservative politicians, one of whom (Macleod) was dead.

2. Eric Morley, b. 26 September 1918, Chairman of Mecca Ballrooms and noted for sponsoring of Miss World competition.

3. An actor.

4. A former Conservative politician.

5. An actor.

6. Probably a pop singer.

7. This reference, frequently made, has never been explained.

8. Pamela, Countess of Onslow (b. 1915) had introduced Littlejohn, a criminal of her acquaintance, into conversation with her friend, Lord Carrington, the Minister of Defence. The result was that Littlejohn was recruited as a spy by British Intelligence, imprisoned for robbing a bank in Dublin, and informed newspapers of the Carrington connection. Waugh married into the Onslow family in 1961.

9. Johnson-Smith, a Conservative politician, met Littlejohn as Minister for the Army, a post from which he was soon removed, in Lady Onslow's home.

The *Daily Mirror* once sent me round all the capitals of Europe to ask what Europeans wear in bed. The trip lasted several months and must have cost many thousands of pounds. What on earth am I doing in my prime working for mean old sods like Lord Gnome from whom, in over three years, I have received exactly one day trip to Boulogne?

Friday 23rd August

I have not yet seen a British newspaper which has mentioned the opening of the Grouse season. The British Tourist Office in Paris had no idea of this year's prospects, and seemed surprised to be asked. Now that *PHS* and *Atticus* have gone vulgar, I suppose we are all expected to make international telephone calls to the *Daily Telegraph* Information Service before we know whether there is any point in coming back to England before winter. Why do newspapers nowadays assume that we are exclusively interested in the holiday mishaps of the lower classes?

Saturday 24th August

A most interesting agricultural experiment is being made in this part of France[1] which may revolutionize farming methods as we know them and bring untold benefits to mankind. The idea is to feed cattle exclusively on butter, greatly enriching the milk yield so that in many cases it is scarcely distinguishable from Devonshire cream, and easily convertible back to butter.

This is then sold by the farmers to the Agricultural Community at £1.20 a pound and added to the 'butter mountain' which is such an agreeable feature of life in modern Europe.

In order to pay for all the civil servants employed in preserving, weighing and periodically tasting this butter mountain, British housewives have agreed to pay a levy of 50p on every pound of butter they buy from New Zealand. Aware that this process must logically end with the whole of Europe being submerged in a vast mountain of butter, the Commission has decided to release some as cattle fodder at the sensible price of £4.50 a ton. As soon as it has passed through the cow, of course, it is again worth £1.20 a pound plus VAT.

Cows which die of this treatment automatically become eleigible for the Community's £300 death grant (unless they are over 15 years of age, when the grant is reduced to £150). Discriminating Frenchmen have discovered that their livers have a particularly delicate flavour under these circumstances, when sauteed in a light Madeira or Muscat sauce. Where the more elderly cow is concerned, its liver should be diced and simmered for some time in a young Burgundy with shallots, button mushrooms and dill to bring out the characteristically tangy flavour.

1. It is Waugh's usual custom to spend the summer months at his farmhouse in the Languedoc.

Monday 26th August

The most appalling thing about football hooligans is the discredit they bring on that superb game. Mr Len Shipman, President of the Football League, has suggested a return of the birch. Other suggestions include closing all pubs on match days, declaring a state of emergency or martial law and the use of paralysing gas on football crowds as soon as the match starts.

My own suggestion for football hooligans is that after their arms and legs have been cut off their trunks should be covered with HP Sauce and sent to relieve the famine in West Africa. This would be a small gesture of concern for an area which is being pitifully neglected by the British people.

Tuesday 3rd September

Birthdays, birthdays, birthdays. We have scarcely recovered from celebrating Lord Goodman[1]'s sixtieth, and now we must start plans for Cyril Connolly's seventieth on September 10th.

Religion was the central theme of our thanksgiving for Goodie. As the *Jewish Chronicle* so correctly observed, quoting Lord Wigg's description of him as a saint: "Even *Private Eye* invokes religion to describe him lovingly and fortnightly as the Blessed Arnold Goodman. And that he is."

He is indeed. For Cyril, however, I think something more secular is required than the fortnight of fasting and prayer we observed for the Blessed Arnold. I have written to the Queen suggesting that in addition to the knighthood[2] she plans she should make the fountains of London flow with wine and suspend all the Government's repressive anti-hooliganism laws on Merry Monday.

However, she tells me her Government is far too nervous of popular demonstrations at the moment, and plans a little tea time *conversatzione* for Cyril with Sir Alan Hodgkin and other members of the Royal Society to mark the event.

What does this leave for us to do when Sir Cecil Beaton[3]'s seventieth birthday comes round on January 14th? Cecil has always been the teeniest-weeniest bit younger than Cyril and this may well have affected his career, even when at the height of his fame as Royal Photographer he was privileged to take the first official photograph of Prince Charles in his cradle.

Goodness, how Cecil has suffered! At prep school, my father stuck pins in his bottom, and he reveals the wounds still bleed. During the war years the food was "unappetising, surely even for animals". On top of everything that was happening in Eastern Europe, "we, in England, have endured what

---

1. Arnold Goodman, Lord Goodman, a solicitor b. 21 August 1913, noted for his benevolence and sanctity.

2. Connolly died unhonoured the following year.

3. Sir Cecil Beaton, b. 14 January 1904. A bachelor, he had recently published his Diaries. Noted for mannered speech and susceptibility to colds.

must be one of the most uncomfortable phases in modern history. People are under-nourished, yet the food prospect is dark."

Then there was the health problem — a succession of nasty colds, overshadowing the whole decade: "still stricken with a temperature. . . still in bed, but the throat less painful. I was able to read a lot. . . disappointed in myself. My throat again agonisingly sore, and my condition weak. . . no question of getting up".

We must pray he will be spared with all his delightful organs intact to celebrate his seventieth birthday.

Thursday 5th September
Princess Anne is keeping very quiet in Kiev[1]. If she does not watch her tongue carefully, of course, she may wake up to find herself in a wonderful Soviet mental hospital being stuffed with chemicals to convince her she is a fried egg or a teapot.

The next event in the programme of *detente* is a visit by British psychiatrists to a symposium in Moscow where they will learn all about the wonderful Russian methods. This visit should have a profound influence on the doctor/patient relationship in our mental hospitals.

Whenever I visit friends who have taken refuge from Grocer's England in a loony bin, they always seem to be under the impression that they are being poisoned by their doctors. After this jaunt of the World Psychiatric Association it can only be more difficult to persuade them they are mistaken.

Saturday 7th September
Less than a week to go before BBC 2's uncensored screening of *Ulysses* by James Joyce. Controversially, someone called Joseph Strick is trying to add interest to this incredibly boring novel by filming large parts of it in the nude.

A spokesman explained to the *Daily Mail*: "No one gives a damn about nudity, strong language or the presentation of sexual themes on the screen nowadays provided the subjects are presented seriously. . . "

Seriousness, of course, is the supreme virtue. Smiles have now taken the place of pubic hair as something from which the servant classes must be protected. Naked ladies can prance across our screens with foul oaths as they present their sexual themes to general applause, but if so much as a smirk

breaks the deadly seriousness of their faces they will be led off in chains.

Friday 13th September
Torn between the TUC Conference at Blackpool and the Edinburgh Festival as the entertainment highspots for the week, I eventually settled for Edinburgh. One soon tires of laughing at those born less fortunate than oneself and I doubt if it does much good towards one's spiritual development. In any case, one can seldom understand what they say.

Instead, I go to a play on the Festival Fringe called *Lovelies and Dowdies* acted by a Polish company under the direction of Tadeusz Kantor. It is almost entirely in Polish, but beautifully enunciated. As Mr Kantor explains in a most helpful introduction:

"Where there is no 'masterpiece' (this has been replaced by the conception of a 'process'), where form, shaping, presentation, expression have lost their significance (their place has been taken by reality), in consequence the conception of expression vanishes."

To illustrate this interesting theory, he shows us cloakroom attendants setting upon an actor with two additional legs; another actor is rolled up like a pancake in a carpet. Then the audience is made to do gymnastic exercises and forty of them are dressed up as Orthodox Jews and made to make howling noises from time to time.

After a naked princess has been chased into a henhouse where she is violated by a gang of libertines, the forty Mandelbaums, "overcome by lust and jealousy trample down the princess and join in the general dance of the living and the dead, which becomes the last scene of the End of the World and of the programme".

It may well be that the TUC delegates at Blackpool are trying to say the same sort of thing, if only we could understand them.

Saturday 14th September
Back in London in time for the Stones concert at Wembley Pool. What a wealth of entertainment is available in Grocer's England! At 30, Mick Jagger looks as young and as attractive as ever in his gold *lame* jumpsuit for his clever presentation of *Dancing With Mr D.*

I see my old friend Margaret Thatcher in the audience. Her eyes are bright and her cheeks flushed, but her seat remains dry even through the fantastic climax of *Midnight*

---

1. At the Olympic Horse Events, where she fell off, hurting herself rather badly.

Rambler. I confess, I completely let myself go in this song, and so did nice young Charles Vass, who was sensibly dressed in white ribbed Dakron drip-dry rollneck shirt with cream jodhpurs and matching accessories.

Sunday 15th September
One is never too old to learn something new. In the *Sunday Times* John Raymond reveals that J.B. Priestley, who has just written a book about the English, is really English himself. Judging by his appearance and his prose style, but mostly by his extraordinary accent, I always assumed he was a Swede.

Monday 16th September
National Connolly Day again! I am happy to hear that the movement to canonise this most gifted of book reviewers is already well in hand. Anybody having a knowledge of miracles or favours received through Connolly's intercession are requested to send them to the Rev. Thomas Corbishley SJ, Office of the Vice-Postulation, 114 Mount Street, W1.

My own contribution takes me back to the Spanish Civil War and the hell that was Guernica, 1937. Cyril and I shared the same haystack throughout the bombing while from all around came the shrieks and groans of Loyalist ladies being raped by the Fascists. Auden, Spender and Isherwood were crying like babies; Lord Clark of Civilisation was nowhere to be seen.

As a shell fell between us, Cyril started reciting from Leconte de Lisle in his high, tender voice:
Couronnes de thym et de marjolaine
Les elfes joyeux dansent sur la plaine
At that moment the years slipped by and I found myself in my library in Somerset,

apparently having fallen asleep over Cyril's latest collection of newspaper articles and book reviews. By what magic had his words transported me to the homely comforts of 1973, with its pattering of tiny Filipino feet and cellars stocked with dusty bottles of golden wine from the luscious grapes of the Palatinate?

Whether the explanation is supernatural or not I will be the first to buy a plaster statue of St Cyril the Columnist when his canonisation papers come through[1].

Incidentally, a significant passage from *Enemies of Promise* may provide the clue to Cyril's abundant energy in old age, where he says: "I was eighteen and a half. I had never had sexual intercourse. I had never masturbated". I hope that younger readers in particular will take this saintly man's example to heart[2].

Wednesday 25th September
There is nothing odd about a Minister lying to MPs. In five years as a political correspondent, I never investigated a single Parliamentary Answer without finding it contained at least a deliberate attempt to mislead.

What makes it odder is that a select committee should disregard Parliamentary convention to the extent of accusing a Minister of lying, as they have done with poor Michael Heseltine[3] and his ridiculous Hovertrain.

The true explanation, I'm afraid, lies in the personal unpopularity of Michael Heseltine. This derives almost entirely from his unfortunate appearance, which is most unfair and should not be allowed to influence serious judgement of Hovertrains.

1. Connolly died soon afterwards. The cause of his canonisation has never advanced beyond this one prima oratio.

2. A long correspondence ensued in Private Eye, mostly between a psychiatrist and a hospital patient, about whether masturbation was in fact detrimental to artistic or intellectual development.

3. A Conservative politician.

He is unkindly known as Michael Brilliantine by people who are jealous of his natural wavy flaxen locks, but sources close to Mr Heseltine assure me that he never in fact uses Brilliantine. "I don't need to," the sources explain with an impish grin. The only aids he requires are a dab of Lentheric's Tweed After-shave behind the ears, body talc by Dior, *Eau Sauvage* and the slightest touch of Mary Quant Eye Shadow For Men before a television appearance.

Heseltine's public relations people, Playball Enterprises, have just released this picture of their client in order to correct any false impressions and improve his image with young people. I print it readily, believing that both sides of the case should be given, but fear it will do little to clear up the present controversy about Hovertrains.

Thursday 26th September

My son at Eton writes to tell me that bodyguards are now being provided for Eton boys at the weekends. The headmaster, Mr Michael McCrum, has employed a security firm to protect his pupils after complaints from worried parents about a series of attacks by local guttersnipes.

The bodyguards are, of course, drawn from the poorer classes themselves, so now Etonians will be treated to the diverting spectacle of the lower orders bashing each other up at every street corner while they saunter past into a carefree, protected future. The whole purpose of an Eton education is to prepare boys for such a world.

I telephoned McCrum to congratulate him but of course today is the Jewish New Year so the whole place has closed down.

Friday 27th September

To a special tasting of Observer-rouge, the exciting new red liquid which the *Observer* is marketing as "wine" at ninety new pee a bottle. Good old David Astor[1]! Once described by his employee Anthony Sampson[2] as "a kind of intellectual Medici, with a court of exotic contributors reflecting different facets of his own complex character", he is not one to be put off by his failure as a newspaper man. At 61 years of age, a time when many of us are thinking of retirement, he starts an entirely new career as a "wine" merchant.

Soon every house in Hampstead will be displaying its bottle of Mr Astor's preparation, the new "must" for the thinking drinker.

I did not actually taste any myself, being no expert. But its bouquet reminded me strangely of something I met once in Poujade, a little known wine-producing area in the suburbs of Marseilles.

Here it is that the Marseillais bring their empty tins of frogs' legs, their banana skins,

1. A millionaire journalist, b. 5 March 1912. His brother, Viscount Astor, was involved in the Profumo scandal (June 1963) and his half-brother, Bobbie Shaw, imprisoned for homosexual offences. Noted for patronage of Ms Norah Beloff (q.v.).

2. A journalist.

snail shells, horses' hooves and the few other things which that enterprising race has not yet learned tó eat. From these unlikely materials comes this extraordinary wine known as "vin rouge".

A journalist friend, for a bet, once drank three glasses of it. First, his hair fell out; then his blackened teeth fell to the ground. Finally he went into a coma and his skin started exuding a yellowish froth, like a slug which has had salt poured over it. Now he has become a teacher and spends his evenings trying to sell *Workers' Press*, the amusing Stalinist daily, to commuters in the gentlemen's lavatory at Paddington Station.

Saturday 28th September

News that a man has been found dead in bed at Walthamstow who has lain there unnoticed for the past ten years made me turn again to *London Magazine*, that much-loved British institution which is also so tragically easy to forget.

Still unrivalled in its field, it will probably remain our *only* geriatric Pseuds Corner and Retired Pseuds Rest Home until Karl Miller[1] and his nice Cambridge friends on *The Listener* are a tiny bit older.

The current number contains an interview between David Hockney, the boyish 36-year-old painter, and someone called Robert Wennerstein:

Wennerstein: What's the state of English art in general?
Hockney: I suppose the state of English art is not as interesting as American art on the whole. But, to be honest, I don't think American art is that interesting, either. Perhaps American art is a little more interesting but it's like talking about the difference between the numbers 35 and 37. The difference is slight.

Where else could one read anything of this quality? God bless the Arts Council for supporting this delightful corner of our national life.

By coincidence, I was just thinking of buying a diptych by Hockney. The two pictures show some coloured balls and wavy things — probably symbolising the difference between American and English art. They might seem rather expensive at £8,000, but then I think of the laughs I can have over them in the lonely winter months ahead.

Sunday 6th October

Freedom is not having to go to the Labour Party Conference in Blackpool this week. A report in the *New Statesman* assures us that Labour Party members are getting older and fewer, that many have no very clear idea of which Party they belong to, and all are only interested in a higher standard of living. Why, then, do they continue to stage these gruesome rallies where incontinent old fools sit up much too late ogling the few hideous women and drinking the horrible flat beer of Blackpool? What a way to celebrate our wonderful standard of living!

Monday 7th October

At a first meeting of the Spiro Agnew Defence Fund Committee I begin to realise how much idealism still survives in this much knocked country of ours.

Plans, which are still secret, include a huge charity concert at the Albert Hall which will feature a mouth organ recital by Bernard Levin, further readings from *The Imitation of Christ* by Lady Magnesia Freelove, animal and motorcar impersonations by John Wells; a special charity walk by Brighton & Hove Old People's Association (chairman: Mr T.C. Skeffington-Lodge[2]) and we are trying to get as many schools as possible involved in a mass Black and White Minstrels show at the White City Stadium with Sir Gerald Nabarro as Ringmaster and Enoch Powell, hopefully, on the banjo. I hope that as many readers as possible will support at least some of these very worth-while events and show that Britain still cares.

Tuesday 8th October   *Blackpool*

A most disturbing report reaches me on my arrival in Blackpool for the Conservative Party Conference that Grocer — far from being the ebullient figure he seems — is extremely unwell. He is kept going only by frequent injections of glucose and other substances administered by his friend and constant companion, Dr Brian Warren.

Normally, on hearing this sort of rumour, I rush to Grocer's side with many bogus exclamations of concern, but this evening he is at a small dinner of the British Trawler Federation to which, for some reason or other, I have not been asked.

My man who has gone to the Quayside Restaurant, Fleetwood, where this revolting meal is being served, has disguised himself as

---

1. Northcliffe Professor of Modern English Literature, University College, London. b. 2 August 1921. Friend of Stephen Spender. An up-and-coming pseud.

2. Unsuccessful Labour candidate in 1969 Brighton by-election. High Church Bachelor.

1973

a waiter. At 9.30 he telephones with the latest bulletin: Grocer seems to be behaving normally, has eaten large helpings of smoked salmon and chicken; but he has refused even first helpings of potatoes. Grocer off his potatoes? The dossier begins to build up.

Wednesday 9th October

Nothing I had read about her in *Private Eye* prepared me for the radiant, sublime beauty of Miss Gillian Widdicombe, the *Financial Times*'s brilliant music critic. Since the moment of her first appearance at Lord Carrington's reception the conference has turned into a Widdicombe Fair with every thought of Grocer's ridiculous health problem banished from the scene. At the BBC reception all the men huddled round her in a tight group, jingling coins in their pockets and looking wistful.

My old friend Robert Carey[1] has organised the party with much greater imagination and skill this year. He has even asked a "token" coloured guest to keep us amused. This is another old friend, Lord "Grey" Gowrie, Grocer's intriguing Junior Whip in the House of Lords.

"Grey" arrives looking very sweet in a sort of dinner jacket and spectacles, but without the traditional top-hat and umbrella. Unfortunately, everybody is so occupied with lovely Miss Widdicombe that nobody has time to talk to him at all.

Thursday 17th October

When mad Lord Hailsham is next trying to think up unpleasant punishments he might give a moment's thought to the sensation of listening to Mrs Thatcher on grammar schools for half an hour with a bad headache.

In the evening it was the Young Conservatives' Euroball at Blackpool's Mecca Ballroom. A beautiful dark girl I find weeping in a corner explains that she has been waiting all evening for Grocer to ask her to dance. She turns out to be Mary Lynch, slender long-haired daughter of the great Irish statesman[2].

But Grocer is not at all himself. He dances with nobody, and when I go up to remonstrate with him he shakes my hand listlessly and says he very much enjoys my column.

This last statement is most depressing. It might mean that he never reads it, of course. But if Grocer really takes pleasure in reading the sort of scurrilous filth printed on this page, one must doubt whether he is a suitable person to be entrusted with running the country.

Perhaps it is time one revealed all one knows about him. A good replacement might be William Whitelaw, the wise and kindly Secretary for Ulster.

Friday 18th October

For my last night in Blackpool Sir Nigel Ryan, the distinguished Director General of Inde-

---

1. A BBC employee. From previous references, including scenes omitted on grounds of libel, it would seem that Carey was quite a new friend.

2. In fact, she is no relation.

pendent Television News very kindly agrees to give a party in my honour. All the usual people are there — Grocer, Rippon, the Lord Mayor of Blackpool — but also some new faces, beautiful women and handsome men.

Later I see Miss Nora Beloff of the *Observer*, talking animatedly to Mr Geoffrey Rippon, although of course there is nothing particularly interesting or unusual about that. Tony Howard is getting away with Michael Heseltine, which wouldn't be my idea of fun, although I suppose they're both old enough to know what they like.

What a splendid conference it has been! Thank you Grocer, Tony, Peter, Mrs Roy Smith (the Chairman) and everybody else who has worked so hard to make this such an enjoyable, successful and really relevant conference for us all.

Saturday 19th October

Oh dear — another of these distressing articles by Anne Scott-James which kindly William Rees-Mogg prints from time to time in his newspaper. This time, appalled by the publication of the Waugh diaries[1], Nigel Nicolson's amusing portrait of his mother[2], Lord Moran's interesting comments on Churchill's bowel function and by almost everything else being published nowadays, she has gone and burned all her letters.

What a loss! Anne Scott-James, for those who are too young to remember, was the *Daily Mail* columnist who preceded Jean Rook and Linda Lee Potter, pioneering an entirely new dimension in British journalism:

"I am not suggesting for a moment that I have lived in illustrious circles, either literary or aristocratic, or been loved by queues of men whose names will make history. My life has been comparatively humdrum," she writes.

Well yes, perhaps. But it still seems rather an ungallant way to refer to her husband, the 65-year-old Beaverbrook cartoonist Osbert Lancaster, while he is still alive. Now we will never know the secret of their stormy, tempestuous wooing. Keen literary detective work can only hope to reconstruct what these vital letters might have said.

Dear Anne,
I have been thinking about us and, well, I know that I'm not much to look at but I think I carry myself well and have some very nice suits. As a boy I went to Charterhouse, but I should have thought I could pass
as a Harrovian anywhere, and my son, of course, went to Eton.
Also I know quite a lot of people, partly through belonging to the St James's club which many people say is about as good as White's. Women are allowed in for Sunday luncheon, which is another advantage. What do you think?
Yours most cordially,
Osbert.

Dear Osbert,
I was wondering if you would write. Of course I realise that personal appearance can pose problems, and there is also the matter of your moustache which you do not mention in your letter. On the other hand, I think that other things can be more important. It is very easy nowadays to overestimate the physical side, as if this was the only ingredient in marriage. May there not be something in the old-fashioned ideas we were taught as children?
For my own part, I don't even find you particularly boring. This is my private point of view, and many would argue against it. But my feelings are my own, and I think we will have a most fruitful relationship with many interests in common.
Yours in anticipation,
Anne.

Thursday 24th October

The entire West Country must feel for poor Colonel Dugdale, the Axminster landowner whose daughter Rose has been convicted of burgling her own family home. Previously, she had brought her proletarian lover to dinner who had insulted the Colonel by saying that his asparagus tasted of "tough spring onions". Where did the old boy go wrong? Several explanations occur to me.

In the first place, there is the wicked British system of primogeniture. If Rose[3] had owned a decent share of the pictures, she would have been less tempted to burgle them.

In the second place, there is the traumatic public school system, which by making such a large proportion of boys from good homes into sexual and emotional cripples, greatly increases the attraction of working class youths, many of whom are criminals.

In the third place, he might have forgotten to manure his asparagus properly or cover the beds in straw for the winter. More simply, I suppose, he might have forgotten to cook them.

---

1. This almost certainly refers to Evelyn Waugh's Diaries, published in 'Astor's naughty knickers magazine" — the Observer colour supplement — the previous April.

2. Vita Sackville West, gardener and lesbian.

3. Dr Bridget Rose Dugdale. A high-spirited girl who was later imprisoned for stealing pictures from Sir Alfred Beit in Ireland, and accused of helping to drop bombs from a stolen helicopter. In prison, she produced a baby which Waugh seems to claim as his own.

Finally, there was his disastrous decision to let his daughter study economics at St Anne's College, Oxford. Here, in her own words, she "began to worry about what was happening in the world".

Oxford women's colleges are increasingly in the hands of a sinister group of females who, by insisting on utter seriousness at all times threaten to produce a generation of bores, neurotics and criminals in place of the lovely creatures entrusted to their care.

The authorities of St Anne's College must bear a heavy responsibility for Rose Dugdale's plight. They themselves will probably never realise that the only purpose of a university education is to teach people to enjoy life more than they would have done otherwise, but it is high time the Home Secretary stepped in and put a stop to the rising tide of misery and boredom which these conceited, self-important women are creating all around us.

Friday 25th October

Is London cracking up? Some time ago I wrote to the editor of the *Guinness Book of Records* suggesting it was time he included a mention of Mr Cyril Connolly, the important seventy-year-old book reviewer. I drew attention to Connolly's claim in *Enemies of Promise* that he had never masturbated at the age of eighteen and a half. This must surely be a record, and a very wholesome one too.

Three weeks later, I have still not received so much as an acknowledgement of this sensible and humane suggestion. Wake up, Norris McWhirter!

Saturday 26th October

One of the main horrors of journalism is having to produce appropriate emotions for every public event: delighted amazement whenever the Queen has a baby, shock and anguish whenever a Big Dipper runs amok or British holidaymakers are burned to death in their Fun Palaces.

Nicholas Tomalin[1]'s death is a very sad thing. He was clever, funny, brave and kind, and Grub Street has few people possessing many of these qualities. What is also very sad, in its way, is the spectacle of his friends and colleagues struggling for once to describe a genuine emotion: from Sir William Rees-Mogg's manly conclusion, "He is a great loss to English reporting and nobody will cover his kind of story again the way he did," — to Alan Brien, who apparently decided that the best thing to do was to take a bottle of whisky round to the Tomalin household and drink it there in a corner.

I know that I speak for many of the dear wives of Gnome House when I express the hope that in the event of anything happening to their clever, funny, brave etc. husbands, Brien will find some other way of expressing his grief.

Tuesday 30th October

My wine catalogue from Messrs Hedges and Butler has a long introduction about wine critics and criticism: "Their advice is invaluable, but I still see no reason why we, the vulgar throng, should not continue to enjoy what we ourselves like, although it merits their criticism. . . The beauty of wine will

---

1. A former William Hickey man and literary editor of New Statesman, he campaigned as a journalist for free Bangla Desh in the Sunday Times and was killed by an anti-tank weapon on the Golan Heights in Israel.

rest on the palate of the consumer".

Fine, stirring stuff, even if it is unlikely to win any prizes for fearless reporting, but how happy one is to see Reggie earning a respectable living. If only he had thought of writing wine catalogues before he fell in with Hoffman[1], Poulson, Grocer and all his other disreputable friends.

Wednesday 31st October
I have decided to compile a volume of reminiscences about Mr Harold Creighton[2], the brilliant new editor of the *Spectator*.
I should be particularly grateful for contributions from the many young secretaries who have been privileged to work for this engaging man at one time or another, with accounts of their experiences in his service. All letters will be treated in confidence.

Thursday 1st November
Reckless chauvinism will never find a place in this column. We have all grown to accept the need for a German Royal Family, and even for their odious Protestant religion. But they, too, should learn a little tact.

It is announced today that Princess Anne has chosen the refrain to greet her on arrival at Westminster Abbey to marry her hideous young tradesman — Haydn's well-known ditty *Deutschland Deutschland Uber Alles*. A pretty tune, you will say, but when I reflect on how many people died in two World Wars to prevent exactly this sort of thing, I, for one, propose to boycott the whole proceedings.

Tuesday 5th November
Fireworks night, so we join the citizens in their fawning celebration of a brave and good man's death. In our family we always let off our fireworks in celebration of the attempt to blow up Parliament, rather than its failure, and we have never had an accident. If ever the Vatican requires evidence of divine intervention before raising Guy Fawkes, Soldier and Martyr, to the celestial company of canonised saints, it has only to look at the hundreds of men, women and children blinded and disfigured every year in their attempts to mock him.

If only the Jesuits realised how the aims of St Guy Fawkes coincided with those of nearly everybody alive today, they might drop their pathetic, cringing attempts to deny that he ever existed and actively promote the Cause.

Instead they spend their time and energy trying to fake miracles to promote the canonisation of Pope John XXIII. Only one man in the entire Church is standing out against this ludicrous venture, the courageous, wise and holy Cardinal Alfredo Ottaviani, but he, alas, is blind and nearly 93.

Thursday 7th November
In accordance with his wishes, I last night burnt all the letters I had received over the years from W.H. Auden. But I would be doing less than my duty to posterity if I failed to reproduce this letter I received less than six months before his death, which seems to me to give a good idea of the warmth and generosity underneath the poet's slightly austere manner.

My dear Waugh,
I don't mind anything you choose to say about me — God knows, I have done enough in my 66 years to justify your criticism of "wrinkled American bachelor" — but I do beg & implore you to be more careful what you say about my friend Stephen Spender.
It is all too easy to suppose, just because Stephen has no poetic talent nor any imagination to speak of — and little feeling for words — that he is also insensitive to personal slights. As one who knows him perhaps slightly better than you — I beg you accept my word that he is extremely sensitive, as well as being, at the moment, far from strong in health. In his present state any trifling remark, even made in a spirit of levity — like calling him Stephen Spender-Penny — can cause him the greatest imaginable agony of mind.
I cannot believe that anyone so plentifully endowed with talent as yourself — who has already, in his brief career, if I may say so, produced enough of lasting value to justify the accolade of greatness — can be devoid of compassion for those older and less fortunate than yourself.
Yours sincerely,
Wystan Auden.

The oddest thing about this letter is that I had never referred to Mr Spender as Stephen Spender-Penny. In fact I had never thought of it; even if I had thought of it, I doubt whether I should have done so as the joke seems to me in doubtful taste. Now the letter has been burnt, we may never know what was Auden's purpose in writing it.

---

1. An American swindler who appointed Mr Maudling President of his Real Estate Fund of America (REFA) swindle before being caught and sent to prison.

2. Creighton was proprietor of the Spectator when Waugh was dismissed as Political Correspondent in February 1970, but had re-employed him as Chief Fiction Reviewer long before Waugh's successful action for wrongful dismissal was heard. Substantial damages were paid to Waugh, who plainly bore no malice.

1973

Friday 15th November

Lord Snowdon's accident in the invalid chair he had designed will come as a bitter blow to the country. As a matter of fact, I was the friend to whom he was demonstrating the machine's handling characteristics when it overturned outside Kensington Palace, but he did not seem eager that I should give my name to the press. I never believed that it would work anyway.

Poor old Tony. Nobody asked to put his face on the postage stamps when he married the Queen's sister in 1960. Now he has to see the grinning face of Princess Anne's hideous, semi-articulate stable-lad[1] wherever he looks. No wonder he is under strain.

Monday 18th November

I always try to be in the House of Commons when the Minister for Posts and Telecommunications is answering his Parliamentary Questions. Today Sir John Eden revealed that the number of incidents involving vandalism of telephone kiosks declined from 29,000 in the quarter ending June 1972 to 20,000 for the same period this year.

Whatever the reason for this sad decline I hope it does not mean that the British public is losing its taste for breaking things. There was a time when the sound of breaking glass was a pleasure restricted to richer members of society who could afford it. One of the most agreeable features of social progress in our time is the way the Government has built these kiosks for even the humblest members of society to try their hand.

The pleasures of telephoning are obviously much over-rated, but various people have suggested that destroying these kiosks is a mistake from the point of view of members of the lower class who have no telephone themselves and wish to summon help in the event of an emergency — suddenly finding themselves being murdered, for instance, or on fire.

On the other hand, they are not accustomed to these luxuries, and I should have thought that by now they must have found some more dignified way of drawing attention to their distress. I confess I can never see an unvandalised telephone kiosk as anything but a challenge.

Wednesday 20th November

Having decided to boycott the capital this week as a gesture of sympathy towards the Royal Family in their distress over their daughter's shameful wedding, I naturally turn to the *Daily Telegraph*'s informative *London Day By Day* column to see what I am missing.

In today's newspaper, I discover that Hilda Lady Brabazon of Tara is having a gay old time entertaining Cabinet Ministers to lunch at 96. Sadly, I see that Dame Margaret Corbett Ashby, who is 91, is flying to New Delhi this week for a Congress of the International Alliance of Women, so I shall probably miss her.

However, I learned that the Queen Mother, 73, is attending a repeat gala performance of my friend Herbert Wilcox's film *Sixty Glorious Years*. How well I remember the first gala performance of this amusing film in 1938, attended by the then Queen Mother, Queen Mary, looking a very youthful 71. Herbert tells me he was 81 this year. How time flies! His dear wife, Anna Neagle, who plays Queen Victoria in the film, has not aged a day.

There was an amusing piece about Mgr.

1. This is a further reference to the Royal Wedding of 1973 when Princess Anne married Capt. Mark Phillips of the Royal Dragoons, an accomplished horseman.

Gonzi, the Archbishop of Malta, who is over 88. Unfortunately he does not seem to be visiting London at the moment. The best item tells about Major W.H. Standen and Major W.A. Bailey of the Indian Army Ordnance Corps Association, both of them over 100. I love reading about majors.

Ignoring the nine people mentioned in today's Peterborough column who are already, alas, dead, I worked out the average age of the twenty-two living people named as slightly under 72½. I exclude Dame Anna Neagle from this calculation on the grounds of chivalry, and also someone called Jeffrey Sion, an art dealer whom I don't think I've had the pleasure of meeting.

Monday 23rd November

Parliament will never be the same without Gerald Nabarro. We shared an enthusiasm for a certain type of experimental theatre and spent many happy afternoons together in various clubs devoted to these activities in and around Soho, drinking the Portuguese *bagacera* or *bagaci* he enjoyed so much in his off-duty moments.

He once confided to me that if anything should happen to him, all he asked was for Parliament Square and New Palace Yard to be made into a Nabarro Memorial Roundabout, with a largish statue of himself in the middle. It does not seem much to ask, but I should be surprised if the egotistical men left in charge of our destiny will have even enough generosity for this small gesture.

Tuesday 24th November

A small private lunch party on the ninth floor of the *Daily Mirror* building given by my old friend and former patron, Sir Hugh Cudlipp. Its purpose, so far as I could judge, was to introduce his Editors to people of consequence before his retirement at the end of the year.

The room was much changed since my memories of it under Cecil King[1]. King's handsome mahogany desk had been sold and replaced by a sorry affair of pine and plastic. I suppose this sort of thing is inevitable where newspapers are losing circulation, but if I had known the desk was going for only £16,000 I would have been happy to purchase it for my own office in Greek Street.

However, the food and drink were excellent. Halfway through the meal, one of Cudlipp's younger Editors became overexcited and emotional on learning that *Private Eye* was the only newspaper represented in the room whose circulation had shown a steady increase for the past four years. But Hugh was as engagingly indiscreet as ever. I didn't want to promise anything, but I should have thought we could find a little corner of the *Eye* where he can contribute a regular Press column, so long as he keeps it clean, free from libel, and up to our rather exacting standards of accuracy.

Wednesday 25th November

Once again the British public are treated to pictures of Peter Walker's unusual son, Jonathan, in today's newspapers. It was Walker himself who drew attention to the national peril represented by his offspring's controversial habits. This was during the sewage strike of October, 1970, when he told the Conservative Party conference at Blackpool:

"I warn you of the magnitude of the task ahead. It is enormous. At present, I have a great interest in a chap called Jonathan, my seven-months-old son. By the time he is my age, we will have needed to build more waterworks and more sewage works than have been built in the whole history of man."

Jonathan Walker's amazing output, which already occupies the undivided attention of

1. Former Chairman of Daily Mirror and employer of Waugh. King was ousted by an office coup in Cudlipp's favour after he became extensively alarmed about the state of the economy in 1968. Born 20 February 1901, noted for interest in the supernatural.

eight sewage farms full-time, is only obliquely referred to in today's *Daily Mirror*, where petite, 24-year-old Tessa Walker, wife of the 47-year-old monster, makes this highly significant disclosure: "Peter happily takes over any chore with the children, *short of changing nappies, that is.*" (My italics.)

Her main purpose is to draw attention to the terrible strains on a politician's marriage, which is, indeed, a matter of general concern to us all. Sir John Eden, for instance, the likeable Minister for Posts and Tele-communications, tells me he has run through fourteen wives in the last two years, with six more in the pipeline. Tessa's solution is to have her husband present whenever she has a baby — "it forms an incredibly close link between us and is really exciting," she reveals.

This may work for her, but not everybody would like to have a grovelling 57-year-old Secretary for Trade and Industry present on these occasions. I hope she is invited to be present when Peter has his vasectomy.

Mrs Walker, in any case, is an exception. The sad truth about the general run of MPs' wives is that they are nearly as ugly and as boring as their husbands, and constitute a serious threat to the public by being left un-attended for so long. Their children, of course, are even worse.

The obvious answer is for all MPs' wives and children to be shut up with their hus-bands in the Palace of Westminster for the duration of every Parliament. None of them should ever be allowed out, nor would any-one else be allowed in, except members of the Parliamentary Lobby who have patriotic-ally agreed to be castrated as a token of their good faith and belief in the British Parlia-mentary system.

Thursday 26th November
Claire Tomalin's decision to accept the literary editorship of the *New Statesman* was bound to be a difficult one. She has announ-ced she hopes to continue the tradition of her predecessor, John Gross, and was swayed in her choice by Paul Johnson, who urged her to shut her eyes and think of her whole sex.

If all they wanted was more of John Gross, the obvious choice for successor would have been John Groser, the portly former cleric who covers politics for *The Times* and prob-ably thinks about little else but his whole sex. Unfortunately, the women's lib faction

would not hear of it.

Next time there is a *New Statesman* re-shuffle, a sensible compromise candidate might be Danny la Rue[1], who would bring a welcome spark of liveliness to the book pages. Tomalin could go and take Charles Vass's job on *The Times*, while Charles would be free to fulfil a lifetime's ambition and take over from Danny at the Prince of Wales Theatre.

Friday 27th November
Sir Robert Bruce Lockhart's diaries, which have been generously sent to me by *Books and Bookmen*, provide an abundance of important historical information which may cause historians to revise all their opinions on the three decades leading up to the last war.

For instance, we learn that the Astor fortune — the source of so much misery ever since — is founded on pirates' gold which the Astors stole from a neighbouring land owner. We learn that Professor Joad[2], the notorious sexual braggart, was impotent; that it was not the *People* newspaper which thought up the amusing description of Randolph Churchill as a "hack" journalist — although it cost them £5,000 in libel damages. It was Winston Churchill, Randolph's revolting old father, who said it on 4th October 1932.

But by far the most important revelation is on the delicate matter of Somerset Maugh-am's sex life. "Maugham has had relations with women," claims Sir Robert, who goes on to reveal that "because of his homosexual nervosity he could not perform alone. The liaison was *a trois*. The third was Godfrey Winn[3]."

What an august sandwich! The tragedy is that our libel laws prevented anyone from knowing it at the time. I feel sure that the distressing obituary notice which appeared in *Private Eye* at the time of Winn's death would have been more generous if it had been known that he was providing these useful services to a major writer as well as writing such drivel himself.

Tuesday 30th November
I hear Paul Getty[4] is most distressed by the kidnapping of his grandson. It is hard to know what advice to give him. If the kidnappers were slightly more reasonable, one might be tempted to strike some sort of bargain with them — about £25,000 seems a reasonable sum to me — but as Mr Getty himself has pointed out, he has 24 other grandchildren to consider.

1. A stage performer specialising in transvestitism.
2. A wireless 'personality' of the Second World War years.
3. A journalist, bachelor, and originator of women's magazine journalism.
4. A millionaire, b. 15 December 1892, his oil fortune led to the description of him as 'richest man in the world'. Noted for extreme misery. d.1976.

So far as I know, I have never had the pleasure of meeting Paul Getty III, as he is wittily called. But when I look at photographs of the young man and then think of all the amusing and delightful things one can still buy for £1,400,000, my advice is to stand firm. No good ever came of succumbing to blackmail. An issue of principle is at stake. Fight, fight and fight again.

Wednesday 7th December
A panic-stricken telegram from Dame Harold Evans, the gritty 17-year-old train driver whom Lord Thomson made Editor of the *Sunday Times* in order to improve its image: would I go down to the Ship Inn, Brighton, and tell a conference of *Sunday Times* "executives" (as the editorial staff are called) what they should do to stop their dreadful newspaper getting even worse.

I told them to sack everybody connected with the Arts and Books pages. They have become the preserve of a tiny clique of conceited second-rate hacks whose pretentious drivel, churned out week after week, has contributed significantly to the artistic decline of the nation and to public indifference about the arts. I told them to send all existing staff on a crash reading course to combat that part of their illiteracy which is the result of environmental problems in childhood, and in future to recruit from something above the level of North Country badger diggers to combat that part of it which can be attributed to hereditary or genetic disabilities.

Unfortunately, I think they were all too drunk and too stupid to take in a word I said, but sat looking self-important and overpaid and thinking wistfully about sexual intercourse.

Thursday 8th December
The Australian Rugby League has beaten Great Britain 15-5 for the Ashes at Warrington. So. Normally this is the sort of information one passes onto one's colleague, E.J. Thribb[1] for a poem, but the situation has already been brilliantly summed up by Alan Thomas, fearless sportswriter of the *Daily Express*:

"Albert Fearnley, former Halifax tough-guy and now Bradford Northern manager, put British sport in a nutshell when he said: 'We are breeding a nation of pansies'."

The former Halifax tough guy surely had a point when he drew attention to the sad increase in male homosexuality. In the past two years I can count no fewer than six people in the small and shrinking circle of my friends who have suddenly announced that they are homosexual.

I really don't know what should be done about this. One's first reaction is to persecute these unfortunate people in various small and subtle ways, but I think a better idea might be to appeal to their sense of duty.

It is true, of course, that many women are boring and even more nowadays are mad. But there is surely something to be said for the stern path of duty, for traditional values and ancestral practices.

Friday 9th December
One blessing of the fuel crisis is that we should hear no more of the *Concorde*, Grocer's ridiculous toy airplane which burns more petrol than the entire fleet of London Transport's double-decker buses at full throttle simultaneously. Mr Wedgwood Benn assures me he is developing a model of this futile machine which can work on chicken shit, but I think we can disregard him. The important factor is whether unemployment in Bristol will do anything to help with the servant problem in the West Country.

Saturday 10th December
Asked to appear on the late night Ludicrous Kennedy Show[2] with a handful of pundits whose names I never caught to discuss the State of the Nation. Discussion so boring I keep falling asleep — goodness knows how the audience were supposed to stay awake if the performers couldn't. Afterwards the BBC sent me to the Kensington Hilton. All the notices are in Japanese, and one can't sneeze without knocking over 20 Japanese businessmen come to buy up our remaining Edwardian chamberpots.

The bath towels, made of some synthetic substance which repels moisture, are not much bigger than a gentleman's pocket handkerchief — probably specially designed for visiting Japanese businessmen. Is this a hotel? No, it is a concrete hecatomb, a prayer to heaven for another atom bomb to come and take it all away again.

Sunday 11th December
Further light is thrown on the fascinating debate about Captain Eric Grounds's trousers in today's newspaper. Grounds, it will be remembered, was best man at Princess Anne's wedding and shocked my colleague Jilly Cooper[3] (who's seen a thing or two in her

---

1. E.J. Thribb, author of Polynesian Pantomime, is the resident poet of Private Eye.

2. Midweek, a television news-magazine programme, was chaired by Mr Ludovic Kennedy, b. 3 November 1919, a writer and unsuccessful politician, noted for impressive way with his spectacles.

3. A journalist.

time) by his tight trousers which appeared to make him walk oddly.

Then an indignant lady wrote to say Jilly was wrong: Captain Grounds-for-Divorce only walked like a crab with wet pants because he was wearing spurs, for some reason best known to himself. Today brings an amazing letter from the controversial Captain himself.

He rebukes Jilly for "trying to be witty in a scathing sort of way", but makes the astounding confession that these trousers are, indeed, "considerably tighter than any other pair, military or civilian, which I own." He reveals further that he has made a practice of wearing these trousers at formal occasions over eight years, and boasts that he has "never experienced any embarrassment when required to sit down".

Nobody is interested in whether he is embarrassed or not. What we want to know is why he chose his tightest pair of trousers to wear for Princess Anne's wedding. Was the Palace informed of his decision in advance? Had the Home Secretary, with his anxieties about "soft porn", been consulted? Why was he wearing spurs, and can trousers which are too tight harm a man's physical development? This is the sort of thing the *Insight* hacks should be investigating, instead of attending ridiculous conferences in Brighton.

Monday 19th December
In all our present troubles, the government has chosen to declare a French Letter Day, appointing Jim Prior, the ruddy-faced Leader of the House of Commons, to be Minister for Contraception.

Jim will certainly have a thing or two to teach us. He tells me that among the farmers of Suffolk where he comes from, people often use an old sock, inner tube, or halpenny piece for this most delicate of purposes. There is

also something called the Beccles Bolster which he hopes to demonstrate on television, although I had no difficulty in understanding its function from his rough and ready description.

Tuesday 20th December
To Westminster, where I hear MPs greet the two-day debate on "the most serious peacetime crisis in our history" with screams, jeers and giggles. The two front benches were horrified, and I think I see their point. Although MPs are showing a welcome independence of spirit and also an unusual maturity of judgement in their response to this bogus occasion — as if the House of Commons could do anything whatever in the present situation — there is one over-riding consideration which they seem to have overlooked: Grocer's sanity.

Grocer takes offence terribly easily, and might do anything in a fit of pique.

At this moment of time it is rather important that he sees sense and gives way to the miners' blackmail[1], even if it means he has to resign gracefully in favour of his lovely, oyster-eyed Secretary for Employment, Mr Whitelaw. But, like a gorilla in the zoo, he might do anything if he thinks we are laughing at him. All together then: Nice Grocer! Clever Flexible Grocer! Statesmanlike Grocer!

Wednesday 27th December
I hope none of those tiresome left wingers ever learns about the fun we had at the Palace last night. In these times of austerity and crisis it really did the heart good to see about 200 of the nicest people in London sit down to a nine-course meal in honour of the President of Zaire and Madame Mobutu Sese

1. A reference to the threatened miners' strike which eventually brought down the Conservative Government (February 1974) when Mr Heath called a General Election to support his handling of it. The choice was who governs Britain — Parliament (i.e. Mr Heath) or Unions? The country chose the Unions.

Seko, a most engaging woman.

After the Royal Party had retired, we held an impromptu dance. I saw Sir Thomas Brimelow[1] climb under his wife's skirts in their famous imitation of a pantomime horse, in which position they raced Admiral Sir Michael and Lady Pollock round the room. At this, the wife of the Zairean Minister of Transport appeared to have a fit, so we threw all the glasses in the middle of the room and rolled her in them, which is apparently the way they always cure these things in Zaire. I haven't laughed so much for ages.

Thursday 28th December
A letter from Mr Norris McWhirter, editor of that indispensable and beautiful publication, *The Guinness Book of Records*, in answer to my suggestion that the achievement of Mr Cyril Connolly in never having masturbated at the age of 18½ (see *Enemies of Promise* by C. Connolly, Deutsch £2.75, p. 250) should be recorded as a wholesome example to future generations.

Mr McWhirter, who has spent a long time researching Connolly's claim, refers me to Professor Darlington's study of the subject in his *Evolution of Man and Society*, where it is pointed out that among the 900 million male humans there are some with almost nil libido. So it's unlikely that Connolly holds the record, but I still think it was a jolly good show on his part.

Friday 29th December
A busy day exercising the horse. We may come to rely on them more and more as the working classes withdraw their support for the agreeable way of life we have organised down here in Somerset. In the afternoon, more rifle and bayonet practice, against the day there is a threat to our beloved Constitution.

Many people seem to be similarly concerned. Today I hear of a nasty accident which has befallen Clive Jenkins, Britain's wittiest and ablest Trade Union leader, who would make a very competent Prime Minister, I always thing, when Grocer is finally thrown in the Thames.

Clive was exercising his thoroughbred in the grounds of his Essex stately home, Mutton Row, when the horse threw him. As he lay on the ground moaning softly in Welsh, another brute gave him a vicious kick in the side. The result might have been even more serious if the blow had not been broken by the silver spirit flask which Clive sensibly carries in his hip pocket on these occasions.

Saturday 30th December
A telephone call from my old friend Stan

Gebler-Davis of the *Evening Standard*, another of those journalists who seems a little uncertain of his own name, writing for *Harpers-Queen* under the strange pseudonym of Len Berger-Jones.

Stan is one of those journalists of the old school: black-toothed, cross-eyed, with that indefinable air of never having quite washed behind his ears, he nevertheless knows how to dig for his information. This grand tradition has nearly disappeared now as the Stans are replaced by over-educated, over-washed young men from the universities who think they can get by on their brilliant intellects.

Stan tells me he is writing another article for *Harpers-Queen* about Andrew "Jesus" Sinclair, the Soho mystic-genius-prophet-Redeemer for whom he has a touching hero worship.

Well done, Stan, I say. Then he asks me if I can help him out with any illuminating quotes from the great man — anything amusing, original or clever which I may have read or heard.

I think hard. I must have known Jesus, man and boy, for the best part of 20 years, but I can't actually remember having read or heard him say anything which quite fits into any of those categories.

Sunday 31st December
After my note on the Arts and Books pages of the *Sunday Times* in the last *Eye*, it is encouraging to learn that Julian Symons is going to give up novel reviewing there after six years. He describes his symptoms thus:

"Signs of stress having recently become apparent, a gradual running down of the machine indicated by the gasket blown. . . an insistent **carburettor** clogging. . . even the standard three-star fuel of historical fiction . . . had made the engine begin to stutter. After all, aren't we being urged to save fuel?

"To shift gear out of metaphor, questions about the State of the Novel present an irresistible lure to any departing novel reviewer."

The state of the novel might be considerably healthier if newspapers like the *Sunday Times* did not employ seedy old motor mechanics as critics. Those who have met Symons say he has a pleasant manner, but he was a bad and boring reviewer. He may never have reached the heights of absurdity scaled by resident pseuds like Dr George Steiner, but his judgement was just as bad as Steiner's and his writing even less distinguished.

Having said which, I hope he will accept my best wishes for his future prosperity as Motoring Correspondent or wherever the Dame[2] decides to send him next.

---

1. Brimelow had succeeded Greenhill as Permanent Head of the Foreign Office. Born 25 October 1915, noted for part in forcible repatriation of two million Russians after World War II.
2. Harold Evans, Editor of the Sunday Times (q.v.).

1974

In the months before the first General Election, and in the tense few days after it while Heath tries desperately to hold on to office, Revolution looms. Harold Wilson is returned in two elections, dedicated to a "fundamental and irreversible shift in the balance of wealth and power in favour of working people and their families". In effect, this means government by Mr Len Murray of the T.U.C. and a handful of cronies. Murray persistently refuses to observe the conventions of democratic government and reveal what type of knickers his wife prefers.

The Conservatives obstinately delay over jettisoning their disastrous leader, Edward Heath. Mr Wilson makes his secretary a Life Peeress and opens the Great Debate about whether her children are entitled to be called "Honourable". Waugh supports proposals for a Currency Commission to take currency management out of politics and put it into the hands of a Committee to include an artist, a psychiatrist, a woman, a Negro and a dwarf. Healey warns of social strains which may be too violent for the fabric of our democracy to withstand.

Nixon resigns and Princess Anne's horse, Doublet, has to be destroyed after a fall. Trade Unionists are to be found at every dinner or luncheon party in Downing Street. Michael Foot's odious Industrial Relations Act requires every Englishman to stop and talk to a strike picket if called upon to do so. An alarming rise is discerned in the numbers of male homosexuals around London.

Monday 1st January

A strange telephone call asking me to be photographed for a new women's magazine without any clothes on. I am rather intrigued by the idea until the young lady mentions the names of some other people whom she hopes to interest. She sounds hurt when I refuse, pointing out I would be earning more dollars for Grocer. Why doesn't she ask him?

Tuesday 2nd January

Who should I vote for as a founder member of Peregrine Worsthorne's soft underbelly of the bourgeoisie[1]? On the one hand, Grocer has some solid achievements behind him in the three-day-week and the miners' go-slow, both of which seem sensible and humane measures full of hope for the future[2].

Again, there is a danger that if the Labour Party is elected in its present silly mood, the lower classes will take away all my Wealth. Which might lead one to give Grocer another chance.

But then one thinks of all the annoying things he has done: putting Lieutenant Phillips's face on the postage stamps at the time of Princess Anne's shameful wedding; allowing Captain Grounds-for-Divorce to make a mockery of the ceremony with his tight trousers; introducing museum charges, detente with the Russians and Sunday football. No, I don't think I will be voting this time, either.

Wednesday 17th January

In Berwickshire, staying with the Vasses at their rather dingy home called "The Hirsel" for the historic trial of Miss Eleanor Donaghy, accused of cruelty to prawns. She is alleged to have put them on a hot plate and watched them jump around.

Eleanor's defence is that prawns are not animals and so do not qualify under the Protection of Animals (Scotland) Act 1912. She thinks they are insects, and as such unprotected in law from anything she might choose to do to them.

If her case is upheld, and cruelty to prawns is declared legal, an entirely new vista of sport opens up through the long days of leisure ahead. Less well-off people living in our towns and suburbs, with few opportunities for stag hunting, can join in to their hearts' contents.

From young Charles Vass — he is a nephew of the Baillie who works for *The Times* —

I hear of plans to give up weekly Tupperware parties at his Neasden villa in favour of Prawn Evenings.

One amusing trick is to bemuse your prawn with strong drink and then, by dangling radish leaves (which it mistakes for seaweed) in front of its face you tempt it to jump off the end of the table into a cauldron of boiling *sauce mousseline*. Others shoot at them with grains of rice from pea shooters, but one of the best ways of annoying a prawn is simply to put it in the middle of a room and laugh at it. Prawns have very little sense of humour and hate being laughed at. But we must all await the Court's decision before deciding on further refinements of this sport.

Thursday 25th January

A solid hour of Soviet propaganda on Independent Television's *World at War* last night, couched in such crude and adulatory tones as surely not even Russian viewers can still be expected to take seriously. When the fawning English commentator started referring to the unanimity of the Ukraine under Stalin and the "liberation" of Poland by the Red Army, I had to leave the room to be sick.

Friday 26th January

One sinister — and completely unremarked — feature of Grocer's government reshuffle is the way Lord Gowrie, 34, has suddenly been catapulted into ninety-sixth place among the ninety-nine Parliamentary appointments. Soon he will be within sniffing distance of Supreme Power.

---

1. This refers to a characteristically challenging article which Mr Worsthorne had written in the Sunday Telegraph.

2. Heath had imposed a three-day working week throughout the land in response to the coal and power shortage. It was very popular.

As the only full-blooded Asiatic in the present government, "Grey" Gowrie (as he is cruelly nicknamed by his fellow peers) has been employed welcoming Afro-Asian heads of state on their arrival at London Airport.

Poor Grey! I knew him well at Balliol, where he was one of those vulnerable, self-important, quaintly ambitious young men from the developing world who still put their hopes of fame and fortune in a political career. But things are looking up at last.

Saturday 27th January

The Chinese are quite right to denounce Beethoven as a class enemy seeking to reverse the decisions of the Great Cultural Revolution and undermine the dictatorship of the workers by encouraging certain "spontaneous tendencies towards capitalism", especially in the rural areas. I confess that I seldom find my warm admiration for the working class much enhanced by listening to Beethoven.

We should all be on our guard against any middle class backlash. Already I have found three fascists under my bed and had to whip them soundly before they would agree to be dosed with Syrup of Figs — although I disapprove of corporal punishment in principle, of course. For my own part, I shall listen to nothing but the pop group called Slade[1] while the present uncertainties last.

Monday 2nd February

Both the BBC and ITA seem to have imposed a ban on all mention of the word "revolution" in current affairs programmes[2]. This is grave dereliction of duty. Here are a few precautions we should all take against the day when the workers threaten to invade our homes and take our womenfolk.

1. Never have less than a month's supply of food and wine in the house.
2. Ask the head of your local militia to dinner.
3. Keep all ammunition in a dry place, separate from firearms.
4. Keep your dogs hungry and tied up, throwing lumps of coal etc. from time to time.
5. Promote an awareness of the problem by public readings from *Workers' Press* in every saloon bar you visit.
6. Never travel on a train without a good length of rope in your attache case, in case it becomes necessary to hang the driver.

Tuesday 3rd February

A very sensible suggestion from the Archbishop of Canterbury in our present prerevolutionary situation. Writing in *The Times* he urges that the workers should be encouraged to learn Greek.

This may seem hard, but in fact Greek is a much easier language to learn than it looks, despite a proliferation of tenses in the conjugation of verbs — there is an optative mood as well as the indicative and subjunctive moods we know so well in our native English.

As against this, they will be relieved to learn that Greek has no ablative case in the declension of nouns. This saves an enormous amount of work, and should make the proposition particularly attractive to our "workers" as they are still laughingly called.

Dr Ramsey is appealing for £40,000 towards this urgent and humane end. I hope readers will send him as much money as they have got.

Thursday 5th February

The first meeting of the Chapman Pincher[3] Vigilantes group to smash the working class was held at the White Tower in Charlotte Street. Our membership is largely composed of MI5 men and senior officers of the armed services, so I fear I cannot reveal their names. But I can reveal that the bill for wine and food came to £66 a head, kindly paid by a gentleman from the American Embassy whose name I never caught. One of the high spots of the evening was when a certain Air Chief Marshal read out the menu of Joe Gormley[4]'s £19 a head dinner at the White House restaurant in Albany Street, to jeers and derisive laughter from the assembled company.

1. A proletarian group.
2. The miners' strike and three-day-week are still in force, with Mr Heath's disastrous General Election looming.
3. A journalist.
4. President, National Union of Mineworkers 1971. Born 5 July 1917, noted for cuddliness.

Sunday 8th February

Poor old Solzhenitsyn[1]! I thought his last book possibly less good than its predecessors, but he has certainly done nothing to deserve being shut up with Heinrich Boll, the 56-year-old German novelist and Nobel Prize winner. Germans, of course, can generally hold their own when it comes to producing champion bores, but Heinrich Boll is in a class of his own.

His last full-length novel, *The Clown* (*'Ansichten eines Clowns'*), about the mental breakdown of a wretched music hall entertainer in Bonn might serve as a university text book on how to achieve maximum boredom and depression with minimum content. Soon Solzhenitsyn will be screaming to be allowed back to his cell in the Lubianka. I would ask Solzhenitsyn down to Combe Florey like Anatoly Kuznetsov[2] before him except that I fear he might frighten my poor wife.

Monday 9th February

The blowing-up of the National Defence College at Latimer, near Chalfont, Bucks., which I am told is planned for tomorrow[3], should draw attention to the vile architecture which the Ministry of Defence has been allowed to put up all over the country, under cover of the Official Secrets Act.

I remain neutral on the matter of IRA aims and methods. But if the army will take this opportunity to look at the appalling collection of huts and jerry-built atrocities with which it disfigures the face of England, it will realise that they constitute a provocation to anybody with views on any subject whatever.

Tuesday 17th February

To the Palace to receive my CBE[4] from a smiling Queen Mother — the Queen is apparently in Uganda or somewhere. It is a very handsome bauble and becomes me rather well. Thank you, Grocer.

A disadvantage of these agreeable things from many people's point of view is that they can only be worn with full evening dress, that is to say, white tie and tails. This does not worry me particularly, because of course in Somerset we still do wear the more formal evening dress for dinner unless we are dining with the middle class.

But it occurs to me that as these awards are increasingly made to people from quite ordinary backgrounds (quite rightly, in my view), many of the recipients may only possess a dinner jacket, and will never have an opportunity of wearing them unless they hire evening dress at considerable expense to themselves and some risk of contagious disease.

If Labour wins the election on the sort of left-wing ticket which they have shown so bravely throughout the campaign, they might pluck up courage to introduce legislation allowing Commanders of the British Empire to wear their insignia with an ordinary dinner jacket. At any rate, I pass the idea to Mr Wedgwood Benn, who seems the most anxious to get things done. But if past experience is anything to go by, they will forget all their radicalism as soon as they're in office and we'll have to wait until Paul Foot comes to power for this sensible and humane reform.

Wednesday 18th February

On Monday I went to the Aldwych Theatre for a world premiere of David Mercer's new play, *Duck Soup*. It was a miserable and pointless collection of stale attitudes and affected, silly little jokes, unconnected by any logical argument. One suffered for the poor actors and actresses of the Royal Shakespeare Company, lumbered with this drivel by some doped-out pseud in the Department of Creative Planning.

In today's *Times* Irving Wardle[5] devotes about 700 words to discussing the play's possible meaning. He praises it for its "muscularity, witty writing and some vigorous comic reversals"; he speculates that a half-witted Red Indian who lopes across the stage from time to time muttering, like Lord Gowrie, about the wrongs of his people may be "another absolute of political purity in place of the fallen East European ideal". But Wardle has doubts about the play's ultimate destination.

In the name of truth and justice, I challenge the Editor of *The Times*, whom I believe to be an educated, intelligent and fair-minded man, to go and look at this rubbish. If he agrees with what I say about it, and if he feels that he has any moral obligation as Editor of *The Times*, to rescue the English theatre from the raddled clique of pseuds who are slowly throttling it, he will send for Mr Wardle and sack the brute.

---

1. The Russian author had just consented to being deported from the Soviet Union.
2. An earlier Soviet literary defector whose interview with Malcolm Muggeridge was televised, under conditions of great secrecy, at Waugh's home in Somerset.
3. A bomb there next day did little permanent damage.
4. Commander of the British Empire. A middle-rank award.
5. A journalist and pseud.

Thursday 19th February

Hats off to Mrs Jean Rook, the much malign-
ed star columnist of the *Daily Express.*
In that organ she describes her first meeting
in a pub with Grocer Heath. Instead of asking
him timidly and sycophantically about his
Relatives Report, as any miserable, cringing
member of the Parliamentary Press Lobby
would have done, she demands to know why
he is so fat.

This is far more interesting, and far more
germane to the election. Grocer replied:
"Yes, I must say I am. The trouble is I don't
get any swimming now. We had to turn off
the pool heating at Chequers — it's oil — and
the boat's laid up so I have to make do with
walks at the weekends."

Then Grocer starts to laugh — the bit
Mrs Rook had been dreading — and provides
her with one of the finest pieces of descriptive
reporting I have yet seen in this election:

"His shoulders heaved, his teeth break.
'Ee-uck, Ee-uck,' sweeps over like a gale
blowing the froth off his supporters' beer.

"Actually, when you're in the centre of
the whirlwind. . . it's not so bad. You feel a
bit seasick, but you can survive so long as
you bob up and down with the shoulders."

Because, tragically, so few people read the
Daily Express nowadays, I have decided to
reproduce this scene.

Friday 20th February

Electors of Newham, North East, have an
agonising choice to make next week between
Vanessa Redgrave, the hideous, boring actress
who represents Gerry Healy's Revolutionary
Workers' Party, and John Ross of the International Marxist Group, whose platform includes solidarity with the miners, advocacy
of more strikes, support for the IRA and
agitation for the release of the London
bombers.

Vanessa, according to Healy, believes that
the government is conspiring with military
chiefs of staff to introduce a new order if the
Tories win. "Airfields in Britain are now being prepared as potential concentration
camps," explains this balding, dwarf, Liver-
pudlian twit. For her own part, Vanessa
hopes by her frightful presence to shock the
workers out of apathy. "I am standing to
bring the clearest and starkest warning to the
working class of what would happen to them
if the Tory government is returned," she says.

Saturday 21st February

I now have £2,400-worth of lavatory paper
stored in my cellars[1]. If unrolled, it would
stretch 80 times round every Chinaman laid
end to end from here to Helsinki. It is possible, of course, that my economic analysis
has been completely wrong and we will soon
be back into the good old days of growth and
the Stop-Go cycle. If so, the Chinamen might
as well go home.

---

1. This was a period of sudden shortages and panic buying.

Sunday 1st March
Canvassing for my old friend Gerald Kauffmann, the Labour candidate for the r the
Ardwick division of Manchester, I am again
impressed by the extreme ugliness of English
people and places which one only sees at
times such as these.

The problem, I fear, is insoluble.
Give them more money, and they use it to
build tower blocks of even greater hideous-
ness, where they grow depressed and take to
vandalism and more serious crimes against
each other. One answer, I suppose, is not to
canvass at General Elections. Certainly, there
could be no other reason for coming to this
sort of place.

Meanwhile, I am offering a prize of a
week's supply of Kennomeat to whichever
elected candidate most resembles his consti-
uency. So far, my curly-headed friend Gerald
is miles ahead[1].

Tuesday 3rd March
In a last minute effort to whip up indignation
against the Government, Paul Johnson pro-
duces some terrifying figures for price rises in
the *New Statesman*: a fortnight's salmon fishing now costs £800; shooting in Morayshire
is now £550 per gun per week; in Banffshire,
Lord Seafield is charging £1,100 a week for
his grouse; deer-stalking in Inverness is £90
a day.

He has a point, of course. There must be
many people around today who simply can't
afford these new charges at all. It is easy to
accept Mr Johnson's argument that the
Government should do something about it,
even if this means a subsidy.

Elsewhere he reveals that things are now
so bad that the Duke of Buccleuch and Lord
Hamilton both need head-keepers and the
poor Duke of Wellington is even having to
advertise for a junior water bailiff.

But I see light at the end of the tunnel.
This country has gone through the most unhappy period of acute labour shortage while
everybody went to work in factories. Now all
this looks as though it is going to sort itself
out. Very soon, the country will be back to
normal, with one third of the labour force
employed in domestic service, as it always
used to be.

In our new mood of quiet optimism, we
should feel grateful to the leaders of both
Parties, who have brought this about. It must
be a moment of particular pride for Mr Heath

whose mother, of course, was in domestic
service in the good old days, to have brought
the country back to its senses.

Wednesday 4th March
A very strange telephone call from Baillie
Vass, our beloved 92-year-old Foreign Secretary. If I did not know him so well, I might
suppose he was suffering from the effects of
tiredness. He rang me all the way from his
drab, cold house at Coldstream to tell me
that by a decision of the Duns Sheriff Court
it is now perfectly legal to torture prawns[2].

I suppose this is quite interesting, and I am
always in favour of anything that extends
the boundaries of human freedom, but I
really would have thought this senile old
fool had more important things to worry
about in the middle of a vital election campaign.

He wanted to ask me whether, when a
prawn waves its arms in the air, this means
that it is angry or in great pain. I couldn't
answer this question and referred him to the
Daily Telegraph Information Service.

Thursday 5th March
I refused all invitations to celebrate this gruesome night[3] at Badger Hall and went instead
to my Lady Fartwell's in Cowley Street, but
was driven out by her idiotic cries of delight
at every Liberal victory. Silly woman.

So I swallowed my pride and went to the
Badgers'[4], drawn by the most horrible smell
of pipe-smoke, sweat and human excrement.
What a place to be, and what company to
find oneself in at the moment of civilisation's
collapse!

None of the girls was pretty, none of the
men was clever. Suddenly the reason dawned
on me — childhood deprivation. Richard
Briginshaw, the fearless General Secretary of
SOGAT, has appealed for a "genuinely independent body. . . to report on any bias, class
control and onesidedness in the Press and
mass media in this country". As soon as it is
set up, I shall report the *Sunday Times*.

I counted two train drivers' sons in the
room and at least one miner's daughter,
although there were no miners on this occasion, thank God. Nobody present was what
might be called a gentleman, although poor
Frank Giles, I must admit, always tries very
hard. But this control of what was once a
great national newspaper by people who are
exclusively from the lower class is plainly the
sort of thing Mr Briginshaw is worried about.

1. Kaufman a Labour politician, was noted for baldness and adulation of Harold Wilson.
2. c.f. 25 January 1974 for details of this case.
3. The first General Election of 1974.
4. Ruth and Ron Hall (q.v.).

Friday 6th March
The only useful result of this fraudulent
election has been the return of Ernle Money
in Ipswich with his majority up from 13 to
259. He can now proceed with his excellent
campaign for authors' Public Lending Right
in the months ahead. The most disappointing
result has been Jeremy Thorpe's success in
North Devon. Thorpe was already conceited
enough and now threatens to become one of
the great embarrassments of politics. Soon,
I may have to reveal some of the things in
my file on this revolting man[1].

Saturday 7th March
I feel I ought to warn my readers against a
very dangerous and unpleasant book which
has just been published by Allen Lane: *An
Opposing Man,* the posthumous autobiography of an Austrian communist called
Ernst Fischer.

The objectionable part comes in the introduction by John Berger, the brilliant art
historian and charlatan. Writing about himself, Berger says: "One wants to make love
with fish, with fruit, with hills, with forests,
in the sea".

One would have thought our countryside
has been raped and polluted enough without
encouraging further assault on it from trendy,
half-witted left-wingers, trying to be artistic.
Quite apart from this it is a serious criminal
offence to make love with a fish (see Sexual

Offences Act, 1956). Incitement is similarly
an offence, and anybody who buys this book
may well be abetting Berger's criminal
behaviour.

Sunday 8th March
Very little was heard throughout this campaign of the Rev. Andrew Hallidie-Smith,
rector of Arlesford, Essex, whose solution to
our problems, given from the pulpit a short
time ago, was that union militants should be
executed.

I wish my own church had given clear
instructions at this difficult time, but
Cardinal Heenan seemed hopelessly confused
so I didn't vote. If executing union militants
would really do some good, I am sure many
of them would be prepared to volunteer for
this in the national interest. Like most
moderates, I have an unshakeable belief in
the basic patriotism of the trade union movement, but experience has shown that a voluntary approach has far more chance of working
than any attempt at compulsion.

Friday 13th March
I was disappointed by gritty, boastful Dame
Harold Evans's Granada lecture on *The Half-
Free Press.* I had hoped that as editor of the
Sunday Times — on the publishing side of
the Thomson Travel and North Sea oil
empire — he would tell us how he success-

1. In April 1976, Thorpe started threatening Private Eye with prosecution for criminal libel.
   He resigned only a few days later.

fully resists pressures to influence news and comment on Travel, North Sea oil, etc., and how he champions freedom of expression among those who work for him. Instead, we had the usual heavy bragging about how brave and clever he was to think of publishing an article on the Thalidomide affair which he never, in fact, quite dared to publish.

Now the *New Statesman* has decided to reprint a version of the lecture. Oddly enough, I remember reading an amusing Diary piece in the *New Statesman* some months ago by that great journalist and very wonderful man, Richard West. West revealed how a profile of Rupert "Dirty Digger" Murdoch[1] written for the Colour Magazine had been "held over" on the Dame's intervention. He revealed the existence of a memorandum from Digger arguing that the article was inaccurate and starting: "Point One; I do not like sausages".

Recently — more than six months later — a friend who works for the *Sunday Times* asked West into his office for a drink. West looked embarrassed and eventually admitted that since his little joke appeared in the *New Statesman*, not only is he forbidden to do any work for the *Sunday Times* but the Dame has even forbidden him to set foot on the premises.

Saturday 14th March

Tomorrow being St Patrick's Day, I have been asked to what might be quite an amusing party. Its highlight will be the burning of a picture by Vermeer, the Dutch artist, and guests are asked to "cavort about in true lunatic fashion"[2].

However, I am a little suspicious. The lavishness of the entertainment smacks of Public Relations, and I don't know what makes them suppose the picture will burn. Last Connolly Night[3] I tried to burn some deeply sensitive canvases by David Hockney and Nolan but they only smouldered and gave off an offensive smell.

Sunday 15th March

News of the Archbishop of Canterbury's retirement will come as a sad shock to all satirists. The problem of finding a successor seems almost insurmountable: Baillie Vass is far too old; Tom Corbishley, the dreaded Jesuit preacher, is too ugly; Jimmy Savile[4] may look the part but his accent is wrong; Sir John Gielgud[5] has the right speaking voice, but he is unmarried and that could raise problems.

The best solution would be to ask King Faisal of Saudi Arabia to send us an Imam. The Arabs have made it clear that their main reason for being difficult about their oil is religious — to secure the triumph of Islam over the Christian infidel.

This seems a perfectly reasonable point of view and there is nothing in the history of the Church of England to make one suppose that many people would object to any minor shift of doctrine involved in acceptance of the Koran.

1. Australian newspaper proprietor, b. 11 March 1931. Noted for once employing Waugh as chief political commentator, News of the World. Waugh always refers to this period (1969/70) with great affection.

2. This picture was being held to ransom by thieves who threatened to burn it.

3. September 10th, Connolly's birthday.

4. A wireless 'personality' given to charitable causes.

5. The actor. Born 14 April 1904. Noted for bachelor idiosyncracies.

A few of our more elderly clergymen will object to climbing their church towers to call the Faithful to prayer, and many more will object to the ban on alcoholic liquor. But somebody in this country has got to take his jacket off and get down to work.

It is for the Queen to set an example. I think she would look very fetching in a yashmak, and an early marriage between Prince Charles and some member of the Royal House of Saudi Arabia might go a long way towards answering the tricky question of who will pay for our next round of general increases.

Monday 23rd March
How nice that Wislon means to keep the Wank Tank. This quaint old British institution was charged with warning Grocer about the energy crisis which Grocer now says came as a complete surprise to him. That is why Britain is in so much worse trouble than everybody else. Hats off to Lord Top Wank[1] and his merry men.

One appointment yet to be announced is who will take over Jim Prior's responsibilities as Minister for Contraception. The obvious choice is our one and only "Foot and Mouth" Fred Peart, now happily returned to the Ministry of Agriculture where he caused such devastation among the nation's cows and pigs a few years ago.

There is talk of sending him on a crash course to the Lovecraft Centre in Tottenham Court Road to arm himself with materials for what looks like being a very tough Parliament[2].

Tuesday 24th March
In the morning I go to the Royal Horticultural Society in Vincent Square to choose a button-hole for the opening of Parliament. Unfortunately, the best orchid there — a new cymbidium called the Mavourneen Jester — went for £20,000 to a Californian buyer. One has to be prepared to pay a couple of hundred pounds for a really nice button-hole nowadays, but this sort of figure shows how things were getting out of hand under Mr Heath and emphasises the importance of Mr Wilson's prices policy.

After the Queen's Speech I reflect on how much better a Labour government is at handling the drunken toadies of the Parliamentary Press Lobby. Every newspaper will carry the message that the Queen's Speech was "moderate", but listening to it from the Diplomatic Gallery in the House of Lords I seriously wondered whether the Queen had gone mad, with all her talk about the redistribution of wealth as something praiseworthy and desirable.

The present government has already added a footnote to the English language by its use of the expression "national unity" to mean taking away more of my hard-earned income and giving it to the lower classes. The louder Mr Wilson talks of his unity, the faster we should all count our spoons. But I suppose anything is better than Grocer's method of endearing himself to the voters with loud and embarrassing calls for "growth".

So far as any of us have any interest in politics, we should surely direct it towards seeing that the lower classes do not get any richer than they already are and make the country more hideous than it already is with their transistor radios and plastic accessories. I can see it may be my patriotic duty to do no work at all next year.

Wednesday 25th March
Larry Adler[3] has offered me £35 to tell a boring and disgusting story about President Nixon which he appears to find funny. I apologise to readers, but these are hard times for satirists. Here it is:

Mr Nixon was advised that he should be circumcised in order to ingratiate himself with Jewish voters. The appointed mohel *(ritual circumciser) said he could not do it, explaining "There is no end to this prick".*

Mr Adler told this story at a lunch in the office of a certain "humorous" weekly magazine much favoured by the dental profession. Enoch Powell was also present, but did not smile. Since then, Mr Adler has been wandering all over the earth trying to find someone to print this tasteless and unpleasant story.

Monday 29th March
David Wood, venerable Political Editor of *The Times* today becomes the first commentator to have woken up to the fact which has been painfully apparent to everyone else since the election, that the country is now governed by its trade union leaders.

David explains this Social Contract which everyone is talking about. It means that the government does everything the union leaders tell them to do in exchange for the

---

1. 3rd Baron Rothschild (q.v.).

2. Mr Harold Wilson's Labour Government was returned with no overall majority.

3. A left-wing mouth organist. This bribe was never paid, and Waugh never forgave Adler for this act of dishonesty. Later, when Adler was arrested for stealing toffees in Piccadilly, Waugh followed the proceedings with unseemly relish.

union leaders asking their members politely to moderate their pay claims, if that is what they feel like doing, on a voluntary basis.

So Messrs Len Murray[1], Hugh Scanlon[2] and Jack Jones[3] really are our rulers now. I don't object to this on the grounds that nobody voted for them to govern us, since general elections are a farce in any case. I do object that they have not been subjected to the thorough scrutiny which is such an essential part of our democracy. Even Mr Brezhnev has to discuss his smoking habit with journalists, but we know nothing about this crowd. What does Jack Jones wear in bed? Does Mrs Murray wear frilly knickers or none at all?

It is all very well for Denis Healey to moan about how inflation is going to create "political and social strains which may be too violent for the fabric of our democracy to withstand". Until we can get an answer to these simple questions about Jack Jones's bedwear and Mrs Murray's knickers, we must conclude that democracy is already dead.

Tuesday 30th March
A letter from Mrs Molly Hewitt, of Stockport, in today's newspaper suggests Peter Jay[4] for Prime Minister. "I think he's marvellous," she writes. "I could listen to him on television for hours at a time".

At last it seemed we might save this country from the miserable, emotionally deformed generation which is leading it to its ruin. Few of my contemporaries have shown any interest in politics, but this should not prevent Mr Jay from building a Cabinet of All the Talents:

Dominic Horrid[5], Financial Secretary
Winston S. Churchill, Jr., Sport
Lord Gowrie, Contraception
Paul Foot, Working Classes
Piers Paul Read[6], Food
Jawn Wells, Animal Noises

Perhaps I shall think of some more, but that is quite an impressive list to be getting on with. Unfortunately, when I tried telephoning Mrs Hewitt to discuss my plans, I was told that there was nobody of that name listed in Stockport. I fear it must have been another practical joke by young Charles Vass, the puckish editor-elect of *The Times*.

Wednesday 7th April
I was a little upset, on reading the Duchess of Bedford's autobiography, *Nicole Nobody*,

published today by W.H. Allen, to see her description of an encounter we had at the Midland Hotel, Manchester, some years after the war. One always hopes that one's lady friends will preserve a decent reticence about these affairs, if only to avoid frightening other men away, but I suppose that those who become Duchesses must learn to sacrifice everything for publicity.

I can't complain, as she says nothing to identify me and describes me as a "superb lover". My own recollection of the event is only slightly different from hers. As I remember it, I knocked on a bedroom door at random to ask if I could borrow some toothpaste, and one thing led to another.

Nicole does, however, reveal the mysterious fact that during the three days I spent with her I never once stopped smiling. I think it would be unchivalrous, after all these years, to mention what I was smiling about.

Thursday 8th April
Readers of the corrupt national press may have been puzzled to learn of a leadership debate inside the Conservative Party. What is there to debate about? Grocer has been a disaster. Not only is he an unattractive, almost universally disliked man, but he has learnt nothing from his mistakes and seems determined to make them all again.

The obvious replacement is William Whitelaw, Grocer's lovely oyster-eyed lieutenant. Yet for some extraordinary reason people are now talking about other choices. The reason for this is the sad fact that Oyster Eyes has become increasingly tired and emotional since his return from Northern Ireland.

According to worried friends, William now spends his time braying like a donkey and declaring his loyalty and love for Grocer in the most extravagant terms between convulsive sobs.

With less than six months to go before the election he had better pull himself together, but even a tired and emotional William would be a better bet than the other contenders, and much better than the doomed Grocer. Colleagues should urge the Grocer to die and let his friend grow out of this unfortunate infatuation, wonderful as it may be, and passing the love of women.

1. General Secretary of TUC.

2. Head of Engineers' Union.

3. Head of Transport and General Workers' Union.

4. A journalist.

5. Dominick Harrod, a journalist.

6. A good novelist, who had recently written a non-fiction book about South American footballers who ate each other after a plane crash.

Friday 9th April
Another person who should think of dying
soon is the Pope[1]. One quite understands
that prolonged sexual abstinence can have an
effect on the judgement, but after 76 years
his problems are plainly beginning to get out
of hand. His latest claim that the Mother of
Christ was a thoroughly Modern Mary and
early apostle of women's lib will put a heavy
strain on the credulity of the faithful.

At the same time, he warns us against
"sterile and ephemeral sentimentality" in our
devotion to miraculous statues and the like.
This suggestion cuts at the very root of the
Church's survival. In fact all his doctrinal
difficulties are met in the new Miraculous
Mary Holy Year souvenir kit, produced by
Gnome Enterprises (in association with the
BBC and Phuwatascorcha Inc., Japan).
This assembles to become your very own
miraculous statue to take home with you.
It glows in the dark, bleeds once a month,
and can perform an unbelievable Cha-Cha-
Cha to the music of Max Jaffa on the silver
strings. Every set contains a certificate of
authenticity signed by Our Lady Magnesia
Freelove herself, and instructions on tech-
nique by the world famous Blessed Virgin
Mary Kenny, Rtd. Hurry while stocks last.

Saturday 10th April
The new law introduced by Michael Foot
that anyone meeting a strike picket has got to
stop and talk to it may seem progressive, but
could easily become another instrument for
oppressing the masses.

The great problem for the ordinary, law-
abiding citizen is going to be what he can
talk about to these people. The weather
always seems a trifle lame but they seldom
have much interest in art, religion, philosophy or literature. Perhaps the government
will produce a green paper suggesting likely
subjects and providing useful information
about football matches, recent television
programmes, etc.

The crunch is going to come when a min-
ority of wreckers decides to engage them in
conversation about Kirkegaard or the novels
of Alain Robbe-Grillet. An uncle of mine who
is a philosopher suggests that what really
enrages the masses is not so much any suggestion that other people may be richer than
they are, but that other people may be
superior to them. So this policy of enforced
conversation may be a double-edged weapon
so far as making them any happier is
concerned. I am not at all sure about this,
but it may be worth trying.

Monday 12th April   *France*
In Paris for a few days in case President Pompidou wishes to see me before he dies.
A good test of the English government is
how many francs you can buy for a pound.
Clever Mr Healey has already got it up to
11.35 — at the height of Grocer's disastrous
rule it stood at 9.80, while under Jenkins it
reached 13.00. How nice, at last, to have a
government which is trusted to behave itself.

It is high time the Tories killed Grocer or
forced him to resign. Everybody accepts that,
drunk or sober, William Whitelaw is the only
remotely trustworthy figure in the Conservative Party, but there is a feeling that the
Tories are bound to lose the next election
anyway; far better to let horrible old Grocer
take the rap for that and let William (or the
unspeakable Robert Carr) start with a clean
sheet.

But it is by no means certain that the
Tories need lose the next election. Five

1. **Pope Paul VI.**

months is a very long time in politics, and if my French friends are to be believed, the English are in for some very nasty shocks before then. What is absolutely certain is that no party will ever be elected again with Grocer as its leader. My French friends will be rather hurt if the Tories manage to lose the election by keeping Grocer after everything has been set up for them to win it[1].

Tuesday 13th April

Tomorrow I must fly briefly back to London to hear Lord Snowdon's maiden speech in the House of Lords on the vexed problem of self-propelled invalid chairs. Of course, Lord Snowbottom, as we must all learn to call him now he is so important, has his own views on this subject which may not coincide with my own, but we must all be prepared to listen to the other side.

The Sharp Report on the mobility of disabled people, which is the subject of this debate, takes the line that invalid cars are unsafe and should be replaced by adapted small cars. For my own part, I do not see why invalids should be treated as second-class citizens and confined to small cars. I would like to see an adapted version of the *Concorde* aircraft made available as a matter of first priority.

Snowbottom's approach so far has been to design various invalid chairs which turn over whenever the invalid tries to go round a corner. This certainly makes its contribution to national entertainment, but can be a grave nuisance for more serious-minded citizens who wish to travel from one place to another. Probably there is no ideal solution and the problem, like so many others, is insoluble.

Wednesday 14th April

Why have neither Harold Wilson nor Mrs Williams dared issue a writ against me? Why am I practically the only journalist in Fleet Street to have been singled out in this way? I daren't show my face in *El Vino*[2] while this embarrassing situation lasts and am taking the next plane back to Paris.

Thursday 22nd April

At Easter, the French kill thousands of suckling pigs and roast them whole to celebrate the Resurrection of their Saviour. Even at my favourite restaurant on the Avenue Marceau I find I have no appetite, as I keep thinking of poor Alan Brien back in England. My Easter resolution is to say nothing beastly about Brien for twelve months, and perhaps I will enjoy my luncheon more on Maundy Thursday next year.

Friday 23rd April

The death of Richard Crossman removes the last survivor of the notorious libel case where three Labour politicians sued *The Spectator* over an article by the late Jennie Nicholson (or Clifford or Cross) which described them as being drunk at some conference or other, held, I think, in Venice.

The trial was heard by the Lord Chief Justice, the late Lord Goddard of evil memory, and the plaintiffs were awarded £5,000 each. They were Crossbum, the late Aneurin Bevan, a well-known drunk of the time, and someone called Morgan Philips or Phillips, a Labour Party bore, also long since dead.

In his later years, Crossbum cheerfully admitted that all three of them had been as pissed as newts throughout the entire conference. But the law of libel, alone of all torts, assumes that the defendant is guilty of telling a lie unless he can prove to the contrary, and how can anyone prove that?

Goddard, of course, has long since gone to meet his deserts, but there are other judges just as stupid, as rude and as biased as he was. The paradox involved in actually helping out these unscrupulous and evilly-disposed men by giving them unjust laws to administer was one which clearly tickled the imagination of this Labour intellectual.

He will be sorely missed by those who value the occasional spark of honesty among their politicians. *The Times* obituary points gloatingly to Crossbum's total lack of achievement as a politician: his reform of Commons procedure has been abandoned; as Minister of Housing, he did not build many houses; his ambitious plans to stuff our old age pensioners with more sweets and digestive biscuits than formerly came to nothing. It recalls the classic obituary of the actor Laurence Harvey (ne Skikne) who died last November. I learned it by heart as a model for the day I am reduced to writing *Times* obituaries:

"In general, one has the feeling that his career was never quite clinched. He was always on the point of doing better, appearing in better films than he actually did. On the other hand, he probably made the most of what he was given in the way of talent, and remained somehow a figure to be reckoned with, even if it was often hard to say why."

It is the kindest thing one can possibly say of a politician that he changed nothing. Goodbye, old friend.

Saturday 24th April

At the Requiem Mass for President Georges Pompidou in the Cathedral of Notre Dame I find myself placed next to President Jean

---

1. Heath was retained and the Conservatives lost in November, 1974.

2. A Fleet Street hostelry. Wilson and Williams (soon to become Lady Falkender) had issued writs against many London newspapers alleging libel in reports of Mrs Williams's commercial dealings — the Slag Heap Affair.

Bedel Bokassa of the Central African Republic. As we kneel side by side I realise that he is drunk and appears to be suffering from crabs. Poor Pompidou! I never cared much for him myself, but as a politician he has probably gone to Hell and deserves a better send-off than this assortment of mass murderers and professional liars can offer.

President Nixon seemed distracted and rattled. He could scarcely wait for the end of Mass to start sucking up to President Podgorny[1], but kept waving his place-card at him in a vulgar way. General Bokassa saw me sticking my tongue out at them and asked who I was, but I wished to preserve my incognito and said I was the King of Sweden.

After the Service, Bokassa asked me if I would like to visit some unusual nightclubs he knew in the Central African quarter behind the Gare du Nord. I made my excuses.

Sunday 25th April

Today David Frost[2] is 35. Yesterday, Andre Previn[3] was 45 and the Duke of Northumberland, 60. All that is brightest and best in this country of ours is growing older. How can we stay in the game?

The opportunities are there, of course. I wonder how much the *Sunday Times* has paid Jan Morris[4] for the very wonderful, searing story of how she changed sex. It is little known that I am the only human being in the world who has changed sex and then changed back again.

My reason for changing sex in the first place was a general feeling that at 34 it was time for a change. My reason for changing back was the ghastly boredom of women's conversation after dinner. If Dame Harold Evans or Mr David Astor disputes my claim I am willing to submit to a medical examination in their presence, which will prove that the change-back has been complete in every particular without even a scar to impair the classic proportions of my private parts.

If, on the other hand, they shirk this challenge, one can only draw one's own conclusions about the genuineness of their interest in the surgical sciences.

Wednesday 28th April

I am sad to see in my copy of *Socialist Worker* (a most stimulating newspaper) that Paul Foot reveals the identity of Mr Y and Mr X in the Janie Jones case. This must put an end to all reclamation[5] on the subject, which is a great pity.

For many weeks now I have been asked to private dinner parties to name the guilty men, and there is scarcely a man in public life whose name has not been circulated in whispers from mouth to mouth as a result of my confidential briefings.

I can't see that Foot's action does anything to help the working classes, for whom he has such an irrational passion. Most of us knew the true names all along but suppressed them on the ground that they were extremely boring. Foot has merely spoilt a lot of innocent fun, for which he must be prepared to be rapped on the knuckles in such responsible organs as this Diary.

On the other hand, Judge King Hamilton goes too far in his bungling attempts to send Foot to prison. Foot was not even the editor of the *Socialist Worker*, but someone called Protz whom I do not think I have yet had the pleasure of meeting.

Even Protz should be spared. It is not yet a criminal offence to spoil another person's after-dinner story, and I agree with Harry Evans that it is more important to introduce laws making it a serious offence for anyone — judges and MPs, as well as journalists — to criticise the press in its sacred duty of exposing the Evil Men in our midst. This is especially necessary for more intelligent, thoughtful newspapers like *Private Eye* and *Socialist Worker*.

Nevertheless, I think it is time Protz was relieved of his editorship, and will drop a hint to Tony Cliff, chairman of the International Socialists, at the Confederation of Revolutionary Leaders meeting which I have been asked to chair this evening at the Hyde Park Hotel.

Thursday 29th April

Mrs Castle's decision to introduce free contraceptive devices "without regard to age or marital status" is criticised by the Bishop of Norwich on the grounds that it "must surely encourage the lecherous to harm those below the age of consent". I worry much more about the effect it will have on female old age pensioners.

Most of these live a fairly decorous life nowadays on reaching the age of 80 or so, but who is to tell what orgies of licentiousness will not break out in my own Somerset village where the average age is 92 years 3 months? My life will become unendurable.

It is time we had a sex election here as they are having in France. Chaban Delmas stands for more abortion, Giscard d'Estaing

1. A Russian politician and mass-murderer.

2. A television 'personality'.

3. A popular conductor of the London Symphony Orchestra.

4. A writer, b. James Morris, she changed sex and name in 1973.

5. Reclamation. This word was used by Mr Wilson in defence of his secretary, Mrs Williams, who was charged with speculation over the Slag Heap Affair. For a time it was normal for satirical writers to say 'reclaim' and 'reclamation' where normally they would have said 'speculate' or 'speculation'.

for female elegance and refinement, Jean
Royer for less contraception, more restraint:
"The best contraceptive is 'no'." Madame
Royer goes even further: "My husband and
I believe not only that girls should be virgins
when they marry, but that it would be even
nicer if the husbands were the same."

Is that not exactly what one is saying
when one votes for Grocer? Compare this
clean living man, his reputation unsullied by
any breath of scandal, with the alternative:
Mrs Castle's naked appeal to geriatric
promiscuity. Grocer is 57 and has never said
or done a dirty thing in his life. Mrs Castle is
62.

Friday 30th April
Artists should not be required to take 'O'
levels, argues John Bratby, on the grounds
that creative geniuses are "driven to make
pictures compulsively" and as a result are
frequently unable to pass exams.

It is true that no education is required to
produce paintings nowadays. On the other
hand, we can be sure that if artists are not
made to take exams, every little kiddie in
the country will announce it is driven to
make pictures compulsively; the slow national slide into illiteracy will accelerate and
professional writers like myself will all be
out of a job.

The answer is surely that everybody
should still take 'O' levels as now, and those
who would normally be said to have failed
should instead be declared Artists. They
should be given a hopelessly inadequate
pension and encouraged to slosh around
producing works of genius out of everybody's
way.

Saturday 1st May
I am not one to take offence easily, but even
I can't help noticing that the James Callag-
hans did not ask me to dinner at Lancaster
House for the Polish foreign minister and
Madame Olszowska.

Of course I do not mind in the least.
A glance at the English guests confirms that
this dinner must have been one of the dullest
on record.

Obviously, no calculated affront was intended as I saw Mr Callaghan only the other
day on a certain matter and found him as
friendly and helpful as ever. But this sort of
oversight can only add weight to the question
which is being asked more and more: Does
James Callaghan quite know how to behave
as Foreign Secretary?

The question was asked after his fracas
with Common Market foreign ministers.
One somewhat magisterial answer was offer-
ed by the increasingly eccentric Michael
Leapman, my opposite number on *The
Times:*

"There is a case for Britain's renegotiating
Community membership and there is a case
against it. Neither case is helped by peevish
and erroneous insinuations against Callaghan's
manners and breeding."

Oddly enough, I have seen no insinuations
about Callaghan's breeding. So far as I am
able to discover, his father was a Chief Petty
Officer in the Royal Navy, his grandfather
a silversmith in Coventry, his greatgrandfather
a schoolteacher in County Cork. An admirable lineage, by any reckoning. Sadly, the
family seems to have lost its Faith — possibly
from the admirable example set by their
Protestant Majesties at sea — but I see

nothing in the main line of descent which
could explain the boorish or neglectful
behaviour of any descendant. Yet Leapman
certainly gives us food for thought.

Sunday 2nd May

Atticus, my opposite number on the *Sunday
Times*, written by the pleasant and gifted
Allan Hall, today draws attention to the
atrocious condition of English authors,
beggared by the Free Library system. He was
commending my own recent volume of essays,
Country Topics, excellently witty but beyond
the resources of *Private Eye* readers at Michael
Joseph's exorbitant price of £3.50.

The most distressing feature of the present
situation is the degradation to which prominent writers are now reduced. Poor Lord Snow
(alias C.P. Snurd) may have to hire himself
out as "humanist in residence" at St Barna-
bas Hospital in New York, making daily
rounds of wards where patients lie recovering
from an ugly new form of brain operation.

Obviously, this idea of confronting seriously ill patients with some hideous caricature
of a human face marks a return to the shock
treatment used in primitive African witch-
craft. It may work or it may not. I have an
open mind. I only ask whether this is a
reasonable way for us to expect widely
regarded English novelists to earn a little
money in their old age.

Wednesday 5th May

Who can Hartley Shawcross mean when he
says that he knows of a corrupt politician,
now dead, who is held in high esteem?
Labour chauvinists keep pushing the name
of Ernest Bevin at me.

Nobody under the age of 35 has ever
heard of Bevin, let alone holds him in esteem.
And many people over that age confuse him
with Aneurin Bevan, the well known drunk.
It is rather like asking one's wife or children
to distinguish between Richard Crossbum[1],
the amusing journalist who is unfortunately
dead, and Anthony Crosland[2], the serious,
peach-like, rather conceited Labour politician of 55 who is, I think, Secretary of State
for the Environment or something like that.

In any case, the prospect of uncovering
yet another Labour crook — and a dead one
at that — is too depressing at the present time.
The problem is not to find a politician of
either party who is corrupt, but to find one
who was ever held in high esteem. The only
man who fills the ticket is the late Sir Winston
Churchill KG, PC, OM, CH, FRS etc.

Younger readers may not be absolutely
certain who he was, but there can be no
doubt that he was held in high esteem by the
generation of women who were left behind
in the last war, and even by some of their
simple-minded menfolk. I always thought
they were wrong in this, and in Churchill's
last years conducted an unsuccessful campaign to have him hanged for his part in the
Yalta Agreement. But he evaded me.

The odd thing about this is that so far as
I remember Churchill had nothing to do with
contracts for land clearance in the Ground-
nuts Scheme. Never mind, it looks as if we
may have found another opportunity to take
vengeance on the old brute for his persecution of P.G. Wodehouse.

Thursday 6th May

Pressure is constantly being brought on me
to use this column's not — ah — I hope
entirely inconsiderable influence in world
financial circles to urge a return to the Gold
Standard. There is much to be said for this
course of action but the main objection, it
seems to me, is that we do not at the moment
actually happen to have any gold. It was all
pledged several times over by the Grocer in
the course of his mad struggle to stay in
power.

But I certainly agree with the wise and
good Sir William Rees-Mogg that our currency
is too serious a matter to be entrusted to
politicians. Ideally it should be looked after
by a Committee which includes at least one
artist, a psychiatrist, a woman, a Negro, and
a dwarf.

On the other hand one sees that Francis
Bacon[3] might be considered too common,
Ronnie Laing[4] too tired and emotional, the
lovely Tina Brown[5] too distracting, Mr Mark
Woodnutt[6] too enterprising, and Lord Snowbum too small, so we are left with my original committee of four wise men: Sir William,
Master Peter Jay (to speak for young people),
myself and Lord Balogh. Harold Lever may
be permitted to attend from time to time in
order to protect his very considerable interests in this field.

If MPs object to having the currency and
money supply taken away from their political control they must be ducked in the Thames
until they agree to it. This is no time for the
usual courtesies.

Friday 7th May

I hope Rose Dugdale had nothing to do with
beating up the Beits and stealing their pictures

1. Richard Crossman (q.v.).

2. Anthony Crosland (q.v.), noted for having a pretty, gifted wife.

3. A fashionable painter.

4. A fashionable psychiatrist.

5. A lovely young lady.

6. A Conservative politician of dusky hue who died soon afterwards.

from Russborough. She used to be a most attractive and engaging girl before she went to St Anne's College, Oxford, and allowed the dons there to fill her poor head with a load of boring rubbish about economics.

Some millionaires undoubtedly invite outrages of this sort. Jocelyn Stevens[1] (about whom I am writing a treatise) may be a case in point, and I quite understand why Beaverbrook workers found it necessary to pour salt over his nice, curly white hair. But the Beits have never hurt anyone in their lives, and on the many occasions I have been the guest of this kind and friendly couple they seemed to interpret their role in life purely in terms of providing food and drink for other people.

If St Anne's allows elderly folk to be beaten up and robbed simply because they are rich, then Rose and her fellow idealists had better watch out for a backlash against the poor from Christ Church and Magdalene. Soon we will see drunken gangs of rich young bloods in Bullingdon coats invade the modest homes of old age pensioners to smash their plaster ducks on the wall, tear up their Peter Scott prints and pee over their plastic flowers. Nobody will gain in the long run.

Saturday 15th May

I am sure I was right to refuse to put up the £65,000 needed to get the engineers back to work[2]. There is a certain amount of entertainment to be derived from the spectacle of other people working, it is true, but surely not £65,000-worth. For that sort of money I could invite the whole County to lunch with a brass band and a special performance of *Iolanthe* or *Yeomen of the Guard* thrown in.

If only Grocer was still in charge, there would have been a General Strike. Many of us could have our first opportunity to drive a bus or hit some workers on the head with a truncheon.

But it is no good pretending that Grocer can achieve anything now. The longer the whey-faced poltroons of the Conservative Party delay sacking him, letting "I dare not" wait upon "I would", like the cat in the adage, the more certain it is that Enoch will eventually succeed him. This may be good for a giggle from the rest of us, but it will be very bad for Enoch's character.

Until Grocer is replaced by lovely, oyster-eyed Willie Whitelaw we must leave the government of our country to Hugh Scanlon, and start worrying seriously about whether Mrs Scanlon wears frilly knickers or plain ones. The Central Office of Information, which I have been telephoning daily for the last eight weeks, has still to make an announcement on this important matter. Until it does, I think we must decide that democracy in this country has been superceded by the dictatorship of the proletariat in its customarily brutal and repressive forms.

Sunday 16th May

I am afraid I may have been premature in congratulating Cyril Connolly on his proud boast (in *Enemies of Promise*) that he had never masturbated at the age of eighteen. Reviewing Jan Morris's distressing book about how she changed sex, he goes into a long maunder about his own private parts:

"It's bad luck on her that the reviewer chosen for this book should have a castration complex, for there is nothing I dread more than injury to those parts whose activities are still in the private sector and which I regard as the source of so much intellectual authority, lucidity, judgement and visual pleasure."

Visual pleasure indeed. If this horrible old man can't keep his eyes off himself at the age of 70 he might have been better advised to experiment a little earlier like everyone else.

Monday 17th May

At a Reunion of the Victoria Cross and George Medal Association in London last week — I gatecrashed it, saying I was from William Hickey — they asked me who I thought was the bravest Englishman alive. I replied without hesitation that it was Ian Ball[3].

We hear a lot about the heroism of the victims of violence on these occasions, but very little, for some reason, about the heroism of the criminals. If Ball had succeeded in outwitting all the armed policemen and brave chauffeurs protecting Princess Anne, if he had managed to evade all the public-spirited passers-by and heroic journalists of her invisible bodyguard, he would still have had to spend anything up to a month closeted alone with the young lady and her speechless, smiling husband until the £3 million ransom money arrived.

It was this sort of courage, this willingness to take risks and face unmentionable horrors in the cause of profit which once made the foundation stone of our country's commercial empire, as I remarked in the course of a brief speech in reply to the Association's toast of The Guests: "It may be true, as our detractors say, that Great Britain has only got one Ball, but at least we should be proud of the one we've got," I concluded, to polite murmurs of assent from the company.

1. A rich journalist.
2. This was the sum at stake in an industrial dispute.
3. A madman who attempted to kidnap Princess Anne in the Mall wounding her police bodyguard. Princess Anne was awarded the DGCVO and Captain Phillips also honoured for alleged bravery.

1974

Tuesday 25th May

Yesterday was Peter Shore[1]'s fiftieth birthday, and I find myself this morning with a splitting headache, furry tongue, spots before the eyes etc. How time flies! Most of my friends seem to have committed suicide this year, and it seems only yesterday that we celebrated Peter's fortieth birthday.

On that occasion, he wore a blue romper suit and his hair was tied up in pretty blue ribands to match the startling blue of his frank, instantly likeable eyes.

But how many of my readers have ever heard of Peter Shore today? Who is this haggard, long-haired, degenerate figure with fanatical staring eyes who bores on and on about the Common Market, a subject everyone else lost interest in four years ago? If he asks me to his sixtieth birthday in ten years' time, I am very much afraid I will have to say that I have a previous engagement.

Wednesday 26th May

Next week there is to be a most exciting event at the Institute of Contemporary Arts as part of the Poetry International festival. It is called *The Politician as Poet* and it involves "a distinguished group of political figures" who will introduce and read their own poetry.

The "distinguished group", I can reveal, in fact consists of two former MPs and two members of the House of Lords who have lost their jobs: Enoch Powell, Uncle Tom Driberg, Lord Hailsham, and the great Lord Gowrie. Their "poetry" may prove rather embarrassing but the political significance of the event should not be overlooked. By bravely agreeing to appear on a public platform with Lord Gowrie, Enoch triumphantly disposes of the *canard* that he, personally, suffers from any sort of colour prejudice.

Lord Gowrie, who was a Junior Whip in the Lords for much of Grocer's disastrous government, often refers ruefully to his dusky hue in his poetry. One is reminded of William Blake's famous line: "And I am black, but O! my soul is white." Here is Gowrie writing about his father in the bath:

> "He turned the hot tap on so water ran
> in cataracts down his knees, floating the
> dark gland beneath."

Not quite up to Blake's standard, perhaps, although it should clear up many arguments about what colour these people's things are. But the important factor is that here we have a young man without any of our advantages of colour or cultural background who is sitting down to try and write poetry instead of blowing things up with postal bombs.

I hope that as many *Private Eye* readers as possible will go along to the ICA on June 4th to give him a good hand.

Thursday 27th May

This evening I found myself debating some fatuous motion or other at the Oxford Union. Apart from a good speech by Lord Longford, it was one of the most boring and frustrating evenings I can remember.

My friend and mentor Alan Watkins has advised that we should all refuse to speak at universities until the National Union of Students has withdrawn its outrageous ban on right-wing and racialist speakers. Unfortunately I had accepted the invitation already in a moment of mad conceit.

So I arrived in Oxford armed with a number of extremely unpleasant racialist jokes with which to punish the "students" for their intolerance and assert my dignity as a self-respecting liberal. On arrival I was told that Oxford University had already disassociated itself from the NUS motion, so I was left with nothing whatever to say.

Never mind. Here is quite a good racialist joke for those who find themselves similarly placed. I print it in the hope that students will now stop asking me to address their miserable societies.

Q: What is black inside, red outside and
    bloody funny?
A: A busload of West Indians driving over
    cliff.

Saturday 29th May

A most thoughtful leader in today's newspaper raises the old question: is socialism sinful? Does it lead inevitably to debauching the currency and similar offences against the Holy Ghost? Plainly, as the great Sir William Rees-Mogg points out in discussing the sad case of Edward Short[2], socialism can create the *occasion* of sin, which we are bound to eschew no less vigorously than the sin itself:

> "In such circumstances, men do yield to
> temptation; their sense of honesty is destroyed, their careers are destroyed. Others are
> almost equally damaged by their friends and
> colleagues yielding to temptation, even
> though they have not given way themselves."

On balance, I think we must all decide that socialism is something we should all endeavour to put behind us, whatever its surface attractions.

---

1. A Labour politician.

2. A Labour politician, noted for receiving large sums of money from from T. Dan Smith..

Monday 1st June   *Olbia, Sardinia*

Olbia, the Sardinian fishing port where I seem
to find myself at the moment, has recently
been the scene of a most distressing international misunderstanding, after a civic reception for the officers of a Japanese fishing
fleet which put in.

The men had been at sea for a long time
without any of the comforts of alcohol or
female company. In northern Sardinia, it is
normal for middle-class ladies to say "Chin,
Chin", with Edwardian conviviality as they
lift their little glasses of sweet wine to their
lips.

The civic matrons of Olbia were not to
know that in Japanese the words "Chin,
Chin", roughly translated "Fuck, Fuck", are
generally interpreted as an invitation to sexual intercourse. The scenes which followed,
and over which I think it prudent to draw a
discreet veil, will be remembered in Olbia
long after the visit of Tottenham Hotspurs is
forgotten in Rotterdam[1].

Tuesday 2nd June

The Rotterdam incident has increased the
prestige of Englishmen abroad quite measur-
ably. Waiters are more attentive, barmen
prompter with orders, and such foreigners as
one meets more respectful. I never thought
I would find myself beholden to any crowd
of English football fans.

Much has been written about the problems
of football violence, but nobody seems prepared to discuss the benefits. Plainly, many
people of the lower class occasionally feel the
urge to bash each other up. Should they not
have special arenas set aside for the purpose,1
or even be sent abroad to bash up their
opposite numbers in foreign parts, rather
than be allowed to disturb the tranquillity
of everyone else?

A similar remedy should be applied to the
so-called race problem in America. If these
people can be taught to play football — and
there is every reason to suppose they can —
then any racial tension or frustration can be
worked off in pitched battles staged somewhere in the Arizona desert between supporters of Detroit Hottentot Spurs and Harlem
United All-Blacks.

Wednesday 10th June

In an amazing letter to *The Times,* discussing
Wilson's ennoblement of Marcia Williams[2],
Sir David Hunt bluntly denies that Caligula
ever made his horse a Consul. The most interesting thing about this obvious lie is that
every schoolboy in the country knows he is
lying. Is there no untruth so absurd that this
wretched man is not prepared to utter it in
order to ingratiate himself with Wislon?

Hunt it was who as our High Commissioner
in Lagos perpetrated one of the ghastliest
diplomatic balls-ups of modern times, assuring
Wislon that the Nigerian Civil War would be
over in a matter of weeks if Britain supported
the new military regime in Lagos. Hunt had
just married a Nigerian millionairess and was
understandably delighted when Wislon accepted his advice, although he was on his honey-
moon at the time. Three years and two million
deaths later, it was left to a tired and emotional Foreign Secretary called Michael Stewart
to announce that the British policy had been
triumphantly vindicated.

And this is the man who would now lecture us about Caligula's horse! For my own
part, I am not in the least bit worried about
whether Caligula called his mount 'Consul',
but I have not been able to sleep for several
nights worrying whether Lady Falkender will
be able to call her children "Honourable".

This dignity is reserved for children of
certain degrees of the peerage, born in wed-
lock. If Lord Chalfont, for instance, or Lord
Caradon, had been sowing his wild oats
around (a most preposterous suggestion), the
resulting offspring would not be entitled to
this distinction. But I know of no recent
precedent which relates to the children out
of a peeress in her own right who is unmarried.
What would be the position, for instance, if
such a peeress declared her children to be the
result of virgin birth?

I must consult Garter on this ticklish matter as soon as I get home. Meanwhile I can
only warn all my friends who are Honourable
— Dame Katy Macmillan, Bobbie Corbitts,
Paul Foot — to be on their guard against any
assault on their ancient privileges.

Thursday 11th June

Whenever an Earl dies I feel in some way
diminished myself, but Lord Rosebery's death
makes the whole country smaller. I thought
I saw him only last week eating a whole side
of salmon alone at White's Club, no mean
feat at the age of 92, although I may have
been mistaken.

My last meeting with him was rather embarrassing. I was one of a small deputation
which went up to Mentmore some ten years

---

1. A football team, many of whose supporters had been imprisoned for acts of hooliganism after a foot-
   match in Rotterdam.

2. She was created Lady Falkender.

ago to beg him to accept the leadership of the Conservative party when it became painfully apparent that Sir Alec was not up to the job. He listened to us patiently, but neither Willie Whitelaw's tearful appeals to his patriotism nor my own eloquence on the theme of class solidarity, nor even Oliver Poole's tactful reference to the large sums of money at stake could alter the deep contempt he had always shown towards the Conservative party.

As he shook our hands at the door, he allowed his natural gruffness to abate and I swear there was a twinkle in his eye as he said: "I'm sure you'll be able to find some greengrocer or male hairdresser who'll be pleased to get the job. He'll probably be grateful for the money."

"Primmy", as we used to call him in the Regiment, was never short of money, as his father, the Liberal Prime Minister, married a Rothschild. This may not be the sort of thing you or I would care to do, but I can see one would be eternally grateful to any parent who did it. The death of this admirable man is a sad blow to the nation, already reeling from the loss of Doublet[1], but he would probably not want me to go on about it. His son, I am told, is a beast.

Friday 12th June
Poor Spike Milligan[2] is up before the beaks for shooting a marauder at his home with an air rifle. His mistake was to let the brute get away. Every house of any size in Somerset has its graveyard of would-be burglars. Usually their graves are unmarked, but some landowners with a sense of humour put up rather touching little headstones: FIDO, a faithful friend; DAFFODIL, not forgotten; PUSSIKINS, the best mouser ever.

Saturday 13th June
In all that has been said and written about the Price sisters[3], nobody has yet suggested that it might be the quality of the food in prison that accounts for their strange behaviour. This omission is typical of the extraordinary complacency of the English on the subject of their disgusting food, which drives so many Englishmen like myself abroad for most of the year.

Yet when I examine my own motives for not planting bombs in public places — it seems, in many ways, such a logical reaction to the challenge of modern life — I find that horror of prison food ranks even higher than

distaste for the company of my fellow prisoners or the torture of constantly blaring television which is, I am told, the cruel and unnatural punishment which society prescribes for those of refined or philosophical bent who infringe its laws.

If, by their deaths, the Price sisters could have achieved some slight improvement in the standard of prison catering, their lives would not have been wasted.

Monday 15th June
I know who is responsible for the House of Commons "bomb" incident[4], but am not sure whether to tell the police, as it is all rather embarrassing. The guilty man is called Rear Admiral Sir Alexander "Gay" Gordons-Lennox, Wislon's dreaded Serjeant-at-Arms, but on this occasion his outrage was almost certainly unintentional.

The narrative of events is as follows. Recognising that the price of liberty is eternal vigilance, I have had someone watching Gordon-Lennox night and day for the past four years. This precaution was against the day when, not content with excluding *Private Eye* (which has the largest circulation of any political journal) from the Press Gallery of the House of Commons, the old brute tried to seize power and destroy all vestiges of democracy in the land.

Recently my spies told me that this frightful man had been looking pastier than ever and was plainly suffering from constipation. Despite constant applications of All-Bran and Sennacot, it was fully a month before the hiccupping old fool finally made his way to the Serjeant's Convenience, sensibly situated at some distance from the Chamber of the House in a converted cellar under Westminster Hall.

I learned of his intention at 8.23 this morning. Within two minutes I had telephoned the Press Association to warn them of the danger. By 8.29 a.m., "Shandy" Gordon-Lennox, as Gay is known to his cronies, had done his worst. Maybe the country will allow itself to be lulled into a sense of false security by official explanations about an IRA bomb conveniently placed over the gas main. But I know the truth.

Tuesday 16th June
A letter in my copy of *Socialist Worker* (very good value indeed at 5p) is signed by eleven workers at Redfern National Glass, Barnsley, and asks whether workers and progressive

---

1. Princess Anne's horse, which had to be destroyed after a fall.

2. A comic.

3. Two Irish terrorists who had gone on hunger strike in prison.

4. A bomb under Westminster Hall had caused considerable damage; the Irish Republican Army claimed credit.

intellectuals - people like you or me —
ought not to disassociate ourselves from
groups like the IRA on the grounds that
they are always murdering innocent people
for no very good reason.

The point is answered in a longish editorial note:

"The IRA is not made up of 'murdering
scum' whose sole aim in life seems to be the
out-doing of one another in the number of
innocent men, women and children they can
mutilate'. Rather, it is made up of ordinary
working men and women. . . "

The editors go on to point out that these
'ordinary working men and women' are probably worried about poor housing, low wages
and the unemployment problem in Derry.

This column has sometimes expressed
concern about 'ordinary working men and
women'. Gone are the days when they doff-
ed their caps and wreathed their simple faces
in happy smiles whenever one addressed
them.

But despite their surliness I am far too
timid a man to describe them as 'murdering
scum' in the way *Socialist Worker* does.

Wednesday 24th June

I had an unpleasant experience today in the
church of St Martin's-in-the-Fields, Trafalgar
Square, where I sometimes go to eat my
cheese sandwiches and have a quiet snooze
in the lunch hour. It turned out there was a
memorial service going on for Duke Ellington, the musician, whom I do not think I ever
had the pleasure of meeting.

Every out-of-work musician in Shaftesbury
Avenue had turned up to add his bit to the
disgusting noise, no doubt hoping for some
free publicity. Poor 'Duke' Ellington, whoever he was. I can't believe all that din did
him any good when he was trying to argue
his case in front of the Pearly Gates.

Through the crowd I caught a glimpse of
Larry Adler playing his mouth organ in a
moony sort of way behind Cleo Laine, who
was pretending to sing a song called *Mood
Indigo*. I was about to go and tell him to
stop it at once as he was making himself look
ridiculous when I remembered that he was
the only person who had ever offered me a
bribe during my career as a journalist — £35
to tell a particularly disgusting story about
President Nixon's penis.

Needless to say, I accepted the offer in a
flash and told his boring, tasteless story in
my column, much to the dismay of my

older readers — but the rat never paid me my
£35. I went outside to find a policeman and
have him arrested, but by the time I got back
he had vanished. He is probably in Israel by
now, but Interpol has a long arm and I doubt
whether this evil man will be at large for long.

Thursday 25th June

Today I agreed to see someone called Kenneth Harris so that he could report an 'exclus-
ive conversation' with me in his pathetic
newspaper, the *Observer*. He drove himself
down to Somerset, a plump, slightly common
young man, but obviously well intentioned
and anxious to please[1].

He gave me a list of questions he proposed
to ask me. They were of such embarrassing
banality that I almost wept on his grey
padded suiting as I answered them. Did I feel
I had enough opportunity to mix freely with
ordinary people? What did I feel about
music? about young people? about the press?
How did I reconcile my way of life with the
way ordinary people thought and lived nowadays?

Poor man. Obviously, one has all too
much opportunity to mix with ordinary
people. The great problem of modern life is
how to avoid them. As I rang for him to be
shown the way out, I reflected that David
Astor has a lot to answer for, sending his
minions on these humiliating errands which
must represent at least one nadir of human
degradation.

Friday 26th June

After everything that has passed between us
I was rather touched that the Prime Minister
and Mrs Wilson should have thought to ask
me to a *souper intime* in Downing Street for
Princess Chichibu of Japan. The only guests
apart from my dear wife and myself were Alf
Allen of USDAW and his nice wife, Ruby;
a young Englishman to whom the Princess is
apparently attached called David MacEwans
and a Foreign Office couple whose names
I did not catch.

Alf Allen told me he had no particular
interest in Japan but that part of Wislon's
Social Contract with the unions involved at
least one union leader being invited to every
free dinner served in Downing Street or
Carlton Gardens.

The food, of course, was disgusting: cream
of asparagus soup out of a tin; fish-cakes with
a poor apology for parsley sauce; mutton
chops with reconstituted potatoes and fruit
salad with ice-cream.

---

1. **This interview has a curious similarity to one reported in the Observer between Harris (a journalist)
and the Prince of Wales.**

I made a lot of jokes about Grocer Heath's two pandas from China and how they were a particularly appropriate gift in view of his well known difficulty in mating. Everybody· agreed I was the life and soul of the party,· and even Princess Chichibu tittered delicately into her hand.

Oriental ladies have always held a fascination for me, but it would be indelicate to go into that now. I restrained myself with difficulty from saying "Chin Chin" as we drank toasts in the thin yellow wine provided, pledging eternal friendship between the Japanese and British people or some such rubbish.

Saturday 27th June
Madame Soekarno is a very lovely lady and Anthony Blond[1] is revoltingly ugly by any standards, so perhaps we should rejoice in her successful libel action against Blond & Briggs who mendaciously suggested that her late husband, the Indonesian dictator, once had it off with Norma Levy[2].

But successful libel actions are never cause for celebration and I can't help feeling that Blond allowed his heart to govern his head when dealing with this beautiful widow.

Soekarno was famous throughout the whole of southern Asia for the voraciousness of his sexual appetite, and it was a perfectly reasonable mistake on Norma's part, when finding herself with a furious black midget on top of her, to assume it was the ex-President of Indonesia.

At any rate, my sympathy to all concerned. I suppose Blond would not understand about these things.

Tuesday 30th June
As the storm clouds gather and the threat of proletarian dictatorship looms ever nearer, many of my neighbours in Somerset have been building machine gun emplacements and investing in anti-personnel land mines for their parks and *parterres*.

This puts me in something of a dilemma, as I do not want a bloodbath but obviously can't leave my dear wife and children completely unprotected against the day the working class marches up my drive to take possession of my marbled halls. Probably the best thing would be to invite them in and poison them with paraquat, but this involves always being present to receive them.

After much thought, I issue each of my dependants with a World War II gas mask and a supply of milk of magnesia tablets against the disgusting food they will have to eat in the new era of social progress.

Ear plugs would probably be useful too, against the noises these people make and the terribly boring things they say. But not even the wives and children of the rich can expect everything. What did the good Lord give them fingers for?

Wednesday 1st July
A touching letter in the newspaper today from my old friend Tom Skeffington-Lodge, the only human being I know (I don't count Gerald Kauffmann) who has never been at a loss for a kind word to say about Harold Wilson.

Nor does he let us down this time: Mr Wilson's 'very able Cabinet' has evolved policies of 'fairness and foresight' which are 'widely endorsed as those needed in a situation grave but not irretrievably so'.

Well done, Tom. I wonder why Wilson has not yet rewarded this amiable man with the peerage he so richly deserves. No doubt there were old debts to be paid to Lord Kissin-and-Kuddlin[3], Lady Forkender and so on — but Wislon had better move fast. Of all the crimes of the detested Grocer Heath, the meanest and most contemptible for which he will always stink in the nostrils of educated Englishmen through the ages — was his refusal to honour P.G. Wodehouse on his 90th birthday in October 1971.

Thursday 2nd July
Another very beautiful letter, this time in the *Daily Telegraph* from General Sir Walter Walker, my neighbour at South Petherton, in Somerset. Walter asks: "Why is the country in such a mess. . . What on earth has gone wrong?"

He thinks that we lack "dynamic, invigorating, uplifting leadership," adding that "the communist Trojan horse is in our midst with its fellow travellers wriggling their maggoty way inside its belly". He argues that the country is yearning for a leader like Churchill, and thinks it "inconceivable that we should not be able to produce such a man before it is too late".

He may be right. I would be only too happy to offer my services to the country in this capacity, but I'm afraid I simply haven't the time to spare at the moment. If some of my readers are less pressed, the correct thing is to go to the nearest post office or labour

1. A publisher.
2. One of the prostitutes involved in the Lambton scandal (q.v.).

3. Harry Kissin, a businessman of East European origin, b. 23 August 1912, raised to the peerage for mysterious reasons by Harold Wilson in 1974. Noted only for being unknown.

exchange and apply for the necessary forms.

Reggie Maudling was not too hopeful at lunch today. I invited him more for old times' sake than anything else, but it was not a great success. He seemed to spill most of his lunch down his waistcoat and was emphatic that we could not recall Harold Macmillan from retirement, as some of my brilliant friends on the *Daily Express* have been suggesting.

He didn't think Lord Avon was the right man either — nor even the late Duke of Gloucester! I suppose we will all have to search our attics to see if we've got any old baronets up there who might take the job.

Friday 3rd July

Lunch with Denis Healey[1] at the White Tower. After a 17-course meal, Denis tells me that the greatest danger facing the Labour movement and everything we believe in comes from Wedgwood Benn, who is trying to set himself up as a leader of the left without the proper intellectual equipment or administrative experience for the job.

He thinks his Wealth Tax will be a wonderful thing to fight the election on, but is worried that James Callaghan doesn't possess the proper intellectual equipment or vision for the post of Foreign Secretary. This saddens me as I'd rather hoped that Jim would take over the leadership if anything were to happen to Harold, as we all rather think it might.

After lunch, which cost £94 for two, he confirms that the meeting has been on lobby terms. Obediently, I get into the approved 'lobby' position and start licking his shoes. They taste, curiously, of *creme de menthe*.

Saturday 4th July

Roy Jenkins was late for lunch at my hotel and said he couldn't stay long as he was expected for tea in Berkshire with the Wothschilds. I rather grudged him the large glass of Hine '29 which he demanded at the end of the meal.

I asked him whether he was going to take up Paul Johnson's suggestion to re-introduce hanging and, if so, who he thinks we should start with. He says Paul Johnson.

I put forward my own scheme to combat terrorists — that every man and woman in Britain should be obliged to carry firearms, just as they will soon be obliged to wear safety belts. Allowing for unavoidable accidents, this rule should have a wonderful effect on our population problem too. Jenkins says he prefers to use the condom.

He refused my invitation to spend the afternoon in Highgate Cemetery, London's new fun scene[2]. He is a profoundly second-rate, unimaginative man, and a greedy one at that.

Sunday 12th July

Spent the day mooning around Highgate Cemetery looking for fun. To think that Swinging London should come to this. The imposing memorial to my great-great-great-grandfather, the Reverend Alexander Waugh, who died in 1827, has not yet been able to attract any attention from these voluptuaries.

He was a worthy man, but I confess it might be difficult to find him sexually exciting after all these years, even if we weren't related. For myself, I could scarcely raise a *frisson* even in front of Karl Marx's grave.

1. A Labour politician, newly made Chancellor of the Exchequer.
2. There had been reports of vandalism, orgies and necromancy in Highgate Cemetery.

Perhaps I am getting too old for these new fads. Back to Rupert Street for a sauna and most stimulating massage.

Monday 13th July

The Finer Report on single parent families which I've now read from cover to cover, recommends vastly increased assistance for unmarried mothers, as one would only expect. But it ignores the most crucial issue: have the children of unmarried mothers the right to describe themselves as 'Honourable', if their mother is subsequently given a life peerage?

King Charles II's bastards certainly used courtesy titles as well as inheriting their mothers' honours. But perhaps that is not an exact parallel. Until Mr Wilson sets up another Royal Commission to investigate the matter, the nation will remain in doubt.

Monday 20th July

Lady Stocks's desertion of the Labour Party is the unkindest cut of all. If this doughty 82-year-old Vice President of the Association of Joint Sewerage Boards can't take it any longer, can any of us hope to stay the course?

Yet the Labour movement means so much to me. It was in the milk I drank at my mother's breast while dad worked his 148-hour week down the coal mine, emerging only on Christmas Eve; it is my bones and my blood, it is the air I breathe, it is the opening of the flowers in the morning and the cawing of the rooks in the high beeches at the bottom of the park in the evening. Must we all despair?

At least there is Lady Falkender's induction to look forward to. I can't think why anyone thought she would have any difficulty finding sponsors, since Marcia has created more peers in her time than Lloyd George and the Moncreiffe of That Ilk[1] combined. With her enormous wealth[2] she could have bought herself a couple of royal dukes, if that was what she wanted.

When the Countess of Slagheap[3] takes her place among her peers in the Upper House I like to think a little ray of sunshine will settle on our unhappy island again. We *will* find a way out of our balance of payments difficulty and nagging industrial relations problem. It *can* be done.

Tuesday 21st July

Rather an awkward meeting of the Tuesday Club at Tony Benn's London home this eve-ning. This is a new idea — a small, informal group of fairly senior people with progressive leanings, who gather in each other's homes to discuss matters of mutual interest, like how to push our spineless wreck of a Prime Minister into the occasional pretence of a forward-looking posture.

Tonight there was Caroline Benn on my left (as rich as Mrs Harold Lever, I believe, and very nearly as attractive in a sort of American High School way), then Michael Foot[4], whom she rather seems to fancy, though goodness knows why. After him came Barbara Castle, looking very fresh after her recent operation but talking too much for my taste. Then Tony Benn, Betty Shore, Ted Castle, Judith Hart, Peter Shore and Jill Foot on my right.

It could have been such an enjoyable occasion. We were all university people, all good conversationalists, and all *involved*. The food, it is true, was a little odd — first some tinned mandarin oranges, then a sort of cereal with Complan sprinkled on top, then a huge mug of tea with vitamin pills in case any of us were feeling deficient. I chose vitamin G which tasted rather like cow-cake. Michael was being very embarrassing with shouts of "Delicious, absolutely delicious," after every pill.

But I am afraid I rather spoilt the happy atmosphere by suggesting we should invite Eric Heffer and Stan Orme — two very nice senior Ministers with progressive views on most subjects. My suggestion was not well received. It isn't exactly that they hadn't been at university or that they might not know how to hold their spoons and forks correctly, but... well, you know, I wish I'd never raised the matter.

Wednesday 22nd July

Everybody says I should have gone to the House of Commons yesterday evening to watch them all making fools of themselves. I don't blame Harold Lever for staying away from the Palace of Westminster until the appallingly dangerous Sergeant at Arms has been securely corked.

But it is not the very real danger that this constipated old brute will cause another explosion which keeps me away. I don't even mind the noise which MPs make — the yells, grunts and groans of the affluent or the poor whistling noise of those from modest back-grounds. It is the *smell* of 640 over-excited

1. Sir Iain Moncreiffe of that Ilk, 11th baronet. A distinguished, if occasionally overtired, genealogist and Albany Herald; April 1919, noted for monorchism.

2. Possibly a reference to her role in the Slagheap Affair (q.v.).

3. Certainly a reference to her role in the Slagheap Affair (q.v.).

4. Another Labour politician, or his wife.

MPs which I can't quite stomach as I grow older, and that is the shameful truth of the matter.

Thursday 23rd July
Two very good jokes I learnt from Arnold Goodman at tea with the Droghedas: Karl Miller[1] MA is going to be appointed to the Lord Northcliffe Chair of Modern English Literature at London University; and Penélope Mortimer[2]'s ridiculous new novel is being seriously considered for the Booker Prize.

Laugh? I did the nose-trick with my *Patum Peperium* sandwiches all over Joan Drogheda's lovely Aubusson carpet. Arnold really ought to go on television.

Friday 24th July
Today my review edition of the new *Encyclopædia Britannica* arrived — thirty volumes costing £279 to members of the public who wish to improve themselves, but free as sunshine to diligent reviewers. In about four months I should have completed my study, weighed each of the 44 million words in the scales of Truth, Charity and English grammar, analysed all its major propositions for evidence of Marxist bias and be in a position to deliver my considered judgement to *Books & Bookmen*, Britain's only serious literary publication.

Imagine my amazement, on opening the *New Statesman*, to find a review already written by someone called Sir Peter Medawar, a zoologist from Watford Road, Harrow, Middx. Medawar must have felt able to pronounce on the whole £14 million, 15-year

project within minutes of receiving his thirty volumes.

He complains about pictures of a giraffe on the grounds that everybody knows what a giraffe looks like. It does not occur to him that most of us enjoy looking at pictures of giraffes much more than we enjoy looking at the revolting photograph of Sir Peter Medawar, zoologist, on page 743 of Volume VI.

This is surely the sort of horror we might have been spared. But Medawar's main complaint is about the inclusion of entries bearing upon classical mythology — Chimæras, Gorgons and the rest. "In the opinion of many impatient young moderns," he opines, "most classical mythology. . . is a load of old codswallop."

If this conceited oaf could lift his horrible, rheumy eyes from the tubes of elephant sperm and embryo hippopotami in Watford Road for one moment he might see some things in the world around him which would persuade him to keep his crass opinions to himself.

Saturday 25th July
The death at 90 of Dame Sybil Hathaway, the Dame of Sark, removes the only person in the British Isles whom I still wanted to meet. Unfortunately, she rejected all my advances.

She was a model ruler for our times, forbidding not only cars and aircraft on her island, but also trade unions, taxation, female dogs, divorce, and most of the troublesome manifestations of our age. I had always hoped to persuade this admirable lady to take England under her rule when our parliamentary system finally disintegrates. Now she is

1. A pseud (q.v.).
2. A novelist.

dead I think I shall leave the country for a time — probably for a very long time.
I can see no hope.

Tuesday 28th July *Languedoc, France*
Far away from the hectic political strife of London one begins to see things in perspective.

To everyone outside Britain it is quite obvious that Len Murray[1] is slowly emerging as the Philosopher-King and national leader the country is crying out for. He alone sums up what everybody is thinking when he says there is nothing wrong with unemployment so long as the unemployed suffer no financial hardship. "The difference between work and leisure," he says, "is that work's what you don't like doing."

He describes every man as a battlefield. "Within him at any moment there are conflicts of interest" — between desire for money and reluctance to work for it. "We must stop worrying about inflation and grow to love it," says this reasonable man who holds Britain's future in the palm of his hand.

At present we have the ideal compromise, with nobody working and everybody being paid while our clever politicians raise huge loans from the Shah of Persia to pay for it all. These loans are given on the strength of oil deposits in the North Sea which most Englishmen know in their heart of hearts to be non-existent. Even if they exist, they can be re-nationalised without compensation as soon as the Sheikhs have bought a controlling interest — surely one of the great international confidence tricks of all time.

Of all politicians, only Len Murray has the wisdom to see we have reached the ideal point towards which all civilization has been striving since time began. I just wish he could behave as other democratic politicians and tell us a little about his wife's underwear.

Wednesday 29th July
Today's newspaper carries an item which threatens to drive out even the perennial, nagging problem of Mrs Len Murray's knickers. A huge underwater mountain has been discovered thirty miles off the African coast at Port Elizabeth which is alive with rock lobsters. About 36,000 lbs are being pulled in every day and the supply looks like lasting for ever.

The only trouble with Len's philosophy is that other countries who don't subscribe to it may walk off with all the good things of life. A world in which Japs drink all the claret, Americans eat all the lobsters and Germans guzzle all the wild game would scarcely be an improvement on the dreadful slums of the Industrial Revolution.

Now it looks as though there will be enough lobsters for all in the years ahead. I can't help seeing the hand of Providence in this, and will suspend further discussion of why we are not allowed to know whether Mrs Murray wears frilly knickers or plain ones until I am sure that Len is not a reincarnation of Jesus.

Thursday 30th July
Reading John Barron's alarming study of the KGB or Soviet Secret Police (Hodder & Stoughton, £4.25), I am amazed that anyone should ever be prepared to visit that benighted country. Barron describes how every application for a visa — even from half-witted journalists or students on a Thomson Tour — is accompanied by a KGB decision on whether to "neutralize, influence, recruit or merely watch" the applicant.

Nearly every contact a foreign visitor makes with a Russian is arranged by the KGB and all are supervised after the second meeting, if Mr Barron is to be believed. Visitors are liable to be photographed from every angle at any hour of the day or night.

Under the circumstances, I feel we should tip our caps to Mr Harold Wilson, who has made this disagreeable journey no less than eighteen times. And to Lady Falkender, who has accompanied him five times on his Russian visits, according to Caroline Moorehead's study of this amazing woman.

I should expect a dukedom for accompanying Wilson on a day trip to Boulogne. It is time the Government thought long and hard about awarding this courageous lady a State Pension.

Friday 9th August
I never thought to use valuable space on this page in defence of a member of the Rothschild family, who are well able to look after themselves. But when Baron Phillipe de Rothschild publicly implores the Editor of *The Times* to employ as drama critic someone who is less loutish, boring and half-witted than Irving Wardle, he merely expresses what every educated man in England has been secretly thinking for years.

The idea of sending Wardle to review Beaumarchais' *Marriage of Figaro* was an elementary error of judgement. If Rees-Mogg is too timid to sack the brute or move him to the Sports page, he should resign himself and make way for handsome mini-skirted Charles Vass, his popular deputy. Failing this, the Baron and I will have no choice but to put our case before the European Parliament at Strasbourg.

1. General Secretary of the TUC (q.v.).

Saturday 10th August

I refused all invitations to attend Sinn Fein's anti-imperialist festival in Belfast tomorrow on the slightly dishonest grounds that I would probably be refused entry by the immigration authorities. The truth is that nobody who has experienced Presbyterian Belfast on a Sunday will ever go a second time, and I feared I might even find the company of my fellow revolutionaries rather trying in these circumstances.

Today I feel uneasy. There are so many things requiring direct action in politics — even violence, if nothing else works. Fred Peart[1]'s cruel and cynical proposal to dump the European frozen beef mountain on British old age pensioners is such a one.

It is well-known that most OAPs have ill-fitting dentures and could not eat frozen beef from Europe, even if they do not happen to prefer Kit-e-Kat and digestive biscuits with their nice cups of tea. Why should they be made to suffer just because the politicians can't decide what to do with their frozen beef?

Owing to a similar miscalculation on my part, I now find myself with five warehouses full of lavatory paper. Without boasting, I can honestly claim that it simply never occurred to me that OAPs should be forced to eat it. Senior citizens should not be used as scapegoats for commercial errors of this sort.

Monday 12th August   *Languedoc, France*

A disturbing letter from my friends in the army who have been looking after things for me in my absence abroad. Apparently Grocer Heath has been sniffing around our organisation, hoping to find himself returned to power when we decide the time is right for a move.

I hope that no group of my fellow-conspirators, whether military, para-military or civilian, will take a second look at this worthless man. Grocer has been a disaster for the country. The only serious charge against Wilson is that he has done nothing to improve the mess which Grocer left behind.

When I return to England to take over the leadership of the country I shall be marching in front of the banners of all that is healthiest in our national life: The Boy Scouts and Girl Guides Association; the YMCA, the Latin Mass Society, the British Legion (Somerset Branch), the Federation of Women's Institutes and the Council for the Preservation of Rural England (Somerset Branch). I do not want to see any Grocers trotting along behind.

Tuesday 20th August

Day trip to Marseilles, where I had been asked to open the World Naturist Congress at Port Nature with a few well-chosen words. Although I have never been a nudist myself, believing, like Cyril Connolly, that some things are best left to solitary contemplation, I have the greatest sympathy with those who find the cost of old-fashioned modesty prohibitive — especially in France, where a pair of swimming trunks costs £11.

Everybody was very excited about the proposal to hold Olympic Games in the nude, as they were in the golden days of Greece. I am not sure that this would add to spectator appeal and might well embarrass some of the "female" athletes from Soviet Russia. If the idea is extended to lacrosse matches,

1. **Labour Minister for Agriculture, proposed beef vouchers for OAPs.**

Miss World contests and suchlike it will spoil a lot of fun for my friend Charlie Vass, who very nearly got into the finals last year as Miss Costa Rican Pygmy 1973.

Wednesday 21st August
The only sane response to Denis Healey's Savings Tax is to see it as a challenge. Friends who sit around moaning that even quite modest savings of £5 million or so will nearly disappear in 40 years at 2½% are missing the point.

Denis has done nothing to deserve the extra money, nor have any of his so-called "working classes". If they are determined to eat the nation's seed-corn, then it is our duty to eat it first ourselves. The only problem is one of human capacity, as the terrible example of poor Mama Cass[1] shows.

But it is the duty of the well-to-do to set an example without flinching from the dangers. Soon I shall take my family to join the rows of British millionaires who are bursting open like ripe melons up and down the Cote d'Azur, their delightful brown-skinned travelling companions popping like toy balloons beside them.

Thursday 22nd August
Dreadful as Sir Lew Grade[2]'s marathon television series *The Life of Jesus* may prove to be, it is our duty to support it. Not even my friend Mary Whitehouse should object to the overt violence of the scourging and crucifixion scenes, scripted by the great Anthony Burgess and directed by Franco Zeffirelli.

Asked why he had chosen Christ, Sir Lew remarked: "I am a Jew. Jesus was a Jew.

I happen to have been born on the same day, but that is not the reason."

The real reason, of course, is that the series will be good for humanity. When I think what the Jews have suffered since the crucifixion, it seems the least we can do to help them make a little money out of it now. We are all guilty.

Friday 23rd August
The news from England gets worse and worse every day. Housewives are tearing each other's eyes out for sugar in Derby. Undefended libel actions have been "won" by Arnold Weinstock[3], Cecil Beaton, David Coleman, Hugh Scanlon and the Church Commissioners, and many of these appalling people have been given "substantial" damages. My heart bleeds for the old country.

The Church Commissioners sued over an article by Iain Scarlet in the *Spectator* which concerned the administration of brothels on church property. For my own part, I don't care whether these brothels are well administered or not, although if the administration of church fetes is anything to go by, they are probably lousy.

But if the Church of England does not want some very rude things said about it in the near future, it had better get a grip on the Venerable John Hayward, Archdeacon of Middlesex. This frightful man is trying to block proposals to put up a memorial in Chelsea to the 15,000 Polish officers murdered by the Russians at Katyn Wood in 1940.

The Rector, called Prebendary Harold Loanby, argues that most of the Poles were

1. A fat musician who ate her last sandwich and exploded.

2. A vulgar television magnate.

3. A businessman.

Roman Catholic and shouldn't be commemorated on Church of England ground, and that nobody wants a lot of Poles visiting the garden where old people sometimes come to sit. He doesn't object to the monument on principle, but thinks it should be sited elsewhere. Archdeacon Hayward, however, says he would prefer a more reconciliatory monument than an obelisk "which is more a finger pointing to the sky asking for justice."

My consolation is that when the working class finally seizes power in England, when these wet and repulsive men have themselves been taken into a wood and despatched with a bullet in the neck, no monument will ever be raised to their foul memory.

Saturday 24th August

When I was last in Washington, Richard Nixon let it be known that he was too busy to see me. I knew then that the rat had something to hide, and it comes as no surprise to learn that he is a liar, a thief and a charlatan.

Now I will have to make the journey again to inspect Mr Ford. I hope he has better manners, although first impressions are not favourable. But I suppose it is the duty of the responsible world citizen nowadays to try and talk the President out of this craven and half-witted policy of sucking up to the Russians, however boorish his manner. It is the office, not the man, that counts.

Sunday 25th August

Today being the Feast of St Lawrence, the whole neighbourhood is given over to dancing, drink and fornication. The priest who declared the orgy open in church this morning proposed that Wednesday should be observed as a day of fasting and penance in expiation for the excesses of the next forty-eight hours.

After Mass I went round to shake the priest's hand and give him some money. This is always a painful experience. Nobody has ever explained satisfactorily to me why the hands of Catholic priests are so horribly soft. Some say it is a product of their sacramental powers, others that they use cold cream.

My own theory is that they are made to sleep in boxing gloves, although I have never been able to think of a reason why this should be so. If any reader has an opinion on this curious phenomenon, I should be delighted to hear it.

Monday 26th August — *France*

One sad result of the present troubles in Cyprus, where a British housewife in her fifties has just been raped by three Turkish soldiers, is that few British couples will retire there now. More of them will come to Somerset.

God's own county has already been made nearly uninhabitable by regiments of retired people whose bungalows sprout like mushrooms overnight. Every morning they can be seen exercising in singlets and longjohns in preparation for the Great Patriotic Uprising when Sinister Groups of Geriatrics plan to take over the country.

The only defence against this invasion must be for Somerset youths to organize themselves into groups of rapists, calling from bungalow to bungalow and doing their dreadful work before the anguished eyes of the budgerigar while the husband composes a letter to the *Daily Telegraph*.

Tuesday 3rd September

Fortunately I realised that Court Line[1] was going to collapse as soon as Mr Benn announced he had rescued it, and laid in stocks of paraquat against the charabanc tours of stranded Clarkson holidaymakers who now come to my door begging for a cup of milk, a crust of bread, or a little money to get them home.

Nothing could be more irresponsible than to help these people back to England. As Peter Jay has shown, the country simply can't afford them any more. It would be an act of moral cowardice, as well as poor economic management, to encourage them to return and batten still further off the productive endeavour of the bourgeoisie.

One day soon the Government must realise it has found a wonderful new way of syphoning off its surplus population and spreading the burden. Intelligent planners will arrange for the collapse of all cut-price package tour firms every year at the peak of the holiday season. Travellers must be warned in tiny print that in the event of such a collapse, repatriation is not only impossible but also illegal. Otherwise I am afraid these unhappy people will take their holidays in Somerset next year, probably in a caravan.

Wednesday 4th September

The injustice of making Princess Anne a Dame Grand Cross of the Royal Victorian Order

---

1. A package holiday firm which collapsed soon after Benn had assured holidaymakers they were safe, stranding many people abroad.

while the real hero of the kidnap attempt, Ian Ball, languishes in a lunatic asylum like some Russian liberal, demonstrates once again how close we are moving to the sort of society that exists in Soviet Russia.

Ian Ball, as I pointed out at the time, was prepared to risk not only the bullets and truncheons of the police and the impertinent attention of passers-by but also the prospect of three weeks closeted in a Surrey bungalow with this frightful young woman and her speechless, grinning husband while the Queen got together her ransom money. Moreover the absurd Captain Phillips wins an award for "bravery" while poor Ian sits around in a dressing-gown watching his fellow patients pretend to be field marshals or poached eggs.

My first reaction was to return my CBE to the Queen in protest, but on second thoughts it seems to me she has done nothing to deserve it, and it is rather a pretty thing. She should have prevented the whole disgraceful and humiliating marriage in the first place.

Thursday 5th September
If the fashion for shooting American ambassadors catches on, there is a new one who seems ripe for a little attention. Shirley Temple Black, better known as the child film star Shirley Temple, has just been appointed US ambassador in Accra, Ghana.

She is now 46, scarcely to be distinguished from any other American woman of her age. But before the war there was a brilliant English literary magazine called, I think, *Night and Day* — the equivalent in its time of *Private Eye*, or possibly *Books & Bookmen*.

Its film critic, Graham Greene, was unreservedly disgusted by Shirley Temple's performances, as in *Good Ship Lollypop* where the seven-year-old star wiggles her way down an aircraft cabin, parking her cute little bottom on the knees of other passengers — and said so in no uncertain terms.

The resulting libel action closed down the magazine and forced England's greatest novelist into an exile from which he has never returned for any very long period. Perhaps my West African friends will think of more amusing things to do with this hellish woman than just shoot her.

Friday 6th September
Anybody who needs money might like to borrow my idea of founding a children's comic which would be exactly the same as *Dandy* or *Beano* in every respect except that it would include mild lavatory jokes: Desperate Dan the Lavatory Man, Keyhole Kate Knickers etc. Anybody who has any experience of children will know what a fortune is waiting to be made. Few modern parents would object, and D.C. Thomson, publishers of *Dandy* and *Beano*, are inhibited by religious error.

At any rate this is a much better scheme than that of my friend Peter Paterson, who has had the bright idea at 43 of founding a new London daily newspaper of — groan — "independently Radical" outlook.

Apart from anything else, this footling scheme represents a shocking waste of talent. Paterson, despite his rough upbringing and "Independently Radical Outlook" is one of the funniest men in London, with as pretty a line in puns as any I know. I will be happy to employ him on the text for Desperate Dan the Lavatory Man as soon as he has come to his senses.

Saturday 7th September

Tomorrow we return to England and must face the agonizing choice between General Walker's *Unison* movement and David Stirling[1]'s *GB75*. On name alone one would choose *Unison* with its pleasing echoes of *Una Voce*, the international Latin Mass Society to which all people of intelligence and goodwill belong. Colonel Stirling could scarcely have picked a more disgusting name for his organisation if he had been opening a Neasden boutique for the trendier over-70s.

But euphony is not everything. A terrifying article by Sir Charles Vass, heart-throb pundit of the Carnaby Street era in my newspaper last week revealed that standards have slipped so far in the army that only 36 per cent of its officers have been to public school. There is no reason to suppose they will be any better at tackling the country's problems than the present Cabinet, or even the disastrous Grocer himself.

Obviously, Sir Charles wants the Baillie back. First, I should like to know what schools Walker and Stirling attended[2], how many 'O' levels did they get, how many rugger caps etc? Which, oh which, of these well-meaning men can make the greater contribution to helping our beloved politicians out of their desperate fix?

Monday 16th September

In the scenes of mass hysteria over the resignations of Lords Chalfont and St Davids from the Labour Party, no announcement has been made of my own resignation, handed to Wilson at Downing Street by personal messenger this morning. Wilson is obviously trying to suppress the news until after the election.

Well, I'm going to announce it now. It may come as a shock for Labour, but it is meant to be a shock. My reason for resigning from the Party to which I have given a lifetime's service is quite simple. All this week I have been in a National Health hospital, as is my citizen's right from time to time, attended every minute of the day by sweet, gentle, long-legged nurses in their irresistible uniform of black stockings, white linen pinafores and comic hats.

The most poignant thing about these beautiful, doe-eyed angels, as revealed by Wee Willie Hamilton in the House of Commons recently, is that they are so badly paid that many of them are forced to submit to the vile advances of older men in exchange for a meal.

So, when the quacks all formed up on me yesterday morning and said that as they could find nothing wrong with me after ten days I had better stop using scarce national resources and get out of bed, I had my plans ready. I had drawn up a list of possible dinner invitations. Before they could be delivered, the hypocrite Wilson announced that he had doubled — tripled — quadrupled — nurses' pay. Every expensive restaurant has filled up with nurses celebrating their release from slavery.

Only the massage parlours are now left for fun-loving Englishmen who can't face the boredom of modern females for very long. Soon I expect the dangerous left-wing luna-

1. Colonel Stirling was a Scottish eccentric who, like many others, started founding national movements at this time.
2. General Sir Walter Walker KCB, CBE, DSO, went to Blundell's; Colonel Stirling to Ampleforth.

tics who have taken over the Labour Party will start legislating against even this harmless pleasure. For my own part, I intend to remain what I have always been, a Social Democrat.

Tuesday 23rd September

Plainly, *Private Eye* has been going downhill while I was away. At a party in the Torode[1]'s elegant maisonette this evening I was surprised to hear a voice raised in anger at the story in last week's issue of the Conservative candidate for the Isle of Wight who is lucky enough to number a coloured lady among his acquaintances.

"It shows the depths of racist squalor to which the *Eye* has sunk," pronounced the speaker, a man whose proud Afro hairstyle, dusky skin and care-worn face proclaimed the sufferings of his people. With some difficulty I recognised my old friend from Eton and Oxford days, Lord Gowrie — Grocer's inspired choice for spokesman on health in his last, unhappy administration.

We must all try to keep our standards up, including whatever is valid and true, eschewing whatever is false meretricious or in poor taste. I hope Lord Gowrie will accept my sincere apologies on behalf of everyone who works for this magazine, the English people and white races everywhere, for this lamentable slip which occurred while my back was turned. We are all guilty.

Wednesday 24th September

I was sad to read in my newspaper that Baillie Vass now attributes the failure of his disastrous administration to those who worked in the satire industry. Explaining how he was "unlucky enough to hit the time when satire was fashionable", this much-loved elder statesman continues:

"I think it did make a difficult situation more difficult for me than it need have been. It was the height of *TWTWTW* — all that rather nasty debunking of authority."

What he does not seem to realise is that it was the appointment of the 14th Earl of Home (alias Baillie Vass. Recreations: love-making, needlework) as Prime Minister and First Lord of the Treasury which set the whole satire industry on its feet. There was no accident involved. He created the situation in his benign and half-witted way, by being the first totally satirical Prime Minister.

If only any of my readers had the faintest idea who Baillie Vass was or what he did, we would hold a Grand Week of Remembrance and Thanksgiving for the old booby now he has been wheeled out of the House of Commons for the last time.

Thursday 2nd October

Whenever the subject of football hooliganism comes up, I rack my brains trying to think of a punishment which is bad enough for these dreadful people. Not even in Lord Russell of Liverpool's famous book on Nazi war crimes — *Scourge of the Swastika* — could I find an appropriate punishment until suddenly, today, I see the light.

When Franz Stangl, commandant of Treblinka and supervisor of some million murders, was arrested in Brazil in 1967, nobody could think of a bad enough punishment for him, so they just put him in prison. Four years later, he was visited by Miss Gitta Sereny, described as "a slight woman in her early fifties with an abrupt, jarring way of laughing."

Miss Sereny was researching a treatise on the extermination camps which has now appeared — *Into That Darkness*. In it, she reveals how the man who had personally supervised these atrocities without turning a hair was reduced to a shadow of himself by seventy hours of conversation with Miss Sereny. Nineteen hours after she had left him, he was dead. "He had finally faced himself and told the truth," she said.

Obviously, the way to end football hooliganism is to let it be known that Miss Sereny is researching a book into its social and emotional background. Anybody convicted of these offences will be required to spend up to five, or even ten, hours with her alone. Every football ground will carry posters showing her face and, as a special refinement, police riot squads will be equipped with loudspeakers and recordings of her high, jarring laugh.

Friday 3rd October

Normally, of course, I would advise everybody against voting in this ridiculous election between teams of twittish nobodies for posts which carry no importance or authority on the British scene. Apart from anything else, there must be some danger of catching infectious diseases in the polling booths, or whatever they're called. One never knows who has been there before one[2].

But my eye has been caught by generous odds offered by Ladbrokes against the Liberals winning a greater number of seats than any other party — 150 to 1. Obviously, nobody in his senses thinks the Liberals will get there, but these odds might help.

It is often said that we are a nation of punters. If enough of us put our vote where our money is, we might make the killing of all time — even if this means having the absurd Jeremy Thorpe with his peculiar tastes and unsavoury habits as Prime Minister for a while.

---

1. John Torode, a journalist.

2. This refers to the second General Election of 1974, which confirmed Harold Wilson in office.

Monday 6th October
Michael Foot reveals today that when re-elected he's going to give long and serious thought to those who earn more than £10,000 a year. This is encouraging, as the election campaign so far seems to have ignored us completely. How nice of Michael to spare us a little of his generous compassion. It makes me sorry that I ever called him a posturing ninny.

On the other hand, I really think he ought to be thinking more of those unfortunate late people we read about who still earn less than £10,000 a year. We may not know many of them ourselves but there are articles about them every week in the "quality" Sundays. They must be in a dreadful plight nowadays.

It is sad to see how Michael has lost his grip. Once the silver-haired father-figure and pin-up of all nice young women with a social conscience, he can now be seen as just another silly, vain and untruthful politician. I think the decline set in with his hagiography of Aneurin Bevan, the Welsh bully-boy and drunk. But it might be something he's eaten.

Tuesday 7th October
I must be going deaf. Last night at the Drog-hedas' I distinctly heard someone — it may have been Roy Jenkins — say that the Labour Party conference was just about to open in Scarborough.

Hastily packing my toothbrush, flea-powder, condoms and other essential equipment, I arrived here this morning to find myself at the annual conference of the Co-operative Funeral Service Managers Association.

Its President, Mr Alex McKinnon, is worried about the state of the funeral trade. The Social Security Death Grant of £30 has not been increased since 1967, and has in fact only gone up by £10 in the last 25 years.

Many families simply can't afford a funeral nowadays, preferring to keep their loved ones in the deep-freeze until the Death Grant is raised. This takes up space required for essential foodstuffs and may constitute a health hazard.

It is all too easy to forget the nation's undertakers in this hectic election period. My day in Scarborough will not have been wasted if I can help these honest, industrious people to get a square deal.

Wednesday 8th October
The only interesting thing to have emerged from the election campaign is Lord Hail-sham's scheme to hang traitors. Probably no-body can agree what a traitor is nowadays, but historically the word was used to describe any politician who fell from office.

I don't believe in hanging myself, but if the politicians really want to hang each other after every election it would certainly add a note of drama to these dismal occasions. What else will we be able to do with poor Grocer which is equally swift and painless? Sir Michael Fraser tells me that Central Office is thinking of offering a thousand-pound prize for any more humane method.

Thursday 15th October
Party time again. Election parties are becoming ritualised now. Those who aren't invited to the Goldsmiths'[1] go to the *Spectator*'s party, and those who can't even wangle an invitation out of the *Spectator* go to the *Daily Telegraph*'s lovely walrus-like Lady Fartwell. Feeling convivial, I went to all three.

1. Sir James Goldsmith, financier and close personal friend of Lord Lucan.

Christopher Soames was at the Goldsmiths' so I left immediately and Anthony Haden-Guest frightened me away from the *Spectator* with a disgusting story about his adventures in the public lavatory at Victoria Station. So I settled among the waifs and strays at my Lady Fartwell's in Cowley Street. It is just a stone's throw from the Salvation Army hostel in Great Peter Street, and many people apparently went there in error and spent some time sipping meths among the has-beens of that agreeable establishment before they noticed the difference.

In Cowley Street I saw dear Lord Longford deep in conversation with Mervyn Southwark[1], who looked very fetching in a purple cassock with jewelled icon pectoral and matching accessories. A funny old man I at first took for one of Lady Fartwell's amusing chihuahuas told me he was Stephen Spender, the 1930s "poet" and war hero.

Lady Fartwell told me she had only invited her closest friends as she did not wish to upset the *Telegraph* workers with tales of extravagance. They are apparently on strike for more money, which seems to me to be a little ungrateful. But I suppose we put away some 300 bottles of champagne nevertheless, and the evening was enlivened by clever animal impersonations by John Wells. Apparently he does them free for anyone who asks him to a party, bar-mitzvahs a speciality. But I can't see there will be many gay times in the years ahead. It was the passing of an era.

Friday 16th October
What a miserable election it has been. In the new spirit of austerity I take an Underground train from Islington to Tottenham Court Road. One would have thought that at least the lower classes would look happy to have won again, but they look absolutely wretched. Perhaps they always do, but in that case the whole thing seems a waste of time.

Saturday 17th October
Harold Wilson will have a lot on his plate, what with the fruit-gum crisis and the collapse of the economy, but if he really intends to be a reforming Prime Minister there is one thing requiring urgent attention.

Ever since the marriage of Princess Anne to her stable-lad — many people trace the decline of our country's status from that shameful occasion — the Court Circulars have described her as Princess Anne, Mrs Mark Phillips.

This is obviously intended as a reminder of our national disgrace and atonement for false pride in the past. But it means that she was made a Dame Grand Cross of the Royal Victorian Order as a reward for poor Ian Ball's gallant but ill-fated attempt to kidnap her.

The time has surely come to insist that if this young lady must be mentioned at all in the Court Circular, which is almost the only readable part of the newspaper nowadays, she should be referred to as Princess Anne Dame Anne Phillips. Not much less ridiculous or humiliating than the present style, I agree, but at moments of national despondency every morale-boosting gesture counts.

Sunday 18th October
In Church today, I decided to cancel my subscription to the *Daily Mirror*. I will miss The Perishers and Marje Proops, of course, but already I feel a better, cleaner person for my decision. There can be no doubt that the *Sun* is a much better newspaper nowadays[2].

Monday 19th October
Today I drive up to Bewdley, in Worcestershire, a delightful small town with a three-star barmaid in the George Inn. I have come to interview Mrs Mary Whitehouse[3] on behalf of the *New York Times* — an intelligent, articulate and charming woman, not at all the monster we are given to believe. In fact I watch television very seldom and cannot know what she is talking about much of the time, but when she mentions a programme on Florence Nightingale which I happen to have seen I have to agree with her wholeheartedly.

I turned it on — no doubt like many others — because I have an interest in the period, but all we saw was some fatuous rubbish about two moronic twentieth century students rubbing up against each other in bed. If Mrs Whitehouse can do anything to keep these conceited, boring young men of the BBC and ITV in their place she should have the support of us all.

Tuesday 27th October
A very narrow escape tonight. I had thought to dine at Pratts Club in Park Place, but changed my mind at the last moment[4]. Now I learn that Grocer was dining there. Phew! This wretched man drove me out of Buck's Club when he started appearing there 12 years ago, but I never dreamed he would dare show his

1. Rt. Rev. Mervyn Stockwood, DD, Bishop of Southwark since 1959, b. 27 May 1913, noted for Labour politics and bachelor mannerisms.

2. The Daily Mirror had given extravagant support to Harold Wilson throughout the election. Later, many Mirror men were raised to the peerage and given lucrative Government employment.

3. Kidderminster housewife who founded 'Clean Up TV' campaign in 1964; b. 13 June 1910, noted (erroneously) for butterfly spectacles.

4. Heath had been dining at Pratts when a bomb went off in Brooks's nearby.

face in Pratts.

It is a sad commentary on modern life that the bomb in Brooks's found practically no members there at 10.10 pm and only singed the whiskers of a few roistering trade unionists upstairs. Time was when all the clubs were full of convivial people well into the small hours.

Women's Liberation, I suppose, has changed all that — wives now demand that their menfolk report home at six-thirty sharp and spend the rest of the evening listening to their dreadful conversation. Soon there will be nobody left here to drink with in the evenings apart from these embarrassing bachelors.

Thursday 29th October

I don't know why Lord "Manny" Shinwell[1] asked me to his 93rd birthday party at the London Sporting Club. Whenever I have met him as a political correspondent I have found him rude, conceited, and, on the few occasions I could understand what he was saying, extremely stupid.

Nor do I enjoy boxing matches, although I can see that less fastidious people might find it amusing to watch two members of the working class bashing each other's brains out for money. But it was a shock to see Grocer Heath and Baillie Vass grin and smirk at the revolting old fool when they refused to send so much as a birthday card to P.G. Wodehouse, the greatest living Englishman, on the occasion of his 90th birthday three years ago.

Friday 30th October

A black day for truth. In order to clarify Sir Keith Joseph[2]'s amazing suggestions, the Office of Population, Censuses and Surveys has issued a list dividing everybody according to social class. To my horror I find I am listed in the second class as a creative artist, along with publicans, radio supervisory mechanics (whatever they may be) and occupational therapists.

We are judged subordinate to dentists, pharmacists, biological scientists (ugh!) and accountants who are in the first class. Class three includes bricklayers and lorry-drivers; class four, engine room ratings and street hawkers; class five, charwomen and chimney sweeps. These last two are the people whom Sir Keith feels should be visited by well-meaning ladies with chemical and rubber appliances.

The suggestion that I am a second-class citizen is clearly libellous. I am sorely tempted to issue a writ and seek an injunction preventing further publication of this libel. Freedom of the press is all very well, but only if it is exercised with responsibility and restraint, that is to say, by people like ourselves.

Any damages will be given to the Tomalin Award Fund, in memory of a great journalist and very good friend of *Private Eye*, who kept us informed faithfully over the years of all the murky things which go on in the corrupt and sinister recesses of the Thomson Organisation[3].

Saturday 31st October

In India they give men transistor wireless sets as a reward for having a vasectomy, but this

1. A former Labour politician.

2. He had urged greater self control in sexual matters among the lower classes.

3. Private Eye was currently being sued by Harold Evans, editor of the Sunday Times (q.v.) who announced his intention of giving any damages he might win to the Tomalin Memorial Fund.

strikes me as silly. It can only add to the noise, which is surely the greatest reason for being concerned about population explosion. In any case, all the poorer people in England already have transistors and would probably demand colour television sets. The constant sexual stimulation they receive from these machines could not be very healthy, under the circumstances.

Yet Sir Keith is plainly right, that working class children face a grim future with no bourgeoisie left for them to batten on. The correct solution is not to try and prevent them breeding, which is probably immoral, but to encourage the middle class to breed more.

If every baby born was presented with a new volume from Anthony Powell's witty series, *Dancing in the Waters of Time*, bound in hand-tooled Gnomex leatherette, or a signed photograph of Lord Clark[1] with deckled edges, middle class couples would find the idea of having babies much more exciting. And those in socio-economic classes four and five might even be discouraged, feeling — quite rightly — that they were being got at.

Monday 2nd November
A long-standing luncheon engagement with Harold Lever[2] at his agreeable flat in Eaton Square. Tasteful chamber music from the Belgravia Ensemble accompanies every change of course, while naked African boys, gilded all over, offer us their curly heads as hand-towels after the dessert.

My purpose in accepting this invitation was to put Harold in the picture about the British economy. Harold's view is that it doesn't matter how much we overspend because our creditors will never let us go bankrupt for fear of losing the vast sums they have already lent us. The Arabs have much more money than they know what to do with. He should know, he explains with a charming gesture towards his lovely, radiant wife, because he married one.

When I put it to him that elements in the Government are welcoming inflation as a vehicle for social change, he diffidently suggests we should take our coffee in the Green Drawing Room. In many ways, he thinks, we should see social change as something necessary and even welcome.

In the current table of Precedence, for instance, last revised by Mrs Beeton in 1960, it may be quite right that Marquesses' younger sons should rank above all Secretaries of State who are not peers apart from the Prime Minister and Lord President (Mr Short), but it is surely absurd that County Court judges and Masters in Lunacy should rank below the sons of life peers.

As I search Sloane Square for a taxi after lunch, I reflect that I'm really on the side of Mr Wedgwood Benn. These social changes must and will arrive, even if it is necessary to put the entire working class out of what is laughingly called its "work" to bring them about. Our Government is in good hands.

Tuesday 3rd November
All my life people have tried to stop me letting off fireworks. The latest is Andrew Faulds MP, the bearded git from what used to be called Smethwick and is now apparently called Warley East.

Andy thinks fireworks should only be bought from "approved outlets for firing in public or private displays by local authorities or bona fide organisations".

One day he will realise that three times as many children are injured every year by slipping on banana skins and demand that unskinned bananas should only be sold under medical supervision with representatives of the local council and World Health Organisation standing by.

"Old people are often frightened to venture out," whines this dismal 51-year-old, as if there was some pressing reason why old people should not stay at home one night in the year.

The main point, which Faulds is too stupid to realise, is that there is practically no way of having fun which is not dangerous if imprudently indulged. This year the children are joyfully burning an effigy of Andrew Faulds as they dance around the bonfire with lighted rockets in their hands, but if Parliament ever listens to this bossy maniac I give due warning that I shall release the pack of them to descend on Westminster and finish the good work started by that brave and holy man St Guy Fawkes in 1605.

Wednesday 11th November
Old people are becoming more of a menace every day. Sugar workers can't even go on strike like ordinary self-respecting British workmen without promising that "emergency" supplies of sugar will be made available to old age pensioners.

British sentimentality about old age pensioners has always struck me as the most sickening of our national hypocrisies, springing from the cruel British practice of sending old people away instead of keeping them in the family. The applause which greets any public expression of concern for the old always reminds me of the compassionate noise one hears at a bullfight when a bull is being incompetently killed.

1. Kenneth Clark, art historian and television 'personality'. Born 13 July 1903, noted for expression: 'What could be more agreeable?'

2. Labour politician, noted for wealth.

Now we learn that the chief objection to siting a memorial to the 4,500 Polish officers murdered by the Russians in Katyn Wood is that old people like to sit in St Luke's Gardens, Chelsea, and might be frightened by it.

It *could just be* that the long arm of SMERSH has reached into St Luke's Parochial Church Council and tickled up the skirts of the Venerable Archdeacon of Middlesex. But I suppose it is equally likely that old people genuinely would be frightened. I'd already thought of offering the Poles a site for it in my garden, but if these obelisks really scare our senior citizens they're just what West Somerset needs, and I shall start building a chain of them all around the countryside.

Thursday 12th November

In Cheltenham, to speak to the massed ranks of literature fanatics assembled in Cheltenham Town Hall. It is a beautiful town and its younger residents, contrary to popular legend, strike me as particularly swinging.

Dinner is paid for by Guinness, the brewers, yum, yum. Very good for you. Unfortunately, Cheltenham's *Aubergine* restaurant doesn't serve Guinness so we have to make do with rotten old wine. But Guinness's local manager, whose name I never quite catch, gives us miniature bottles of this "most delectable of bibations" (Lawrence Durrell) to take away. Jolly decent of him.

The meal is slightly spoilt for me by the behaviour of Michael Frayn[1] who insists on drinking his soup through a straw and then blowing his nose. I suppose this was the smart thing to do with soup in Cambridge in the 1950s, but nowadays it strikes me as a trifle *vieux jeu*, not to say downright silly.

He would probably look healthier if he drank more Guinness. It's a man's drink.

I hope I now qualify as Guinness Journalist of the Year, if not for a place in the *Guinness Book of Records* as the man who has put more free plugs for Guinness in a shorter space than any other journalist since the great Bernard Levin went to Wexford Festival last week.

Friday 13th November

There may not be much else to look forward to in 1975, but at least there is the Gilbert and Sullivan centenary coming up with a bumper 14-week season at the D'Oyly Carte company at Sadler's Wells.

The company is in money trouble and has not been able to get a penny out of the Arts Council. It is churlish and wrong-headed, of course, to grudge any money which is spent on the Arts, or what are satirically called the Arts, rather than given to the brutish, over-rewarded louts of the Trade Union movement.

We should not object to any of the enormous sums paid to Ian Hamilton's worthless *New Review* or any other beneficiaries, if they did not also withhold subsidies from the very few worthwhile publications in this country, like *Books & Bookmen*, *Private Eye* and *Christian Order*. Similarly, nobody would object to the subsidies for "Moving Being" Dance, the Road to Workers' Power Group, or, most ludicrous of all, *Tribune* poetry readings, if these patronising sods and pseuds did not also refuse money to the D'Oyly Carte Opera Company.

1. A former journalist, bad novelist and bore.

Tuesday 23rd November
In the High Courts of Justice all day.
The bottom-slapping libel action brought
by Colonel Brooks[1] against the *Sunday
People* has been advertised as a show that is
going to run and run — two weeks is the
latest estimate, at a minimum cost, I should
imagine, of £18,000. I will be here throughout to ensure that the money is well spent.

It is hard to know whose side to take at
the outset. Generally speaking, one hopes
that the plaintiff in a libel action will lose,
since there is nothing so funny as a person
demanding money to which he is not entitled
in recompense for an injury to his reputation
which he has not sustained. And on this
occasion, to make it even better, the plaintiff
is a solicitor.

But in this case the defendant's newspaper
has forfeited all claim to sympathy by encouraging its employees to bring libel actions
themselves against *Private Eye*, a smaller and
weaker publication than the *Sunday People*,
in a very similar sort of case. As a result I
have no wish to influence the verdict in any
way.

Under the circumstances, any result of
this excellent suit will cause almost equal
pleasure, although, of course, one hopes that
justice is done. For once we can be truly im-
partial and rejoice in the fact that if the
Sunday People is deemed to have committed
the filthy and revolting offence of libel, then
it is going to be taught a very sharp lesson.

Incidentally, I am puzzled that Miss Carr,
who met the Colonel through an advertisement for "good-natured young ladies" in
Private Eye, should take her complaint to
the *Sunday People*. We have had no complaints, nor have I had any trouble of this
sort from any of the young women who have
responded to the various advertisements I put
in from time to time.

Wednesday 24th November
Courts are an odd place for discussing sex.
When Mr Roger Gray, QC, for Colonel
Brooks, argues that "every healthy, normal,
vigorous male is a bottom-slapper in mind if
not in deed", I feel he is pitching it a little
high.

One can only speak for oneself, but I can
quite honestly say I have never been tempted
to slap a girl's bottom for pleasure. On the
other hand, I can see it might be quite jolly
to pour whisky over them, given the right
circumstances[2]. Perhaps what Mr Gray meant
was that every healthy, normal, vigorous
male *lawyer* is a bottom-slapper at heart.

But when Mr Michael Eastham, QC, starts
his cross-examination today with some very
personal questions to Colonel Brooks, I find
myself even more bewildered: "Do you ob-
tain sexual pleasure by putting your hand up
a woman's skirt when she is not wearing
tights or knickers?" she asks.

In Court, it sounds as if this might be one
of the most perverted and vile things that any
man has ever done to a woman. Yet, ever
since women first started wearing skirts, it
has been known as an agreeable thing to do.
Every normal male, whether healthy and
vigorous or not, has been doing it or thinking
about it for years — except, I suppose, lawyers, who have their own pleasures.

I don't think I can stay here much longer.
Already I find myself eyeing the pigeons in
Trafalgar Square rather oddly during the
lunch adjournment.

Thursday 25th November
The sad fate of John Stonehouse[3] proves
once again, if proof were needed, that there
is Someone Up There looking after us all.
I feared for him yesterday when I learned
that a writ on his behalf claiming damages
for alleged libel had just been received at
Gnome House.

The list of those who have died suddenly,
suffered appalling accidents, committed suicide, or gone mad after suing Lord Gnome
can no longer be ignored by students of psy-
chical phenomena. Stonehouse will be sadly
missed by his many business acquaintances
and creditors, but if by his death he can cast
some light on that half-world we only dimly
perceive, he will not have died in vain.

Friday 26th November
A very boring and hideous young woman
I met at dinner recently told me she thought
the Miss World competition was an insult to
womanhood. She maintained that by asking
them to parade their bodies we were neglect-
ing any possible intellectual appeal these
women might have.

Under the circumstances I decided to
enter the Miss World competition myself to
demonstrate solidarity with oppressed
womanhood through the ages. The only
other male I recognised with the same chivalrous idea was my small but very dear friend,
Charles Vass of *The Times*. He was having
a second shot as Miss Costa Rican Pygmy,
but didn't even get into the semi-final.

I am not by nature a very vain man but
I must admit to feeling distinctly gratified
when Eric Morley kissed me lightly on the

---

1. Colonel Brooks had brought a libel action against the Sunday People for its comments on his behaviour
   in paying a young woman whom he had met through a Private Eye advertisement for taking off her
   knickers and submitting to being spanked on his yacht.

2. Having spanked her, Colonel Brooks poured whisky over her bottom.

3. Stonehouse, a Labour MP accused of irregularity in business by Private Eye, had been announced
   drowned off Haiti. It was also suggested that he had been murdered by the Mafia and sunk in concrete.
   He later turned up in Australia and was arrested.

cheek and declared me Miss World 1974.
I suppose it was my witty repartee to the
compere's idiotic questions which got me
there.

Now I must fly to Auckland, New Zealand to open the National Cheese Fair and
I wish I had kept my mouth shut.

Saturday 27th November
It is no good pretending that my tea-time
sessions at Buckingham Palace with the
Queen are as much fun as they used to be.
We used to gossip for hours on end about
everything under the sun. Today, she keeps
asking me when I think Denis Healey will be
forced to devalue, and doesn't even seem
interested in some rather spectacular gossip
I have about the Lucans.

The truth is she's thoroughly rattled.
She doesn't like the way things are going at all.
In particular, she is scared by the Hudson Institute report on the British economy which
suggests that abolishing the monarchy might
help us survive. Do I think Healey has read it?
When I promised to ask him next time I see
him she does the nose trick with half a scone
and some gooseberry jam. That was not what
she meant, she says.

Next I suggest that the monarchy would
not be in such a bad way if she had taken a
firmer line over the Phillips wedding, as I
suggested at the time. She gets extremely
grand and sniffy, saying that when they
require my advice on such matters, *they*
will ask for it.

A sticky afternoon, made stickier by all
the gooseberry jam thrown around. Next
week I think I'll just send a message to say
I'm washing my hair.

Sunday 28th December
Services in the Roman Catholic Church have
become so inane and so repulsive that I am
seriously thinking of joining the Church of
England. Perhaps it is just that we have a particularly ghastly set of priests in the Taunton
area, but visits to church are now occasions
of sin, tempting one to anti-Christian frenzies
of the sort which once led to Nero's excesses
in the Roman Colosseum.

Obviously, the history of the Church of
England is totally abject, rooted in cowardice, servility and doctrinal error. On the
other hand, it seems to have acquired a certain dignity over the years, while the present
countenance of the Roman church is transcendentally ignoble and reptilian in every
aspect. I would welcome guidance in this
moment of darkness and doubt.

Monday 29th November
Connolly's death leaves only one survivor
from the three judges who awarded the 1972
Booker Prize to John Berger for his boring
and rubbishy "novel" called *G*; but this survivor, the fiendishly stupid Dr George Steiner,
of Cambridge, is only 45, and there's the rub.

One always hoped that natural wastage
would one day remove the Geriatrics Corner
of British criticism which, from the pages of
The Times, Observer and *Sunday Times,* has
lain like a wet blanket on all artistic endeavour in this country for the past 15 years.

But there is a whole new generation of
trainee or probationary geriatrics waiting to
step into their shoes. Men like Richard Hoggart, Raymond Williams, Michael Ratcliffe,
Irving Wardle and the appalling Dr Steiner
himself may not be as talented as their predecessors, being in most cases simply un-

readable, but they have the same fatuous
opinions and the same dedication to that
dismal cul-de-sac of arts and letters known as
"the modern movement". Far worse, they
have bred another generation of artists prepared to pander to their idiotic requirements.

Now I must apply myself to preparing
Connolly's obituary for tomorrow's newspaper. While concentrating on his many endearing qualities, I would not be doing my
duty if I failed to mention his prodigious
laziness, which is the clue to everything else.
It is a shame he never did a spell in the army
where he might have learnt the first lesson of
Officer Cadet School, that an idle man is
a discontented man.

Tuesday 7th December
Poor Princess Elizabeth of Toro! I never
dreamt she was the Foreign Secretary of
Uganda and former mistress of President Idi
Amin when I rescued her from a public lavatory at Orly Airport a few weeks ago. Now
she has been sacked from her job for being
found in these compromising circumstances
with an "unknown European", it is my duty
to set the record straight.

It is quite simple. I was at Orly Airport
waiting for the Air France flight to Gabon
where I proposed to stay with some friends
(the Weld-Potines). I heard a loud disturb-
ance coming from the ladies' lavatories, and
found a crowd of Frenchmen laughing up-
roariously at the plight of an unfortunate
coloured lady who had locked herself in her
cubicle.

The French find anything connected with
lavatories irresistibly funny, but I could see
she was genuinely distressed; so I climbed

over the door and released her. She had been
unable to master the locking device through
an imperfect understanding of the French
language.

It is quite untrue that we were "making
love" as President Amin has claimed. No impropriety occurred, and if this dirty-minded
dictator repeats his smear anywhere outside
his own repulsive country, I shall seek the
protection of the libel laws, like Harold
Evans, William Rees-Mogg, Colonel Brooks
and everyone else.

Thursday 9th December
Today I received the 120th reply to my
appeal for spiritual guidance from *Eye* readers on the matter of joining the Church of
England. I can't answer any of them, but
they will be fed into a computer and I shall
do whatever it decides.

Friday 10th December
George Hutchinson[1] seems very excited today. He thinks he's found a new name in the
hat for the Tory leadership, but on closer
scrutiny it turns out that he's only thinking
of Fatty Soames[2] again.

One day perhaps I'll understand the extraordinary hold this fat man has over so many
of my friends. It can't be sexual, and now he
has lost the services of M. Alphonse Bougainvillea, his masterly *chef de cuisine* at the
Embassy in Faubourg St Honore, it probably
isn't eleemosynary at all. Perhaps his brains
appeal to them, although one shudders at
the thought.

These absurdities obscure the urgent need
to get rid of Grocer. At a lunch for Golda
Meir in Downing Street today I saw my Lady

1. A columnist in The Times.

2. Unsuccessful Conservative politician, later ambassador in Paris. Born 12 October 1920, noted for fatness.

Falkender, as she now so amusingly calls herself. Marcia is the architect of Britain's new South Africa policy and was plainly feeling cock-a-hoop, flanked by Gerald Kauffmann and Joe Haines[1]. She told me that she and Mr Wilson were seriously considering another General Election next autumn on the Common Market issue.

It is high time the Tories realised that until they can pull together for a mighty heave in favour of Mr Whitelaw, they will have Grocer Heath clinging at their throats like a dying rat with lockjaw.

Saturday 11th December
To Stratford where Nicol Williamson's Macbeth had been praised in one newspaper — probably *The Times* — as being free of gimmicks. I suppose the reviewer failed to notice how Trevor Nunn, the Royal Shakespeare Company's 17-year-old artistic director, opens the play with a satanic orgy between monks and nuns, how he suspends the witches like hams from the roof throughout the second scene, how one of the witches is plainly parodying Margaret Drabble[2]. . .

It is a silly and confused presentation, despite a good Lady Macbeth by Helen Mirren and, more surprisingly, an excellent Porter — the part I've always coveted — by Ron Pember. Macduff is rotten, while Williamson (whom I've seen do better in other plays) shouts and gobbles his lines, for all the world as if he were acting in some wretched play of the 1950s by John Osborne[3] about the lower classes.

One problem for Shakespearean actors nowadays is that they are plainly embarrassed by the more famous speeches, like: *"Had I but died an hour before this chance"* or *"Tomorrow and tomorrow and tomorrow"*, both of which Williamson threw away. I see their difficulty, but it seems a shame that we shall never hear these speeches properly delivered.

One solution might be to swap them around a bit. Thus, instead of saying *"Once more into the breach, dear friends"*, Henry V might recite *"Friends, Romans, Countrymen"*; instead of *"Tomorrow and tomorrow and tomorrow"*, Macbeth might break into *"Where the bee sucks, there suck I"*.

Obviously this solution is not ideal, particularly from the point of view of narrative continuity, but it seems to meet two requirements — the actors' passion for endless novelty and the audiences' pathetic hope of hearing a little poetry from time to time.

Tuesday 14th December
In the House of Commons to hear Wislon announce that there is not a shred of evidence for believing John Stonehouse was a Czech spy apart from the first-hand testimony of his Czech paymaster. No wonder Wislon decided to let him stay in the Government.

It is always a relief to hear that any minister or MP is not a spy, although I can't think how some MPs manage to rub along on their measly £140 a week pay and expenses. It must be their sense of duty which keeps them going.

On the other hand, I have never attempted to hide my belief that Wislon is a Russian agent. Needless to say, I have no evidence whatever to support this belief, only intuition. We may never learn the truth, but I think I would be prepared to back my intuition with a small wager. Perhaps I will place it with my old friend Ian Mikardo[4], the House of Commons bookmaker.

Wednesday 15th December
At a lavish party given by Mr Leo Abse, the socialist MP, I am interested to see how this fun-loving man has tackled the servant problem, with twelve rather pretty serving boys, all dressed up in the Abse livery.

Michael Foot, the distinguished-looking Secretary of State for Employment, is among the guests, in a very gloomy mood. He is afraid he has been made to look ridiculous by revelations in *Private Eye* about his involvement with the Crossbum Diaries[5]. He keeps trying to compose a pompous letter to the Editor which will only make him look sillier.

If he had been more collected, I might have suggested to him that Abse is breaking various laws about the employment of children. But probably, if one investigates the matter, one will find that this enterprising host has simply painted some grown-up Filipinos white. This might prove *the* party idea for 1975.

Thursday 16th December
I see the Novosty news agency in Moscow has expressed admiration for Thames Television's series *The World at War,* which I mentioned at the time in connection with a long paean of praise to the Red Army's "liberation" of Eastern Europe.

Thames Television must be proud that their finished work comes up to the very exacting standard required by the Russian

1. Wilson's Press Secretary.
2. A female novelist.
3. Playwright and one-time 'Angry Young Man' exponent of the kitchen-sink school of drama, b. 12 December 1929, noted for intemperate letters to the Press.
4. Left-Wing Labour MP specialising in journeys to Eastern Europe.
5. He was literary executor of Richard Crossman's estate and a member of the Cabinet at a time when the Cabinet Secretary was trying to suppress large parts of the Diaries.

propaganda services. It would be a terrible shame, while so many programmes are having to cut down on their budgets, if British know-how lost the opportunity of leading the world in Russian propaganda films.

Friday 17th December
Morris Finer's death comes as a severe shock. He was a most engaging man — humorous, kindly, indiscreet and, so far as a judge ever can be, honest.

Oddly enough, I had intended to include a small rebuke to him in my column this week. At a wedding a few weeks ago, he was heard inveighing against *Private Eye* and suggesting that some of our information was not as accurate as it might be.

Now it is too late to correct this error. The Curse of Lord Gnome has struck again. So soon after Stonehouse, these unhappy coincidences are becoming a grave embarrassment. I sincerely hope that all those with current writs against the *Eye* will resist any temptation to paddle in concrete over the festive season.

Saturday 18th December
Rose Dugdale's son, born today in Limerick prison, has made me absurdly excited.
All my life I have wanted to have a son called Augustus, but have never yet found a woman prepared to oblige me in the matter. Surely Rose will be brave enough to defy convention.

1. Sir Alfred Beit (q.v.).

The great danger in her present state of mind is that she will give him some ridiculous and unpronounceable Irish name, meaning "Victory for the Irish lower classes in their struggle against oppression by English capitalist landlords" or something like that. This would be especially unsuitable as neither of us is Irish.

A compromise might be to call him Alfred, after the kindly Irish baronet[1] who seems to have seen quite a lot of Rose while she was stealing his pictures about nine months ago. But I can't help feeling the lad would get further in life with a nice name like Augustus.

I have already put him down for Downside in the Christmas term 1987, under the name of Augustus, but that seems to be the limit of a father's authority in these disturbed times.

Sunday 19th December
Is there nothing any of us can do to avert eco-doom, while three out of every four people in the under-developed world are starving, pollution threatens to engulf us all in a rising tide of sexual promiscuity, teenage violence and drug-taking, and even now housewives are tearing each other's eyes out for a cauliflower leaf in Derby?

My dear wife and I decided not to send any Christmas cards this year. This may not make a very big contribution to the world shortage of raw materials. People may laugh at us and call us both "cranks", but at least it is something. We have decided the time has come when those with a concern for the human race must stand up and be counted.

Monday 20th December
A most inconvenient summons to the Palace. The Queen thinks the Conservatives are making fools of themselves and wants to settle the leadership question before Christmas. I say I will only come to dinner if Baillie Vass is not there, but the Palace says that Baillie has made exactly the same condition about me. In the end, we both give in.

Other guests are Lord Poole[1], Harold Macmillan, Norman Stevas[2] and Kenneth Rose[3]. Macmillan is a bit of an embarrassment, unbudgeably convinced he has been invited to form a government himself.

In the end, everybody agrees with me that we must have Whitelaw as Leader, Grocer as Shadow Foreign Secretary, and Keith Joseph as Shadow Chancellor.

Then the Queen announces in her strangled voice that she will never be really happy until Baillie Vass is back in Downing Street, and everybody starts to cry.

Tuesday 28th December
A horrible sight on television of Mrs Castle walking round the ruins of Fairfield Old People's Home, Nottingham. I suppose she hopes to attract the geriatric vote by this belated display of concern.

I see this fiendish woman only as a persecutor of the self-employed. By tripling my National Insurance contributions and imposing her special Self-Employment Tax she hopes to reduce me to a cringeing employee like everyone else.

As Secretary of State for the Social Services it was her responsibility to see that old people's homes do not suddenly ignite and burn up all their occupants. It is no good calling for top-level enquiries afterwards. She has failed in her job and should now be sent to prison like any other 63-year-old hooligan.

Monday 30th December
A party at David Hockney[4]'s fills me with depression. It is not that I have any prejudices against these people but as my friend Enoch constantly says about the blacks, it all boils down to a question of numbers. London seems entirely full of male homosexualists these days, spreading their peculiar gloom wherever one goes.

Obviously, we must strive to see their point of view. More and more of my friends, appalled by the stupidity of modern women, have started announcing their solemn intention to be "gay" next year. I can quite understand that Londoners, as they constantly rub up against each other on the Underground, should grow worried about over-population.

But the last days of Sodom can scarcely have been gloomier than these dreadful London parties. I think I will retire to the country and muse about it all, writing occasional worried letters to the *Daily Telegraph*.

Tuesday 31st December
A feast of poached venison for family and tenants. Next year we will be crouching in the dark, chewing raw turnips as we shoot at any "workers" who show their hideous, grimacing faces through the window.

My New Year's Resolution is to work less hard, so I have sacked the *New Statesman*. Although the official reason for this is Howard[5]'s stinginess in refusing to raise his fees after 18 months of loyal and devoted work from me, the real reason may be that I have been paying too much income tax. This can only encourage the lower classes to batten off the productive elements of the bourgeoisie still further.

---

1. Former Conservative politician, then working for Lord Cowdray.

2. Bachelor Conservative MP.

3. A great literary figure of the time, once allegedly mistaken by Lord Carrington for a Japanese lavatory attendant.

1. A fashionable painter and bachelor.

2. Anthony Howard succeeded Crossman as Editor. Waugh had been writing in the New Statesman fortnightly before his New Year's Resolution to stop. From 1 January 1975 he wrote weekly.

1975

The death of the great Duke of Norfolk strikes new terror. After a year of Workers' Power, the new masters are compared to baboons in the zoo which can't bear to be laughed at. Waugh mentions plans, never revealed before or subsequently, for the CIA to 'destabilize' the Wilson regime. Vietnam and Cambodia fall to the Communists, although Waugh welcomes the Cambodian innovation of shooting politicians' wives, after an embarrassing letter to *The Times* from Mrs Michael Foot about her husband's bottom. A friend of Mr Jeremy Thorpe has a misfortune with his dog.

Wilson, in a generous and memorable moment, knights P.G. Wodehouse who dies almost immediately afterwards. So does Franco, without a knighthood. The Conservatives choose a grocer's daughter to lead them. There is a referendum on the Common Market, Western statesmen capitulate to Moscow in a conference at Helsinki called by the KGB agent and former Nixon associate, Henry Kissinger. Factory output remains well below what it was during the three-day week, and Waugh comments on an epidemic of impotence among English males.

Wednesday 1st January

No newspapers, no post. I am roused from my lethargic torpor by a telephone call from a friend in London with the news of P.G. Wodehouse's knighthood. Well done, Harold Wislon! Whatever the future may hold for this man — whether he will be thrown into the Thames in the Glorious Counter Revolution, or whether he will spend the autumn of his days in the miserable loneliness of an official flat in Pushkin Square, Moscow — he will have earned at least one warm corner in British history.

Whenever I brought this matter up with Grocer he gave me to understand that there were insuperable legal and civil service objections to any honour of the greatest living English writer. I suspected he was lying at the time, but now he's revealed for all the world to see as a liar.

The true reason is probably that he consulted Breadwinner Hogg[1] to whom he frequently went for legal advice. He was not to know that the madman Hogg was one of the most strident persecutors of Wodehouse, already up to his elbows in the blood of this innocent man.

When Grocer refused to honour Wodehouse on his 90th birthday in 1971, it was an act of spite and small-mindedness which set the seal on his electoral chances. If the Tories really can't get rid of this constipated old sod it will be time for the country to rid itself of the Conservative Party[2].

Thursday 4th January

I am reading a most interesting book called *The Next Step* by Sir Richard Acland, the West Country thinker. He has decided that we are all the prisoners of Big Business Fascism.

His group are called the Monists and plan to engulf us all in brotherly love as a step towards common ownership of property. Their mottoes are: "Do your own thing"; and "Come together".

This is plainly the sort of idea one can expect to have if one lives in the country. For my own part, I am quite happy under Big Business Fascism, but anybody interested should write to him at Sprydon, Broadclyst, near Exeter.

Friday 5th January

Last week I had lunch with Colonel Brooks, the respected solicitor who was so viciously libelled in the scurrilous *Sunday People* over his part in the bottom-spanking affair[3]. He did not succeed in converting me to the bottom-spanking idea, but I was interested to learn that he is one of the survivors of the notorious Singapore railway, immortalised by Alec Guinness in *The Bridge on the River Kwai*.

So was Anthony Chenevix-Trench, who retired from the headmastership of Eton at the early age of 51 to take up an appointment at Fettes College, Edinburgh. Oddly enough, if Trench had a single weakness it was for spanking other people's bottoms, although he confined himself to boys. The noble posterior of Lord Brocarse[4] (Jellicohen's boy) still bears the scars, I believe.

It makes one wonder exactly what happened on the Singapore railway. Perhaps Alec Guinness got it all wrong. Before rewriting the history of the Bridge on the River Kwai I would like to hear from all young people who have been spanked, fingered, or otherwise interfered with by survivors from this heroic episode of British military history.

Saturday 6th January

At last I've had time to read the 29th annual report of the Arts Council of Great Britain, explaining how it spent its £17,138,000 of public money for 1973/74.

Very little went to literature in any form — rather less than 1% — but £23,550 of this went to literary magazines. Of this sum more than half — £12,500 — was paid to Ian Hamilton's worthless *New Review*, four times as much as was paid to any other magazine.

To add insult to injury, the Council seems to have given this wretched enterprise an open-ended promise of future subsidy:

"The Council agreed fully to subsidise the new monthly literature magazine *The New Review*, edited by Ian Hamilton who for many years edited the quarterly *Review* (a poetry magazine). *The New Review* was successfully launched in April 1974 and seems likely to establish itself both nationally and internationally as the leading British literary magazine."

It is not true that *The New Review* was successfully launched. In fact they are already selling off back numbers at half price. The main point about this magazine is not that it is any better or worse than any of the other publications struggling to make ends meet in the dusty recesses of Pseuds Corner, but that apart from being more expensively produced it is *exactly the same*. The same

---

1. Lord Hailsham of Marylebone.

2. The Conservative Party eventually heeded Waugh's repeated advice six weeks later, appointing Mrs Margaret Thatcher in his place.

3. Brooks was eventually awarded token or contemptuous damages of £1.

4. Viscount Brocas, son and heir of 2nd Earl of Jellicoe (q.v.), b. 29 August 1950, noted for adherence to the Young Idea.

writers write about the same people just as boringly as they have always done: Robert Lowell, George Steiner, Phillip Larkin, Roy Fuller, A. Alvarez, Julian Symons.[1] November's issue (December does not appear to have emerged yet) even carries a profile of Doris Lessing by C.J. Driver,[2] confirming for the 55th time that both of them are just as boring, just as stupid and just as pseudish as their writing suggests.

I am sorry to say that I think it is time the Literature Panel of the Arts Council was closed down. By feather-bedding a smug coterie of untalented bores it not only wastes taxpayers' money, which would not matter in the least, it also does a grave dis-service to English literature. None of us can be indifferent about that.

Sunday 7th January
A telephone call from nice young Tony Howard of the *New Statesman*, vastly increasing his offer. After all, I have decided that everybody must be prepared to roll up our sleeves and work a little harder for the national emergency.

Sunday 14th January
Alan Brien is back to lavatories again, and all is well with the world. I had been worried about the poor chap, but it was obviously only a short attack of what is sometimes called "writer's block".

Today he reveals that Tweedie, his attractive and engaging wife, who has been working for two years to get him house-trained, has finally succeeded in persuading him to clean up the lavatory after he has used it.

Well done, Tweedie. Well done, Alan. All the news is not bad news in these troubled times.

Monday 15th January
To Grosvenor Square for a meeting with the head of CIA's London Bureau, the gifted and engaging Mr Cord Meyer, and some associates from Washington. It is little known that *Private Eye* has only been able to keep its price so amazingly low thanks to generous assistance from this philanthropic body.

Plans for "destabilising" the Wislon regime in this country are now far advanced, I am happy to report. Our men in the trade union movement have been told to press enormous wage claims while those in London Transport see to it that there are longer and longer delays between trains and buses etc. Only arrangements for the final assault on Downing Street need to be settled.

Washington is particularly anxious that this should be carried out by British troops and suggests various units in the Brigade of Guards stationed in London. Cord and others over here are not quite sure that these picturesque bum boys would be quite up to it, fearing that they might be frightened away by Lady Faulkender or Wislon's dog, Paddy.

I suggest that if US Marines are needed for stiffening, only those of African descent should be used and they should be disguised as West Indian bus conductors. Now I must contrive to buy 3,000 London Transport uniforms before Zero Hour — thirty minutes after Wislon has landed in Moscow[3].

Tuesday 16th January
A visit from Miss Angela Levin, of the *Observer* colour section, who is interviewing the nation's top workers to discover the source of their exceptional energy. My secret is very simple.

For breakfast, I touch nothing except a couple of young partridges (in season) or a fat capon, washed down with a quart of barley wine. I never eat aubergines, scotch broth or shellfish at breakfast.

For lunch, I prefer to sit in a convenient church (or in the churchyard, if the weather is fine) to eat my cheese sandwiches with a bottle or so of whisky to help them down, while I ponder the eternal verities — life and death, beauty and pain, yin and yang etc. After April, I will probably have to make do with a bottle of methylated spirits.

In the afternoon, if my work involves heavy intellectual strain (VAT accounts, for instance, or an important game of bridge), I may drink a bottle of *creme de menthe frappe* on crushed ice. Tea is not taken seriously in any of my houses (thin cucumber sandwiches, followed by a hot meat or eel pie — even sausage and mash at a pinch —and ice cream). Dinner is the most important meal for the intake of energy by essential food supply.

Here one tries to be as varied as possible, but a typical meal might start with pigs' blood pudding followed by *demoiselles* of goose, cold lobster or stuffed carp, roast suckling pig in honey, redcurrant leaf sorbet, roast beef or venison, artichoke souffle, orange or raspberry tart, snipe's entrails on toast, fruit jelly with cream and nuts. Brown rice and sesame seed are available as a small contribution to world problems. I think my agreeable complexion comes from the fruit jellies, while nuts are well known to be good for sexual performance.

1. Six pseuds.
2. Two more.
3. Wilson was making another of his numerous trips of Moscow.

Wednesday 23rd January
Pictures released today of MPs' new accommodation in Old Scotland Yard confirm what I have learned from eight years' bitter parliamentary experience — that however much fuss these overpaid buffoons make about "Members' interests", they are only interested in one thing: sex.

True, the rooms do contain a little desk where the Member can pretend to be getting on with his "work". But a far more important piece of furniture in each "office" is a huge and luxuriously upholstered divan, which can only be intended for seductions.

But before all the frustrated young women of London rush round there they should learn that most MPs are permanently drunk, and would almost certainly get no further than a boorish fumble at their shirt buttons. Another distressing feature of MPs is that most of them have bad breath.

Thursday 24th January
Any impure thoughts I might ever have entertained about the Church of Rome, or fleeting temptations towards the Church of England, are dispelled today with the scandalous decision to refuse permission for a memorial to victims of the Katyn Wood Massacre in St Luke's Gardens, Chelsea.

Giving judgement for the Venerable J.D.R. Haywood, Archdeacon of Middlesex, who, for reasons best known to himself, does not want the Russians to be blamed for murdering a whole slice of the Polish nation, the Chancellor of London Diocese states that "the monument was intended to be politically controversial, and its symbolism was not restful or consistent with the Church's ministry of reconciliation."

Plainly the CofE is as spineless and as unprincipled as it always was. There may be nothing particularly uncontroversial or restful about mass murder, but the Church's policy is that so long as it does not disturb the Archdeacon and his sodding old age pensioners, mass murder is something better not discussed.

Now that the Americans have been forced to drop the wicked policy of *detente* with the Soviet Union initiated by the criminal Nixon, we might try to bust up all this mateyness between the churches. I think I will pave the way with a succession of unpleasant jokes on the Vicar of Combe Florey, called Mr Bonsey.

Friday 25th January
Prince Philip has asked me if anybody I know would like the job of being his personal valet. His present man, George Tribe — formerly of the Welsh Guards — is retiring and all applicants for the job so far have turned out to be pooves.

Being a simple naval fellow, Prince Philip finds this worrying. If only he knew what the rest of us have had to put up with in the way of domestic servants: drunken Irish cooks who have chased our dear wives around the kitchen table with a carving knife; Italian butlers who have gone mad and tried to murder the daily women; nannies who have grown horns and lost all their hair.

I know nobody who is at the same time neat, quiet, deferential and sexually normal, but anyone interested should write to the Comptroller at Buckingham Palace, SW1 for further details.

Saturday 26th January

It is high time William Whitelaw stopped
fluttering his lovely eyelashes and pleading
"loyalty"[1]. I suspect some more sinister explanation for this and if I find out what it is
I shall not hesitate to hint at it in this column.
If Grocer has got some sort of screw on him
he should go to the police and have Grocer
done for blackmail. This is certainly what
that repulsive man would do to him.

Sunday 27th January

I am very worried about my friend Peregrine
Worsthorne who seems to be suffering from
a brainstorm. He seriously proposes Lord
Hailsham for the Tory leadership on the
grounds that he will set the grass roots on
fire and make Mr Wilson cry.

　He mentions that there are a few objections to the scheme, it is true: that the old
brute is 67 and now permanently stuck in
the House of Lords[2]. He might have added
that Hailsham is also mad and unpleasant
with it, a squalid opportunist whose fits of
hysteria make him far more dangerous than
the pathetic, rumbling insanity of Keith
Joseph. I have also read that Hailsham has no
legs, like Richard Wood[3], although I have
not been able to check on this information
which may be untrue.

Monday 28th January

I think I will vote *for* the Common Market
in this referendum. Many people, I know,
are disgusted by Mr Soames's appalling shape
and horrified at the thought that this might
happen to them, but I see it as a symbol of
prosperity and forward-looking attitudes[4].

　Londoners, of course, who are constantly
rubbing up against each other in cinema
queues and at homosexual cocktail parties,
will probably want to keep their skinny, ratlike figures. But I think fat men get just as
much fun out of life, especially if they are
rich — look at Sir George Weidenfeld — and
in many parts of the world fat women are
thought much more enticing. It is just a
question of what is available.

　At any rate, this seems as good a reason as
any for taking part in the ridiculous business.
An even better reason for not holding the
referendum at all is that it will give Ron
"Badger" Hall the excuse for holding another of his revolting election parties.
These are now recognised as a major health
hazard by those concerned with the spread
of hepatitis and kindred ailments.

Tuesday 29th January

Spend all morning outside County Hall singing hymns with some fine people from the
Salvation Army and a nondescript collection
of religious maniacs protesting about film
censorship.

　I have no strong feelings either way about
dirty films and don't really know what I am
doing here, but there is nothing else to do in
the morning in this ghastly city where nobody seems to get up before lunchtime.
If only they would have community singing
on the Circle Line it might keep some of us
away from the massage parlours.

Wednesday 30th January

To Rome for the night with a friend. I hope
there is no truth in the story I heard at dinner
about the death of Pope John. It was told to
me by a Dominican who claims to have been
in Rome at the time.

　It appears that Pope John was found
dying in the Vatican apartment of a nun,
Eugenia Casaroli, cousin to the Secretary of
State and Mother Superior of the Order of
the Immaculate Conception. He was dressed
only in his *tunica brevis*, or papal pyjama
top.

　Nobody knows what he was doing there,
as the holy nun is very old, extremely ugly
and sports a great *uhlan* moustache.
The Vatican information office explains that
he probably mistook her for the Greek
Catholic Archimandrite of Aleppo with
whom he wished to discuss the doctrine of
the Hypostatic Union (a doctrine on which
the Greek Catholics have always wobbled).
His pyjama trousers, it is thought, may have
fallen off on his way through the long Vatican corridors — a mishap which is not
uncommon among gentlemen of his age.

　The Vatican has never revealed this before
in case it should add to the absurd cult for
Pope John among young people. Oddly
enough, I would not be at all surprised if he
had genuinely mistaken the nun for the
Syrian Archimandrite (who has a long black
beard), because however pleasant Pope John
may have been to meet, he was undoubtedly
very stupid.

Thursday 7th February

I suppose there is something to be said for
keeping the names of female "rape-victims"
out of the newspapers, since a great many of
these women are mad and only make their
monstrous allegations in order to draw attention to themselves.

---

1. Whitelaw refused to stand against Heath on the first ballot for the Conservative leadership, and so lost
   the prize to Mrs Thatcher.

2. Hailsham renounced his original peerage, a Viscounty, in order to stand unsuccessfully for the Tory
   leadership in 1963. After the Conservative victory in 1970 he was made a Life Peer to sit as Lord
   Chancellor.

3. A legless Conservative politician.

4. This referendum was won by the pro-Marketeers. Soames (q.v.) was a Common Market Commissioner
   by then.

Nobody seems to have thought of the unfortunate men who are almost always innocent and who have to suffer immensely damaging publicity for days on end in newspapers which never devote quite so much publicity to the verdict as to the lurid allegations made by the depraved women in court.

Nor is there any protection in law for men who find themselves raped by women, although this is a much commoner occurrence nowadays. It frequently happens to me, but being a shy man I dread the publicity and whenever I go to the police with my complaint they laugh in my face.

Friday 8th February

Sad and terrible news about my cousin, the Duke of Norfolk[1]. Although I can't honestly claim to have met him more often than once or twice, I frequently dreamed about this bland and beautiful man, just as loyal subjects are said to dream about the Queen.

In my dreams he always gave me wise advice, moderating the angry passions in my soul and diverting them to wholesome ends. His presence was an entirely benign one throughout the land, and nobody could seriously believe that anything very terrible would happen to England while he was in the background, ready to lead the country back to sanity and justice whenever stern duty called.

When a great nobleman dies we are all diminished. Far too many of the rich and powerful in this country now appear consumed by a mixture of avarice and squalid funk. Bernard (as I feel I can call him now that he's dead) put them all to shame. He was a wise and godly man. R.I.P.

Saturday 9th February

Easter falls this year on March 30 and already my old sow Elsie is in farrow to provide us with her suckling pigs for Easter luncheon.

This tradition goes back to the earliest times, when Christian families used to celebrate Easter by the cruel and beastly practice of eating a Jewish baby. Nobody that I know still observes this custom, and for my own part I am very glad they don't. The new arrangement strikes me as altogether more humane as well as being more oecumenical.

I don't know how the Jews have been able to move with the times in the matter of their own Passover celebrations. They are inhibited, of course, from eating pig by their dietary laws, originally a product of desert conditions in the days before refrigerators when bad pork could represent a serious health hazard. I imagine they make do with chicken.

Monday 11th February

To Arundel for the great Duke's funeral. A melancholy day indeed. Words can scarcely express my disgust at the Queen's absence. She is not only insulting the ducal and illustrious Howards and the entire English nobility who were here thousands of years before her

---

1. Waugh's great-great grandfather, the 3rd Earl of Carnarvon, married in 1830 Henrietta Howard, niece of 12th Duke of Norfolk, and his great grandfather, the 4th Earl, married his own cousin, Elisabeth Howard, in 1878.

own family came to these islands. She also
insults every autochthonous citizen of her
adopted country, down to the meanest
workman.

The new Duke, Miles, looks handsome
and brave, as well as benign. It turns out he
is only as closely related to the great Duke as
I am. If I were not debarred from inheriting
by the despicable male chauvinist system of
primogeniture, I should certainly see to it
that neither the Queen nor any of her snivel-
ing relations sets foot in any of my castles
again.

Tuesday 12th February
So it is to be Mrs Thatcher (146-79-19)[1].
As the only one of the five candidates in the
final round who has ever dared to attend
luncheons at *Private Eye*, she was undoubtedly the one who deserved best. I *warned*
Whitelaw time and again that he could not
rely on his pretty face alone to see him
through.

Obviously Mrs Thatcher owes her election
to the chivalrous instincts of backbenchers.
As a gentleman, I suppose one would be
bound to vote even for an ugly, bald, puking
thing like Barbara Castle if she offered herself
for election. But I can't help feeling that
chivalrous instincts are misplaced in politics
and these new developments may mark the
death of chivalry.

If it is unbecoming in a man to wish to be
Prime Minister and boss the rest of us around,
it is doubly unbecoming in a woman. I blame
Dennis Thatcher, whoever he may be, for
not keeping his wife under control. Anybody
else whose wife showed these distressing
symptoms would shut her in her bedroom on
bread and milk for a few days, sending her to
a nursing home if she persisted. It is this
wretched husband who should be blamed for
all the troubles ahead.

Wednesday 13th February
I decided to ignore last night's reception at
Buckingham Palace for proprietors and in-
fluential members of the Press to meet
Tommy Steeie[2], the Poet Laureate[3], More-
cambe and Wise, Jack Hulbert[4] and suchlike.
I had already met all these people and had
no desire to be seen in the Queen's company
after her disgusting treatment of Cousin
Bernard[5].

The Queen probably thought I stayed
away because she is not going to get her
money after all. I don't care. I hope it hurts.

Thursday 14th February
Sad news from Athens where Aristotle Onassis is reported to be in a "critical, if not
desperate condition"[6], suffering from a rare
disease which causes progressive weakening
of the muscles. I feared something of the
sort would happen when I read in the gutter
press recently that this otherwise kind and
sensible man had issued a writ alleging libel
against my beloved employer, Lord Gnome.

Until recently, there was always a decent
lapse of time before Lord Gnome's Curse
struck. Randolph Churchill lived on for a
number of years before dying prematurely,
so did Lord Liver of Cesspool and poor Bob
Pitman. Even the *Scottish Daily Express*
struggled on after a fashion for a few
months. Bankruptcy, blindness and insanity
generally arrive sooner, it is true, but nowadays the Curse is liable to strike almost as
soon as the papers are served — in Stonehouse's case on the same day.

I hope Aristotle gets better soon and
looks after his health more carefully in
future. I hear that Derek Marks, last editor
but one of the *Daily Express* and another
former litigant, is far from well.

Friday 15th February
Marks has died in his sleep, at only 54.
Too young, too young.

Saturday 23rd February
As I get older I find I think more and more
about rape. A historic ruling in the House of
Lords may alter our ideas on this subject.
"If a woman resists," says Sir Harold Cassell,
"then a man may think she is in fact consenting and giving him the additional thrill of a
struggle." To which Lord Hailsham, the
noted authority on sexual matters, adds:
"If he believes the woman is consenting to
rough treatment because she likes it, it
would not be rape. . . what a woman wants
and what she consents to may be two different things."

Similarly, of course, a distinction must be
drawn between what a woman thinks she
wants and what, in fact, would be good for
her. In many ways, couples would be better
off if they had the family solicitor present
before attempting any sort of sexual hanky-
panky. Long pauses could be introduced for
Counsel's opinion and reading from relevant
judgements. A whole new dimension of
sexual activity opens up for those with
enough money to hire these aids to pleasure.

1. These were the voting figures in the Conservative Parliamentary election as between Thatcher, Whitelaw and a third, frivolous candidate.
2. A singer and pantomime performer.
3. The great Sir John Betjeman (q.v.).
4. Three comedians.
5. 16th Duke of Norfolk KG, PC, GCVO, GBE, TD (c.f. supra).
6. He died soon afterwards. Greek millionaire, b. 1906, noted for marrying Jacqueline, widow of assass-
inated President John F. Kennedy.

The two women who write to *The Times* on the matter today miss the whole point. Dee Wells and Shirley Conran — both old enough, I would have thought, to be spared from frequent importunities of this sort — ask what a woman should do who does not, in fact, welcome friendly approaches.

Such occasions must, of course, be extremely rare — from my own experience I should have thought more or less non-existent. But if a woman really finds herself in this frame of mind, I think her best tactic would be to strike up what she thinks is an intelligent conversation about Vietnam.

Sunday 24th February
Perhaps I am alone in having reacted to the murderous increase in price of *The Sunday Times* (from 11 to 18 new pees) by having cancelled my order for the *Observer*.
I only read *The Sunday Times* for one thing now (apart from occasional contributions from Tina Brown) and that is Alan Brien's notoriously boring Diary.

This may seem a morbid, even an unhealthy taste in one so young. The truth is only partly that I draw gloomy satisfaction from having all my opinions confirmed about how the other half lives. It is also a terrible warning of what might happen to any of us who, from laziness or lack of moral fibre, allow our standards to slip and succumb to the world of unspeakable shits and buggers who, like the hosts of Midian, prowl and prowl around.

1. **Probably a reference to Ms Norah Beloff (q.v.).**

The *Observer,* by contrast, has nothing of the slightest interest in it nowadays. Its novel reviewing is done by a half-witted woman called Lorna Sage. For a time I supposed this was another of the many aliases used by my old, if slightly foxed chum, Norah Bulgeups[1]. But is appears that Sage is a genuine person, a lecturer at some dim provincial university like so many other book reviewers on newspapers whose editors are too mean to employ proper journalists.

Monday 25th February
In today's newspaper there is much sad news. The Dean of York has collapsed and died in York Minster. He was a blameless man who never, so far as I know, contemplated suing *Private Eye* for libel, but spent most of his time in unrelenting efforts to prevent York Minster collapsing.

The Headmaster of Haileybury has also collapsed and died during a ten-minute football match between masters and boys.
To cheer us up after these blows, *The Times* prints a huge picture on page four of a grinning woman called Mrs Polly Wilson of Histon, near Cambridge, who has successfully reached the age of 100.

Is this really such good news? The geriatric explosion is upon us now. Have you noticed how even the tits and bums of Rupert Murdoch's admirable *Sun* are becoming a little wrinkled?

Yesterday's *Observer* Colour Section, which I was horrified to find the cook read-

ing on her day off, carried a delightful photograph showing hundreds of piccaninnies with the stern message that they should have been eliminated by contraception. No doubt this was an attempt by David Astor to maintain the excessive profits of Lord Cowdray[1] and his rubber baron friends, but the true crisis we are facing is exactly the opposite.

Contraceptives are no protection against the rising tide of old age pensioners. It is true that science has given us the wonderful substance called paraquat against which there is no known antidote, as well as a number of ingenious machines which can be relied upon to make sudden, loud noises. But these remedies are only available, as any moral philosopher will agree, in immediate and specific cases of self-defence, and old age pensioners seldom attack one.

Our best hope for a solution is probably the one already set in motion by Mrs Castle, 63, the bald, half-witted Secretary for the Social Services — either to close down the National Health Service or, more properly still, desist from officious efforts to keep it alive.

Tuesday 26th February
To the Church of St Lawrence Jewry to hear General Sir Walker Walker-Walker[2] talk on Remoralising Britain. I'm sorry to say he does not strike me as a fit person to lead the country after the Glorious Counter Revolution. When things start moving, I fear we will have to give this old booby a bit of a push.

Wednesday 6th March
Rather unexpectedly I find myself in Khatmandu with Prince Charles and a party of 14 other Etonians for the coronation of King Bihendra. I never knew Bihendra at Eton, where he was a junior boy when I was Captain of Oppidans, but he seems to think he knew me.

Before we left London we were all given a briefing by a man from the Foreign and Commonwealth office who strongly advised us to be careful during the celebrations on the grounds that a staggering 94% of Nepalese women suffer from hepatitis and related disorders. Can it really be true? Misconceptions of this sort have plagued British foreign policy from the earliest times and probably account for the loss of our Indian empire. But I confess that what little I have seen of Nepalese women has not encouraged me to delve for the salubrious six per cent.

Instead the British party spends an agreeable evening dancing together in the Royal Guesthouse. With typical British improvisation some of us dress up as girls — the Prince of Wales looks particularly fetching in a *yashmak* with blue paint on his eyelids. We all have to call him *Omyhla*, which means Daughter of the Moon.

Thursday 7th March
Still dancing in the Royal Guesthouse at Khatmandu, I have now enjoyed three foxtrots, a military two-step, and a St Bernard's waltz with His Royal Highness, as well as countless whirls with lesser fry. Joking about

---

1. A very rich peer, whose commercial empire was believed to include London Rubber Company, manufacturers of all English condoms and sheaths. Born 27 February 1910, noted for having only one arm.

2. Gen. Sir Walter Walker (q.v.) was persisting in his aim to recruit a force of volunteers to 'assist the civil authority' in the event of General Strike or breakdown of government.

the name of Nepal's three-year-old heir apparent, Charles says he hopes the lad never goes off the Deependra. Great fun.

More seriously, as we sit out a Dashing White Sergeant, Charles tells me that he has no intention of marrying into the Saudi Arabian Royal Family, as I keep urging him to do. Instead of pointing out that Saudi Arabia's oil reserves will be exhausted in 12 years, leaving us with some raddled old *fatimah* as Queen, he gets very pious and says that he could never marry anyone unless he was truly in love.

Luckily, an alternative scheme has begun to formulate in my mind, but I am upset by this new evidence of the younger generation's imperfect sense of duty.

Friday 8th March

On its return journey our plane refuels in Teheran and I lose no time in securing an invitation to tea with the Shah. He is a disconcerting man with an abrupt way of speaking which many may find unsympathetic.

When I suggest (for this is the purpose of my call) that he uses the opportunity of the Queen Mother's visit to Persia on April 14th to propose marriage, his first question is: "What makes you think she will have anything to do with a dirty old wog like me?"

As a matter of fact, this was exactly the aspect of the affair which had been troubling me. He might almost have read my thoughts. Under the circumstances, I didn't feel I could give him an entirely straight answer, but thinking it over afterwards I am confident that our doughty and magnificent royal lady will not fail in her duty at the hour of her country's need. I also happen to know that the Shah has some very nice necklaces and other pieces of jewelry.

Saturday 9th March

The great Alan Watkins has turned the gaze of his penetrating *Evening Standard* column on London to the distressing subject of London women. He reaches the only conclusion possible for an honest and intelligent observer, that they have been "struck down by a collective madness, an epidemic of insanity".

He cites their constant eating of psychotropic pills, their trips to psychiatrists and their occasional suicide attempts. He might also have mentioned their violent and unreasonable opinions, their inability to discuss anything in a civilised or detached manner, their passionate adherence to boring and idiotic causes, their hysterical aggressiveness and increasing tendency to lesbianism.

And yet, and yet there must surely be a soft core somewhere. Hidden inside these monsters are the beautiful, gentle, soft and smiling women of our dreams. But as Watkins observes, there is nothing to be done. A good defence against the more violently aggressive type of lesbian is to throw lumps of coal at her from a safe distance. Very few women are much good at throwing things.

Monday 11th March

Unexpected visit from a delightful Chief Superintendent of police whose name I did not catch. He told me he was in charge of inquiries into Lord Lucan[1]'s disappearance, and wondered if I could help him.

I assured him I had never met the gentleman; if ever I did, I should almost certainly mistake him for John Stonehouse and decide to have a go, attacking him viciously with whatever weapon was on hand. The Chief Superintendent apologised and said he was only working his way through Kelly's *Handbook to the Titled, Landed and Professional Classes* (one of the few really worthwhile publications of our time, obtainable from Kelly's Directories at £8.50).

His next call was on Eugenie, Countess Wavell, widow of the great Field Marshal, although at the age of 87 she seemed unlikely to have played a very active part in these tragic events. I urged him to hurry. His call after that was on Lord Waverley, who I understand practises as a physician in Reading.

One rather poignant story emerged from our talk. On the night of the alleged murder, the policeman told me, Mrs Maxwell-Scott[2] was awakened by a terrible knocking. When she asked who was there, a thin, wind-buffeted voice came through the door:
"Lucan."
"Lucan who?" said Mrs Maxwell-Scott.
"Lucan see what I've done to my nanny."

Tuesday 18th March

I am glad I did not go to the House of Commons today. The sight of Nigel Lawson assaulting Mr Clinton Davis, Peter Shore's unedifying side-kick from the Board of Trade, could only have stirred up unhappy memories.

Generally speaking, of course, we should all be very much in favour of MPs punching each other, stuffing each other's mouths with Order Papers, or doing anything else to show an awareness of what horrible people they all are. It is not as if they do much else to earn their prodigious salary and expenses of nearly £38 per working day.

1. 7th Earl of Lucan, wanted for alleged murder of nanny. He had disappeared on the night the body was found. b. 18 December 1934, noted for strong support of capital punishment.

2. A friend of the missing Earl.

I worked for two and a half years under Lawson when he was editor and I was Political Correspondent of a magazine called *The Spectator*. Lawson never assaulted me, or even, so far as I remember, waved an Order Paper in my face, although he behaved oddly on one occasion. This had the unfortunate result of my summoning him before the County Court for suitable punishment.

For my part, I bear him no malice. The £700 compensation was eventually paid by the *Spectator*'s proprietor, a benign, fun-loving man known as Harry "Secretaries" Creighton — Lawson had long since been dismissed as editor for reasons which were probably quite unconnected with his ill-considered outburst.

The thing that saddens me is that Nigel, for whom I will always have the fondest feelings, should jeopardise his career once again by indulging these reckless passions just at a time when he was beginning to live down the earlier lapse[1].

Wednesday 19th March

Today we took delivery of our new motor-car, a Rolls Royce *Camargue*. At £29,250, it may seem rather expensive, especially as it has only two doors, but in a few years' time that sum will represent the price of a tube of toothpaste.

The truth may be that I was a little drunk when I ordered it. What decided me was when a man I met in the pub last night said that if I didn't buy it he would have to sell it to an Arab. I remember we both cried into our beer glasses as we sang *There'll Always Be an England* together and the barman said it was time to leave. Now I am stuck with this ridiculous car. Perhaps I shall offer it as first prize for the *Private Eye* competition.

Thursday 20th March

My friend Clive Jenkins[2] gets a terrific bloody nose from Bernard Levin today. This is over Clive's silly remarks on the wireless welcoming the Russian mass-murderer Alexander Shelepin[3]. I had already begun to fear for Clive's state of mind when I read that he was suing *Socialist Worker* (a most informative and entertaining journal) for libel over its witty piece about the holidays in Spain being promoted by Clive's union, ASTMS.

I don't think Bernard should be too hard on him. The significant fact about Clive, who is the most delightful of companions with sound ideas on many subjects, is that he had a deprived childhood in Port Talbot and, is still emotionally a member of the working-class. A sad feature of the working classes in power is that, like the baboons in London Zoo, they cannot bear to be laughed at.

After a year of being ruled by organised labour, one might make other, even more austere generalisations about the working class, if this invitation to the repulsive Shelepin did not sum it all up so beautifully. Do these half-witted British trade unionists like Len Murray realise, as they drool over the man who has helped to murder and imprison more Russian workers than Ivan the Terrible, that in the workers' state of Russia one day's absence from work can be punished by ten years in a labour camp, if the KGB have a mind to it? That factory workers who steal from their place of work can face the death penalty?

The sad truth about Workers' Power, as anybody should now be in a position to see, is that "workers" are so stupid, so cowardly and so incompetent, even in the pig-like pursuit of what they imagine to be their own interests, that they create a hell on earth for themselves as soon as they are allowed any say in the matter.

Friday 21st March

A dangerous lunatic is abroad in the land, called Dr Hugh Jolly. For some time he has been amazing readers of *The Times* with his far-out views on medicine; now he comes out with the view that fear of constipation is a "Victorian health myth that should be forgotten".

Children who won't go to the lavatory are simply holding on to what they regard as a "precious object", he claims. Mothers who overdo their praise for a child's shit are making the object still more precious in his eyes. Rather than give them a laxative, we should be prepared for "months or years of waiting".

A cast-iron rule in journalism is never to attribute a motive, so I shall not even speculate on why Dr Jolly chooses to spread this dangerous rubbish among readers of *The Times*. But what does Rees-Mogg, whom I've always thought of as a good and wise man, think he is doing when he allows it to happen? He has four young children himself, for shame.

Somewhere I suspect a hideous plot to destroy the nation's entire upper and middle professional class by one of the most painful and undignified deaths imaginable.

---

1. Lawson, by now a Conservative politician, had wrongfully dismissed Waugh shortly before being dismissed himself.

2. General Secretary, Association of Scientific, Technical and Managerial Staffs, b. 2 May 1926, noted for collection of Victorian porcelain and statuary.

3. A Russian politician and mass murderer.

Monday 24th March

Deeply shocked by the murder of my old friend King Faisal of Saudi Arabia. Faisal once gave me a bath made out of solid gold with platinum taps, studded in *cabochon*, emeralds and rubies for some trifling service. It is not the sort of gesture one forgets in a hurry. Thanks, old pal.

I wish I could say the same for Onassis, whose last days were spent in an unseemly attempt to sue *Private Eye* for alleged libel. I warned him about the Curse of Lord Gnome, but he was deaf to my warning. R.I.P.

In Holy Week, one might also spare a prayer for employees of the *Times* and *Sunday Times*, both losing money hand over fist, and both, in the opinion of many well-informed people, likely to go the way of the *Scottish Daily Express*, which sued *Private Eye* in 1968. Editors of both the *Times* and the *Sunday Times* are suing *Private Eye* at the present time. Oh dear, oh dear.

Tuesday 25th March

To Glasgow for the day, where I have been asked to stand for election as Rector of Glasgow University, in the footstep of that great journalist and very wonderful man, Kenneth Allsopp[1]. Scenes of terrible privation meet my eyes.

The noble citizens, who have been reduced to eating their own garbage rather than break ranks with the strikers, are now left with nothing to eat at all as the Army mercilessly clears away their only remaining sustenance. Many, in desperation, have been driven to eat the rats which now roam the streets in ravening packs, crazed with hunger and seeking whom they may devour.

One is reminded of the legend of Bishop Hatto, a 10th Century Archbishop of Mainz, who at a time of famine was said to have collected a number of poor people in a barn and burnt it down so that the local politicians should eat decently. For punishment, he was eaten by a swarm of mice.

In fact the legend is quite untrue. Hatto was a saintly man who died in his bed like all good bishops. But if I were that fascist stooge Harold Wilson, I would not care to set foot in Glasgow at the present time. Vote for Waugh in the Rectorial elections.

Wednesday 3rd April

Francis Boyd, the much respected 94-year-old former Lobby Correspondent of the *Grauniad*, makes a curious case in defence of Lobby correspondents. First, he reveals that on his retirement he received a present from the late Will Hamling, MP for West Woolwich. It was a book.

Now there is nothing surprising about that. What is distinctly odd is the reason that Boyd gives for publishing this extraordinary boring fact:

1. Allsop lost a foot at the Battle of Monte Casino.

"I am publishing the fact of his gift. . . not only as a personal salute to his memory, but as evidence, which will embarrass *Private Eye*, that not all politicians and Lobby Correspondents are corrupt, or stupid, or both."

Boyd even mentions me by name — "the exquisite Squire Waugh" — as somebody who will be particularly embarrassed by this disclosure. Now I am as much interested in the problems of old age as the next man, and I think it is very compassionate of the *Grauniad* to go on printing the old booby. But I completely fail to see by what geriatric process of reasoning he arrives from point A to point B: Hamling gave him a book *ergo* not all politicians and Lobby correspondents are stupid and corrupt. The usual prizes are offered for any explanation which is not defamatory of this very wonderful old man.

Thursday 4th April

Today's report of the Department of Education and Science that Public Lending Right for authors will take two years to introduce means that the world of letters will be deprived of any more novels from my pen for at least as long as that.

As a result, I have decided to reveal the plot for a novel I am thinking about, and make a present of it to any housewife or Arts Council-support pseud who has the time to write it up.

It is a political fantasy thriller about a Prime Minister of Great Britain who was photographed by the MVD in bed with a secretary on a visit to Moscow during his hot early middle age, when it seemed most unlikely he would ever be Prime Minister.

Once he is ensconced in Downing Street, he surrounds himself with a sinister court of

East Europeans whom he describes as "financiers" and "businessmen", but only one man guesses his terrible secret. This is a briiliant, debonair journalist who is also, as it happens, irresistibly attractive to women. Provisionally, he is to be called Ron Wall, but I think we may improve on that.

Friday 5th April

A new W.H. Auden Memorial industry seems set fair to rival the Churchill Centenary racket. I hear Weidenfeld & Nicholson are seriously thinking of giving away little plastic busts of this wrinkled old bachelor, each one personally signed by Stephen Spender, to anyone who will buy his extraordinarily expensive volume of tributes.

Auden certainly deserves a memorial or two, but I wonder who will be left to pretend that Stephen Spender was a great poet. Yet it really is quite a distinguished thing to have lived for 66 years as a poet without producing a single line which anybody could possibly wish to remember. You would have thought, by the law of averages, he would have written at least one such line, if only by accident.

Saturday 6th April

I see Larry Adler, the controversial mouth organist, has been arrested for allegedly stealing two bags of toffees worth 74p from Jacksons of Piccadilly. The news does not surprise me in the least.

A year ago this man offered me an extravagant bribe to sully the pages of *Private Eye* with a filthy joke about President Nixon's prepuce or foreskin. Much against my better judgement I published this filth, but he ratted on the bargain and never paid the bribe.

Quite possibly he is innocent of the unpleasant crime of which he is accused, but the police are quite right to keep a careful eye on this loathsome, toffee-fingered man.

Sunday 7th April
Our traditional Easter treat of sucking pig was completely ruined for me by the news that poor Alan Brien is to disappear from the back page of the *Sunday Times*. This pathetic newspaper is now entirely controlled by ambitious, semi-literate braggarts whose only claim to fame is that they once spent 18 years on the Doncaster *Weekly Advertiser*.

Without wishing to spoil anyone else's fun, I could not face the reproachful look in the eyes of that poor dead pig on such a day, and ate a poached egg on toast instead. Goodbye, Alan, and thanks a lot.

Monday 8th April
To Congress House for a confidential briefing of the Industrial Lobby on Len Murray's cock-up of Shelepin's visit[1]. One purpose of his visit, it appears, was to urge the Unions to demand that the Government takes a stricter line with Jews and Ukrainians in this country.

But this was only a small part of his mission, and Len is surely right to feel indignant about the way the press has concentrated on this aspect and built it up out of all proportion. Many of the so-called "demonstrators" were not Jews or Ukrainians at all, but out of work actors hired by the CIA to play these parts.

The main reason for the visit was that Shelepin is very worried about the threat to British parliamentary democracy enshrined in the Treaty of Rome. He hoped to co-ordinate patriotic action by British trade unions in protest against the Common Market threat between now and the referendum.

The TUC have not yet decided their policy with regard to this one. Obviously, if the British public are made aware of the industrial unrest which might follow, they will think twice before they vote the wrong way. On the other hand, there is a general feeling that now Grocer Heath has joined the campaign to stay in the Common Market, anti-Marketeers have nothing to worry about.

Tuesday 9th April
If the *Mirror* strikers can only be persuaded to stick it out a little longer, we are told, the *Sunday People* will have to close. That is a cheerful thought.

Most newspapers have something to be said for them — the *Mirror* has Marje Proops, Christopher Ward and The Perishers, even the *Telegraph* has Peter Simple and an occasional leader — but the *Sunday People* has absolutely nothing. It retains the hysterically hypocritical attitude to sex of an earlier age, its politics are half-wittedly sycophantic to Wislon, and everybody who works for it is stupid and vile. Like many doomed newspapers, it also encouraged two of its least savoury employees to sue *Private Eye* for libel a few years ago.

Wednesday 17th April
Four correspondents have written to tell me that Karl Miller, the former editor of the heavily-subsidised *Listener* and now £7,000-a-year Lord Northcliffe Professor of Modern English Literature at University College, London, has joined Ian Hamilton's worthless, heavily-subsidised *New Review* as an associate editor. I agree that this is very funny.

1. Shelepin (q.v.) had to cut short his visit after hostile demonstrations by British Jews. As head of Russian 'trade unions', he had been the guest of the TUC.

Friday 19th April
This evening, to my dismay, I find I have
agreed to give a talk to a combined meeting
of the Lydeard St Lawrence and Stogumber[1]
and Young Wives. I suppose it was the idea
of young wives that attracted me, but on my
arrival in the village hall I find that there is
nobody who answers to this description.

My talk is on the theme, "It is high time:
we had a Civil War in this country'. I point
out the threat which exists to that most sacred of British Institutions, the Strike;
arguing that when our industrial "workers"
find that there is no more work for them to
refuse to do, they will suffer a severe identity
crisis, after which anything might happen.
I warn them that it doesn't matter which
side they're on, but unless they are prepared
to fight they will find their homes occupied
by ferocious dwarves from the Midlands who
will insist on keeping coal in their baths.

It is hard to say how much effect it has.
The only question comes when I suggest that
in order to declare the Civil War open we
should hire a charabanc, go to London, and
hang Mrs Castle (Wislon's revoltingly ugly
Secretary for the Social Services) by the neck
from a lamp-post in Parliament Square.
One of the ladies asks how much a ticket
will cost and whether we could drop her off
in Swindon to visit her niece.

Probably they are more interested in the
second talk, by a social worker, on how to
make your own mince for mince tarts.
I must admit I find it very enjoyable and
informative. Refreshments are done by
Mrs Yarberry.

Saturday 20th April
Tougher penalties for sexual offences are urged by the Police Superintendents Association in a report to the Law Commission
today. They propose a maximum fine of
£400 for flashing against the present maximum of £100.

This depresses me rather, because although
I have never yet been tempted to expose myself I can see that as I get older it might have
its attractions as a way of passing the time.
The new rate will mean that only the very
rich can afford this pleasure, and it could
easily be reduced to a form of status symbol
or financial boasting.

Another proposal is even more far-reaching
— "that the police should have unconditional
powers of arrest in cases of sexual intercourse
and other overt sexual behaviour". This goes
further than Grocer's proposal for a Contraception Police Force under James Prior to knock
on citizens' doors at midnight and ensure that
they are using approved methods.

But I don't suppose they will catch many
people. I'm convinced that much less of it
goes on than people imagine, that there is
great revulsion from ordinary sexual intercourse among town-dwellers at the present
time. This may explain why so many of them
are mad. A co-ordinated police swoop on
the whole of South Kensington on any night
of the week would be unlikely to reveal anything more serious than Kenneth Tynan
masturbating.

Sunday 21st April
Reading Brian Inglis's delightful history of
drugs, *The Forbidden Game* (Hodder &
Stoughton, £4.95), I was pleased to spot the
hoary old legends that dried lettuce juice is
a powerful narcotic and nutmeg induces
visions.

In these unhappy times when all forms of
dope are so ruinously expensive, I sometimes
draw comfort from eating daffodil bulbs.
After a few one has the agreeable sensation
of floating on air; and after a great many one
can sometimes imagine that one has been
turned into a giraffe with a beautiful long,
furry neck.

Monday 22nd April
To the dentist, where I found an old copy of
Punch with an article by Kenneth Tynan
called 'The Time of My Life'. He claims to
have had sexual intercourse with a strange
young woman in an aeroplane without speaking a word, and without leaving his seat.

In his revolting style, he claims that "by
moving against her in what is known as the
spoon position, I was able to achieve an
enchanting slow-motion climax." Ugh!

In fact, anybody who has tried this sort
of hanky-panky in an aeroplane will know it
is quite impossible. I imagine that Tynan's
lying filth was intended for the British
Airways magazine, also edited by Kaiser Bill
Davis[2] ("say cheese') and given away free to
anyone stupid enought to fly by British Airways. No doubt it appeared in *Punch* as a
result of some mix-up between the Kaiser's
out-trays.

But I think I shall write to the Dental
Association and protest about these mastur-
batory fantasies of a deranged mind left
lying around in dentists' waiting-rooms where
they may be seen by unsuspecting children
and old age pensioners. It is time the dental
profession realised that there are cleaner,
healthier magazines than *Punch* to take their
clients' minds off the terrible pain they are
about to endure.

1. Two West Somerset villages near Combe Florey.

2. William Davis, Editor of Punch. Born Gunter Kase, 6 March 1933, noted as first Editor of Punch con-
scripted into Junior League of Hitler Youth.

Tuesday 23rd April

Sad news indeed that Jamie Mar has fallen to his death from a Knightsbridge balcony. I knew him best at Marlborough where we were drawn together by a shared hobby, and *Who's Who* reveals how even after he succeeded to his title as 30th Earl of Mar he kept up the favourite pastime of our youth, kicking pigeons.

As young men we toured Europe together. One of the best Kicks I can remember was among the Civitali sculptures in the Cathedral of S. Martino, Lucca. Perhaps it was the rich red Tuscan wine we had drunk with our *uccellini con riso*, or perhaps the pigeons of our youth always seemed plumper and more available than the scrawny, nervous birds around today. Later Jamie left for Pisa, where I believe he got in a very good Kick outside the Baptistery.

Before this tragedy intervened we had planned a gala Kick from the top of Nelson's Column in Trafalgar Square to celebrate the 25th anniversary of the Festival of Britain next year.

Some may decide it is a cruel sport, but I think the pigeons enjoy it and, from Jamie's sad fate, one can see that it is not without its risks.

Wednesday 24th April

To Belgrave Square to demonstrate for Public Lending Right with the magnificent Brigid Brophy[1] and other comrades of the Writers' Action Group. Magnesia is there looking as ravishing as ever in an apricot suit of drip-dry Tomalin with matching culottes, and I think Angus Wilson[2] looks rather sweet waving a little piece of cardboard with all his demands on it.

I carry the same banner I always use at demos, saying quite simply HANG THE MINISTER. This is a very good all-purpose slogan, and I am surprised that the Protest Industry people have not cottoned on. It certainly seems to scare the wits out of Hugh Jenkins[3] who thought he could treat the event as a great lark until he sees the hunger and naked hatred in our eyes.

Thursday 3rd May

My long-awaited appointment with Denis Healey to ask what he means by his pathetically inadequate Budget, hailed by all the hacks of Fleet Street as the savagest act of government since Stalin's resettlement of the Ukraine.

Although I had not seen him since leaving the *Spectator* five years ago he received me very warmly at his new home in 11 Downing Street. Over Campari and soda he explained his economic strategy in simple, manly terms.

There can be no return to economic health or normal government until the power of the Unions is broken, he thinks. This can't be done by confrontation, as the Unions would certainly win. It can only be done by giving them enough rope to hang themselves — hence the farcical Social Contract, which we must all pretend to believe in long after wage awards have passed the 80% mark.

He's encouraging Michael Foot and Wedgie Benn to play silly buggers, as he puts it, so that when unemployment passes the 3,000,000 mark in 18 months' time, they will be blamed for it. Meanwhile, he expects employers like me and fools like Michael Foot to go on handing out the rope and he

1. **Author and female thinker, doughty campaigner for Public Lending Right whereby authors would receive a royalty on books borrowed from libraries. b. 12 June 1929, noted for vegetarianism etc.**

2. **Novelist and thinker.**

3. **Labour politician and Minister for Arts. For further study, see 13 June 1975.**

will go on making speeches about the terrible
danger of excessive pay-claims.

Friday 4th May

A heart-rending letter from Sonia Orwell,
lovely widow of the journalist George Orwell
and a former friend of Cyrill Connolly, the
distinguished book reviewer. Apparently
Lord Thomson was so mean to this most
deserving of his employees that Cyril not
only had to work as a tout for Christie's in
his last years but also died heavily in debt.

At one time, Cyril had a valuable library,
but I gather he sold all the best books from
it shortly before he died. I hope that even in
these straitened times as many *Eye* readers
as possible will support the appeal which is
not, I understand, being sponsored by Lord
Lichfield. Gifts of any sort — clothes, silver
paper, trading stamps, even old sweet papers
— should be addressed to the Fund c/o
Lord Thomson of Fleet, Alderbourne Arches,
Gerrards Cross, Bucks.

Saturday 5th May

A depressing afternoon spent burning Old
Master paintings in preparation for the new
Wealth Tax. I felt sad about the two Cana-
lettos which used to hang on either side of
the fireplace in the Blue Drawing-Room, but
I think I shall miss Boucher's *Diane a la
chasse avec Apollon* from the old music
room most of all.

But one must do everything in one's power to resist what Lord Goodman has described
as "this policy of pure envy" which is rotting
the soul of the Labour Movement. As that
wise and good man has said, "the impulse of
envy is incomparably more horrible than
greed." Tomorrow, I start on manuscripts,
printed books and incunabula.

Sunday 6th May

So. David Astor has been socked for £35,000
libel damages plus costs by my good friend
Lord Bernstein[1], aged 76. Well done, Sidney.
No editor who helps employees use this
Crooks' Charter, as our libel laws have rightly
been called, against a fellow journalist des-
erves the smallest sympathy when a Shining
Knight like the great and good Sidney
Bernstein uses these same laws against him.

Astor should continue to watch his step.
I doubt very much whether the Curse of
Lord Gnome has been appeased by this
award, which must be chicken-feed to a man
as rich as the Editor of the *Observer*.
Damages will probably be doubled on appeal.
Where Astor went wrong on this occasion
was to take on a man who is even richer than
he is.

Monday 7th May

The most encouraging piece of news in a
gloomy week has come from Cambodia,
where the victorious Khmer Rouge have embarked on a policy of executing the wives of
politicians in the previous regime, as well as
the politicians themselves. This seems
eminently sensible and just[2].

Mrs Michael Foot springs to mind as an
obvious candidate for this treatment, although I hope our soldiers will spare the
lovely and gifted Susan Crosland. Mrs Foot
writes a hysterical letter to *The Times*
today about her husband's mystery illness,
criticising the press for daring to mention
such a tender subject.

She compares him, for reasons best known
to herself, with a female whose menstrual
periods are irregular or who has suffered an
abnormal discharge. Now I yield to no one in
my concern for Michael as a very wonderful
human being, but I'm not sure if this is the
best way to whip up sympathy for the posturing old ninny in his present troubles, especially as she accompanies her confused
and distasteful argument with a sneering
reference to editorial freedom[3]. This, no less
than Michael's nether regions, is rather a
sore area at present.

The plain truth is that Michael's handling
of the trades unions has made a substantial
contribution to the approaching catastrophe
and has virtually ensured that there can be
no recovery until after a total economic
collapse. As a Minister he is a menace and
a national disaster. It is a matter of perfectly
reasonable public interest whether or not this
menace is about to be removed or whether
only a small part of it is.

Tuesday 8th May

If ever I have said an unkind word about the
great Lord Hailsham, describing him as a
slippery old lunatic or anything like that,
I wish to retract it now with humble and
sincere apologies. Hogg's place in history is
secure after his Appeal Court ruling which
makes sense at last of the tangled law on
rape.

I hope he will now address himself to en-
suring that the innocent male victim of a
rape charge does not have his name emblaz-
oned all over the gutter press.

In a recent case before Taunton Magistrates concerning myself and some 16-year-
old schoolgirls, I was able to convince the
Bench I had an unreasonable belief that the
schoolgirls were consenting. So I left the
court without a stain on my character.

---

1. Sidney Bernstein, millionaire television magnate b. 30 January 1899, noted for support of Labour
   Party for which he received peerage in 1969.

2. Vietnam and Cambodia had fallen to the Communists in quick succession. Laos and Thailand seemed
   likely to fall next.

3. Foot was introducing a Bill whose effect was to deny access to the newspapers to anyone not a
   member of the National Union of Journalists.

Then I had to bribe the hacks outside with enormous sums to keep my name out of the papers.

Which is all very well for the rich, but comes rather hard on the struggling middle classes. If, in the interests of editorial freedom, the government won't protect the innocent male victims of rape charges in this way, they should at least provide payments out of Legal Aid for bribing the press.

No doubt it is terror of exposure which makes the Cambridge Rapist wear a leather hood when he is on the job, despite his obvious innocence. This habit of his has caused great distress among my male friends in Cambridge. Many inhabitants of unsullied reputation — George Steiner, Raymond Williams,[1] even the great Dr Leavis[2] himself — may feel themselves under a cloud of suspicion until the man is allowed to unmask himself.

Wednesday 9th May

Tea-party at the Kents' for the 11th birthday of Lady Helen Windsor. A most charming girl — I think she takes after her mother, but my dear wife recognises the Hesse-Cassel features so strong in the lines of her paternal grandmother. We eat fruit salad and cocktail sausages, then play "pass the parcel" and Musical Bumps. On parting, we give her a working replica of Brunel's S.S. *Great Britain* in brass and green enamel. She gives us a Dalek space-gun and thanks us for coming. At such moments as this one realises that there are still a few things worth fighting for.

Thursday 10th May

To Newmarket Races, where I see what surely must be the first stirrings of the Glorious Counter Revolution. Stable lads on strike for more pay are viciously attacked with swinging binoculars and stabbing hat-pins by all my friends who shall be nameless except to say that they include Bernard Levin, Tim Portarlington-Hoogewerth, Gerry Ward, Buffy Frobisher, Bobbi Korbitts and the rest of the gang.

Class antagonism has been a one-way business up till now and I often used to despair of getting my civil war started with the material available. In order to keep the fires burning, I am promoting a new sport in West Somerset. The idea is to let a stable lad out of a box and then hunt him to hounds.

Friday 17th May

So. Baillie Vass is trying to write his memoirs at the age of 72.

Baillie has given no indication so far in his career of being able to write. He does not need the money, so I suppose we must decide that it is vanity which drives this blind old millionaire to make a fool of himself yet again.

There is a terrible danger that in the ghastly years of proletarian dictatorship ahead when we are being bossed around by Jack Jones, Lawrence Daly[3], and his gang of spiteful yobboes, we will look back to the days of Baillie Vass, the affable cricket-playing aristocrat, and decide he wasn't such a bad sort after all.

Let us never forget that Baillie Vass was an unscrupulous, pea-brained opportunist like everybody else, and carries as much blame as Heath, Wislon, Foot, Benn and Healey for the mess our country is in and for the miseries we are about to suffer. They are all guilty, and future generations of Englishmen will learn to spit at the mention of their loathsome names.

Saturday 18th May

The fact that Mr Prentice[4] has suggested universities should sell their art treasures in

---

1. Two pseuds.
2. F.R. Leavis, of Downing College, Cambridge, distinguished critic. Born 14 July 1895, noted for acrimonious letters to literary journals and splendid attack on Lord Snow (q.v.) in Spectator (1962).
3. General Secretary, National Union of Mineworkers.
4. Minister for Education and Labour politician.

order to keep their students means he has paid no attention to the memorandum I sent him three weeks ago. This suggested that universities should sell their "students" in order to preserve their art treasures.

My point was that students are easily replaced, but our art treasures are irreplaceable. The time is past when English pederasts could buy Arab boys for a shilling or two, but Sheikhs have never been averse to the fairer skins of Englishmen.

These students might not do for you or me, but Arabs are in no position to complain if they seem a trifle dirty or stupid or idle. Nobody wants them here, there is no prospect of employment for them, and this may be their only opportunity to make a useful contribution to our balance of payments. They may object to being castrated, but at least this operation is free and we must all be prepared for a period of decisive suffering.

Monday 20th May
Today Mr David Wood, *The Times*'s sharp-eyed 86½ year-old political correspondent, announces that Tony Benn is a "dangerous politician who stirs up and exploits political forces that will. . . bring Britain to economic ruin."

Nearly eight years ago, on 4th August 1967, *Private Eye* devoted a whole cover to making exactly this point, with a huge photograph denouncing him as The Most Dangerous Man In Britain — on account of his obvious lunacy.

That item remains the *Eye*'s only attempt at "responsible" political comment of the sort Mr Wood practises week after week. We gave up the style after readers complained it was too boring.

Tuesday 21st May
How the literary world does buzz and gossip. Today's *canard* is that when Alan Brien takes over from the 108-year-old Harold Hobson as dramatic critic on the *Sunday Times*, the paper's literary and arts editor, J.W. Lambert, will be replaced by Philip Norman, the ageing 22-year-old leather fetishist.

I think we should welcome the appointment. Norman is a better writer than Lambert, although I believe he has unpleasant personal habits. More important, as I believe, he is reasonably well-educated.

It is probably the fact that Lambert never had a university education which explains why he is so impressed by dons, whose sterile and fatuous preoccupations contribute so much to making these art pages at once the laughing-stock of the philistines and the despair of the literate world. Although I must admit that the novel reviewing has improved since Julian Symons left and Jill Neville[1] arrived. Lambert should be appointed Director of the National Theatre where he can do least harm.

Wednesday 22nd May
To the first of the *Evening Standard*'s literary luncheons at Ken Wood. I stand receiving the guests with Magnesia (who is also a most gifted book reviewer on top of everything else). She looks absolutely ravishing in cream-coloured lace. What an adorable woman she is!

The party is in honour of someone called Donald Swann of Swann and Flanders[2] fame. He has apparently written a novel about his own death (as opposed to the death of Michael Flanders, reported in earlier editions). This is rather embarrassing as I keep calling him "Michael", having confused him with Michael Swann, who is chairman of the BBC and a brother-in-law of the Bishop of Truro.

In the evening I go to Tom Driberg[3]'s 70th birthday party in Barbican. All the Fartwell crowd are here, although I miss John Wells. The Bishop of Southwark looks very nice in his luscious robes and quite eclipses Lady Diana Cooper[4]. The appalling Michael Foot is here, making idiotic noises about the Common Market and refusing all offers of a chair to rest his poor bottom on.

So is rather a handsome Constable from the City of London police, but Uncle Tom has made me promise not to write any more about the party, as he is nervous about bad publicity. Really, at his age!

Thursday 23rd May
I was laughing so much last night about Michael Foot's sore bottom that I forgot to insult him for suing Linda Lee-Potter of the *Daily Mail* for libel.

Last week Wislon had to pay his own expenses in the ludicrous action he brought against the *Daily Express* over the Slagheap Affair, but I hear the *Daily Mail* intend to fight this action of Foot's to the bitter end.

Quite right, too. Everything becomes absurd if disastrous Cabinet Ministers like Foot think they can supplement their grossly-inflated incomes by a quick handout from the newspapers every time they are criticised.

It is time this ridiculous man put his bottom away before I decide to put the Curse on it.

1. Quite good female novelist from gifted Australian family.

2. Two television 'personalities'.

3. Retired Labour politician and High Church bachelor, b. 22 May 1905, noted for providing an alibi for notorious East End criminals.

4. Widow of Duff Cooper, persecutor of P.G. Wodehouse.

Friday 24th May

Although I am under 30 years old and under five feet tall, I see no reason to give a specimen of my spittle to police searching for the Cambridge Rapist. They might put it to improper uses.

But there is something distinctly odd in the moral cilmate in Britain today.
I am getting rather fed up with being mistaken for Lord Longford, my godfather.
Wherever I walk in Soho — to my *masseuse*, to my bookseller, to the various places of entertainment I patronise, even to pay a social call on a French lady of my acquaintance — I am cheered and asked for my autograph.

Today an Irishwoman asked me to bless her. Does anybody know where I can buy one of those leather masks with zips to save me from this embarrassment?[1]

Saturday 1st June

Sad news today that *Books and Bookmen* is going up in price again, putting it beyond the reach of many *Eye* readers at 75p.
It is the only British literary magazine of any real value, not to say the only one worth the paper it is printed on.

The May number, for instance, had excellent articles by Enoch Powell (on Isaiah Berlin's *Four Essays on Liberty*); by Lord Snow (on Maynard Keynes); by myself (on language and translation); by Sir Robert Mark (on Sillitoe of MI5); and valid contributions by many others in a glittering galaxy which includes John Betjeman, Edward Blishen, Sally Emerson, A.L. Rowse, Duncan Fallowell, Sir Harold Acton, Tariq Ali, Paul Foot, Oswald Mosley, Osbert Lancaster, R. Ingrams, Lord Boothby. . . .

If anybody doubts that such a wonderful magazine can exist, they should save up and buy a copy.

The great scandal is that while we have one first-class literary magazine struggling to make ends meet, government money should pour out to support a clique of conceited and untalented oafs on another magazine, which nobody wants to read despite its vast annual subsidy. And there are poor old-age pensioners who can't afford a copy of Rupert Murdoch's nice *Sun* to eat with their ketchup.

Sunday 2nd June

Although I have banned the *Observer* from my house in protest against its half-witted novel reviewer called Lorna Sage, I find my cook reading this disgusting newspaper once again on her afternoon off.

This time she is gloating over a news story headed 'Now For Some Good News'. It is David Astor's way of announcing that Britain's population is starting to fall.
In the last three months deaths have exceeded births by five thousand, according to the Office of Population, Census and Surveys.

Foolish woman. I take the rubbish away from her and spend the next few hours explaining that although the vast majority of people born into this world may be as ugly, stupid, mean and dull as she is, there are always a few — one in ten thousand, perhaps — who are beautiful or clever or kind enough to make the whole exercise worthwhile.

By the time I finish she is in tears, so I box her ears and send her off to Evensong in the parish church.

1. The Cambridge Rapist disguised himself thus.

Monday 3rd June

I pulled out of Granada's *State of the Nation* debate in protest against having to sit beside Grocer. One would have thought that if this man really believed in the Common Market he might have had his revolting suntan removed to give it a chance.

As it is, none of the really convincing arguments have been put to the people. A "Yes" vote may be our last chance to export Britain's industrial proletariat to places like Dusseldorf and Frankfurt where, no doubt, some use will be found for its undoubted talents.

The British working class, as we still jocularly call it, has become the sort of luxury which we in this country can simply no longer afford. It is sad, of course, and I shall be sorry to see them go. Our "workers" have always been a picturesque and charming part of the traditional English scene, with their many agreeable qualities, but one can't afford to be sentimental nowadays. And the truth is, I expect Britain will be a much nicer, cleaner country when they've gone.

Tuesday 9th June

I do not normally read *Cosmopolitan*, the Rev Marcus Morris's prick-and-bum magazine for randy housewives, but we had a clergyman staying in the house and thought it only right to offer him the choice. There is an extraordinary article about my friend Melvyn Braggart[1], the plump twice married 42-year-old heart throb of TV's *Fun with Books* programmes.

He reveals how he gets many letters and sexual overtures from women as a result of his television appearance — "some frankly lewd", he says. But he is a person of "natural and very vigorous impulses", and tends to follow them through.

The many hundreds of letters, photographs and other unsolicited gifts I receive every week from hopeful young women are dealt with in the first instance by a panel of secretaries at Gnome House. They interview the more likely candidates, awarding them marks for elocution and deportment as well as taking the more obvious measurements.

Next, candidates are asked to sit a written examination, which may include trick questions like: *'Trace the influence of the early D.H. Lawrence on the later development of Lawrence Sterne.'*

Those who score better than Beta Plus s are then invited to produce their birth certificates and attend a medical examination before being brought to meet me as I recline on my red divan in the executive suite, eating wafer-thin cucumber sandwiches at four o'clock in the afternoon.

Wednesday 10th June

At Ilkley Literature Festival, Yorkshire, I noticed that the enterprising Cambridge bookshop of Bowes & Bowes is trying to sell some of its enormous stock of unsold *New Reviews* at 45p each.

I have a pile of copies of this worthless magazine which I will happily send to anyone for 12½p each plus postage and packing. My copies are considerably improved by quantities of strawberry jam poured on the faces of Anthony Powell, Harold Pinter, Roland Barthes, Tom Stoppard, Doris Lessing and other unidentified pseuds.

Thursday 11th June

To Belgrave Square, where I have an appointment with Hugh Jenkins, Minister for the Arts, to discuss my suggestion that the Literature Panel of the Arts Council should be closed down.

Jenkins strikes me as a mean, shifty little man of no obvious education but he seems agreeably frightened by me. Our conversation wanders to the subject of Public Lending Right and I receive the distinct impression that he favours a disastrous scheme based on purchase price rather than on loans.

I have thought long and hard on this matter, and have decided that the only sanction left to authors whose livelihood has been taken away by the government is to burn down the public libraries. This would have the additional benefit of getting our own back on the librarians.

Already this month I have destroyed two telephone kiosks in protest against Mrs Castle's Self Employment levy and let the air out of a District Health visitor's tyres. When Mr Healey introduces his Wealth Tax, I think I shall burn down the Post Office Tower. There is a great debate down here at the moment about whether old age pensioners count as government property or not.

Friday 12th June

For nearly two months I have been brooding about a rude letter in the *New Statesman* from someone called C. Stallybrass. He is a schoolteacher of 23 Hills Road, Buckhurst Hill, Essex, and accuses me of snobbery. Oh dear. Perhaps it's true, perhaps it's true.

My father was a tram driver[2] in Liverpool in the bad days just after the war. There were

1. Melvyn Bragg, a young novelist, b. 6 October 1939, noted for pretty face.
2. For alternative explanation of Waugh's father's employment, see passim.

14 children in the family and none of us had what might be called a privileged background. My mother took in washing, and I was the only one of my family lucky enough to get to university, where I was senior scholar in Classics at Trinity College Cambridge at the same time as the Prince of Wales was an undergraduate there.

This began a long association — I might almost say friendship — with the Royal Family to which, it is true, I sometimes refer in this Diary. How else is one to give an honest explanation of one's day if one happens to have spent a large part of it at the Palace? It may be true that I spend a little time in front of the mirror practising sentences from by German phrase book before each occasion — *Entschuldingen Sie, bitte* etc. — but then we're all human and it strikes me as a simple question of good manners.

Sometimes I'm asked to a Meet-the-People luncheon and I confess these are slightly less enjoyable, being attended as often as not by what I call the Arthur Askey[1] class. But we've all got to live together. At least one never gets to meet C. Stallybrass[2] there, or any other shit-faced, evil-smelling guttersnipes of the sort one encounters all too frequently nowadays in other walks of life.

Saturday 13th June

It has been a week of radiant sunshine in Somerset at the height of the asparagus season. I assume that television pictures of deep snow in other parts of the country are lies until *The Times* carries another of its lugubrious leaders prophesying the arrival of Another Ice Age. It is a sure sign it has turned chilly in London.

In fact we haven't had a hard winter for 13 years and the weather down here seems to get nicer every time I go out. Perhaps Rees-Mogg has been seeing phantom polar bears and walruses at his north Somerset home. If so, he should take an aspirin and go to bed early. Now he's probably sue me for suggesting he's mad or drunk or both. It is a terrible thing to see a great man go to pieces in this way.

Monday 15th June

In Finland to attend a literary conference, I suddenly realise that this may be my best opportunity to play the practical joke I have been brooding about ever since Rees-Mogg wrote his extraordinary leader in *The Times* warning us of Another Ice Age. My plan is to release a number of walruses and polar bears in the park at his pleasant house in North Somerset.

When he sees them gambolling outside his library window he will sit down and right meteorological leaders of such startling oddness that before long he will find himself taken away to a nursing home for the rest he so obviously needs. While he is there, he might repent his stupid and unpleasant behaviour in suing Lord Gnome for libel.

A hunting expedition I led today from Lahti in North Finland consisted of three

---

1. A veteran artiste.
2. It transpired, through published correspondence, that the author of this letter was a woman.

Russian poets and a Czech novelist, all with their KGB escorts and all drunk. We caught a Lapp grandmother in our walrus-trap and two Karelian Finns in our polar bear pit, but will try again tomorrow.

Tuesday 23rd June
Today is Midsummer's Day in Finland. For three weeks the sun has been shining all day and all night and the Finns do nothing but laugh helplessly and drink themselves into a stupor.

Today we caught an Eskimo midget in one of the walrus-traps. When I tried to see if he had a rigid digit, he bit me in the hand. I think I may dress him up in a white turtle-neck jersey with cream jodhpurs and send him into *The Times* offices disguised as my old friend Charles Vass. He is the man who advises *The Times* on how upper class people behave; he also has a very pretty bottom. Gracious, I will laugh if my midget bites off one of Rees-Mogg's fingers.

Wednesday 24th June
Back to London with three seal pups (which Mogg may easily mistake for walruses), the frozen Eskimo, and another animal which may turn out to be a wolf puppy as I hope, or may prove to be some kind of badger.

I have an engagement to pelt a clergyman with rotten eggs. He is the Reverend John Pellow, Director of Appeals for the Central Council for the Disabled, who has volunteered to be pelted standing in his soutane in a London square. It was obviously not an occasion for any concerned citizen to miss.

In fact, this is something we might all do. Many Anglican clergymen live lonely lives with nobody paying much attention to them. A friendly egg in the face at the right moment could make all the difference to their day.

Thursday 25th June
I have seen Mrs Thatcher several times since her election as leaderette of the Conservative Party and she has never offered me a post in her so-called Shadow Cabinet. This may cause people to doubt whether she ever offered Grocer one, since I at least have not yet proved my hideous unsuitability for any role in democratic government, as he has done.

In fact, I gather from Sir Tim Kitson[1] that Mrs Thatcher *did* offer Grocer a place in her Shadow Cabinet, so Grocer is lying when he says she didn't, but in such an insulting way that no self-respecting fish-monger could have accepted it.

One of the most depressing aspects of the whole affair is how everybody is saying Good Old Grocer, what a Major Statesman he has become. Can nobody remember how disastrous he was, how wrong-headed, how fatuously obstinate in every mistake, how loathsomely conceited? Mrs Thatcher may prove to be as bad, but she could not possibly be worse.

The more I think about it, the more I tend to agree with my friend Kenneth Rose that the person this country needs now is Lord Mountbatten of Burma[2]. He has all the necessary qualities, being rich and German and very very nasty and so old he will probably be dead before long.

1. Former Parliamentary Private Secretary and very good friend to Mr Heath.
2. Louis Mountbatten, created earl by Attlee 1946. Sailor cousin of the Queen, b. 25 June 1900 under name of 'Battenberg'. Not noted for anything in particular.

Friday 26th June

The Parliamentary Press Lobby sealed its own fate five years ago when it refused to admit *Private Eye*'s political correspondent. Ever since then a subtle and unscrupulous campaign has been mounted against this honourable collection of drunks, toadies and walking sausages whose duty it is to print anything a government minister tells them as if they had thought of it themselves.

Now the chickens have come home to roost with the announcement by handsome, Czech-born Joe Haines, Wislon's £150,000-a-year lap-dog, that in future Downing Street will have no further dealings with them.

No doubt considerations of truth, beauty, honour and natural justice played their part in the Prime Minister's decision, but another factor may have been the discussions we had over a matter of some photographs that have come into my possession. They are of an interesting nature, taken in the balmy summer of 1959 when we were all so much younger and less inhibited and there was still sap rising in these withered old branches.

Saturday 27th June

I saw at least three Lord Lucans in Finland. All of them, I am happy to say, seemed in good health, if a little tired. But my most unnerving experience was today on a visit to Bekesbourne, near Canterbury, where John Aspinall[1] has his private zoo.

There was something rather disturbing about the appearance of one of the tigers there, a fat animal smiling quietly to itself in its sleep. One of Mr Aspinall's guests appeared to have taken off his clothes in the cage, leaving a shirt, underpants and little coroneted handkerchief lying all over the place. At a time of economic crisis, this seems a rather careless way to behave.

Sunday 28th June

I warned David Astor that the *Observer* would probably have to close if he continued to employ such a half-witted novel reviewer as Ms Lorna Sage. Conceited ass that he is, he paid no attention.

Today she reviews Pamela Hansford Johnson's novel, *The Good Listener*. Few people will bother to read her review and even fewer to read the book, but these will be amazed that a serious newspaper can hope to get away with printing this sort of drivel:

"It's characteristic of Pamela Hansford Johnson's cast of mind that a modicum of worldly goods plus a measure of disappointment, should turn out to be the necessary recipe for feeling and acting right. . . . The limitation of this brand of irony is that without the follies it analyses so satisfactorily, its dryness would be intolerable — a thirsty desert where nothing moves."

Of course, so long as Astor is prepared to pay £500,000 a year out of his private fortune to print this sort of drivel, nobody need mind. But now he threatens all their jobs and I think it is time the *Observer*'s lift-boys and engine room workers took the editorial management of the newspaper out of his hands.

Sunday 5th July

Today we enter the fifth week of Mogg's New Ice Age. All the rivers in Somerset have dried up under the scorching sun and my fields are littered with the skeletons of cows, sheep and horses who have succumbed to heat-stroke and dehydration.

George Hutchinson makes a valiant effort to cheer us up by listing some of the national assets which he thinks we have not yet destroyed, sold or mortgaged:

"Think of our material assets alone — our great industries, the financial institutions of the City of London, our schools and universities. Think of our farms, most of them set in some of the loveliest landscapes in the world. Think of our new resources in the North Sea."

In fact, he is wrong about most of these things, which we have either destroyed, sold or mortgaged many times already. I myself suggested selling our surplus university students to the Arabs several weeks ago, but nobody took it up.

I have drawn up a list of our national assets which do survive and which might get us through the summer. By then we shall all return from our summer holidays sun-tanned and fighting fit for the civil war leading to next year's Glorious Counter-Revolution.

First and most obvious of all are the Crown Jewels. These should be sold to the Shah of Persia, who's said to have a taste for such things. There is always a chance that we might get them back again if he agrees to marry the Queen Mother, as I keep suggesting.

Next, there are the Elgin Marbles. Plenty of replicas are already available, and although the originals are often described as priceless I am sure Tina Onassis[2] would settle for £100 million without really noticing it. Then we might send John Wells after her to bring them back, or possibly my cousin Bernard Dru[3].

---

1. A gambler and friend of Lord Lucan.

2. Heiress of Aristotle Onassis (q.v.), the Greek shipping millionaire who died after issuing a libel writ against Private Eye.

3. A Somerset farmer. His mother, a Herbert of Pixton, had married Major Alick Dru, a philosopher and student of Kirkegaard. Born 1951, noted for sobriety, modesty, cleanliness and old-fashioned good looks. Cf. 5 September 1975.

Finally, there is Karl Marx's body, which should have been put up for auction years ago between the governments of China and the Soviet Union. Russia will probably be prepared to pay at least half her gold reserves for this nasty, smelly old thing.

Monday 6th July
In the beautiful town of Durham, debating a motion about truth in the newspapers against a man who claims to be deputy editor of the *Sunday Times*. Needless to say, the *Sunday Times* man is trounced in the debate and humiliatingly defeated in the vote.

The visit does something to restore my faith in Britain's young people. Although Durham University is not famous for its student activism, I hear of a mass petition being got up against the ordination of women in the Church of England. This strikes me as exactly the sort of thing young people ought to be worrying about nowadays.

Friday 10th July
Sir Robert Mark[1]'s strictures about judicial leniency to criminals ring very hollow today when we all celebrate one of the greatest triumphs for British Justice since the Winslow Boy. Larry Adler, the left-wing mouthorganist, has been cleared of stealing two boxes of toffees from a shop in Piccadilly.

If he had been guilty, of course, it would have been a most cowardly and despicable crime. Who knows how many children and old age pensioners would have been deprived of their tiny rations by this mean act? However it appears that although Adler *did* take the toffees, he intended to pay for them later. Phew!

I was in Bow Street Magistrates Court to hear Sir John Foster, QC, the stooping, elderly former Member for Northwhich, appear as a character witness. Adler had once offered to risk his life by playing his mouth organ at the beleaguered garrison in Tobruk, Sir John averred.

Hardened as we are to wartime tales of derring-do, this action really does seem to show a reckless disregard for danger. I have only heard Adler play his machine once — during a memorial service at St Martin's-in-the-Fields. None of the congregation was prepared for it and Adler managed to slip out of a side door before I could get at him with my umbrella. If he really offered to play it in front of heavily-armed, battle-weary troops, he must have been experiencing the Death Wish.

Saturday 18th July
July the Twelfth is always a sombre day at Combe Florey, where we mourn those who fell on both sides at the Battle of the Boyne, all slaughtered by the Dutch sodomite William of Orange to further his subjugation of Ireland in 1690.

Since that fateful day there has never been any serious prospect of an Ireland which was both united and free; probably because there seems no end to the price which Protestant Ulstermen are prepared to pay for the pleasures of contraception.

Last week I heard of a new development which can only have a beneficial effect on the Irish question. My source was not a thousand miles from Fred Peart, the fun-loving ex-PT instructor who is now Wislon's Minister for Contraception. He told me of a breakthrough

---

1. A somewhat loquacious Commissioner of the Metropolitan Police, appointed 1972.

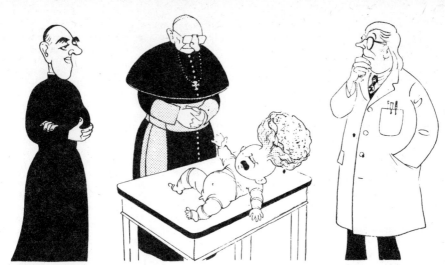

at the Ministry's hush-hush Centre for Contraceptive Studies in Gowrie Road, SW11, where they have developed an entirely new technique, involving a cauliflower and two elastic bands.

The important thing about this new technique is that some theologians who have studied it believe it may not transgress natural law. The results are at present being examined by a panel which includes three bishops, a trade unionist, a businessman, a Negro, a woman and a former Broadmoor patient whose offences included various indiscretions of a sexual nature.

Sunday 19th July
At lunch, there are toasts to Brian Roberts, small but plucky 68-year-old Editor of the *Sunday Telegraph.* He not only had the courage to fight a libel action brought against him by James Roosevelt, son of the American war criminal, but actually won it.

Costs against Mr Roosevelt, who maudlinged[1] Bernie Cornfeld's IOS swindle, are estimated at £20,000. That should teach him a lesson. No cheers for the *Evening Standard,* though, which chickened out of fighting the Forkbender "Slagheap" libel and paid her "appropriate" damages.

The *Sunday Telegraph* gets better every year. It now has practically the only novel reviews as well as one of the few political commentators worth reading. Its editor is that rarest of creatures, a Fleet Street journalist who has never tried to sue Lord Gnome for libel. I think I shall recommend him for a knighthood.

Monday 20th July
On a tour of my factories in the West Midlands I was delighted to discover that production is down by half, well below the level of Grocer's three-day week at the beginning of last year.

Practically no factories produce anything worth having: horrible plastic and metal objects which workers buy because they can't think of anything else to do with the money they earn from making them.

England has been littered with these ugly, useless objects for too long. Now that the workers of this country have very sensibly decided to do no more work we can all settle down to some reading. Matthew Arnold, it seems to me, is a very much under-rated poet.

Tuesday 21st July
There is a most beautiful and excellent article by Bernard Levin in today's newspaper on the subject of bumblebees. It triumphantly confirms what I have always said, that when the nation looks round in wild surmise for a great leader to show us the way out of our present bewilderment and gloom, it need no look no further than the Meistersinger of Devonshire Place.

Now that Ress-Mogg has disgraced himself by his unpleasant behaviour and idiotic remarks about the weather, I can think of no other Englishman possessing the necessary wisdom and moral fibre, except possibly my cousin Bernard Dru.

---

1. This verb is presumably derived from Mr Reginald Maudling, the Conservative politician, whose activities with the Hoffman swindler have already been described. Born 7 March 1917, Maudling was noted for large quantities of food spilled down his waistcoat.

Thursday 23rd July
Going on holiday is much more hazardous than it used to be. Squatters have discovered they have an absolute right to occupy your house, sleep in your bed, drink all your wine, sodomise with your cat and insult the goldfish.

If you try and get back into your house the police will beat you up with truncheons, pull your fingernails out and arrest you under the Vagrancy Act of 1203.

Today I have been busy preparing the house for our departure. I have poisoned the water supply, set lethal booby traps on most of the doors and windows, backed up by a "second strike" battery of unpleasant practical jokes in every room.

Last year, on our return, we found the bodies of two German students, a Norwegian au pair girl and a Birmingham artisan, all hideously disfigured by the guard dogs which must have been feeling hungry.

I buried them unceremoniously under a willow tree after dark.

Monday 27th July   *Languedoc, France*
We have a strenuous regime of physical exercise here, in preparation for the Great Civil War next year. After a small breakfast of yoghurt and honey we go for a five-mile run, followed by twenty lengths of the swimming pool and an assault course.

At the end of it, I have rigged up some dummy figures lounging around with their hands in their pockets. These represent British "workers", and we attack them savagely with night-sticks and hunting knives before coming in for the traditional seven-course lunch and afternoon siesta.

Tuesday 4th August
Problems of over-booking have now reached crisis proportion in my little farmhouse here. Although I suppose it is larger than many less fortunate people's homes in the Languedoc, we now have eight people sleeping in many of the bedrooms.

Today's arrival was a steel-fitter from Solihull. He says he met me in a train going to Leeds. I can't believe I really asked him to stay but he assures me I did and he brought along all his suitcases, an unattractive wife and four odious children to prove it.

When I show him the conditions he will live under, he becomes quite indignant. "This is a ruddy farce," he shouts — I shall not try to reproduce his amusing Midlands accent — "We came here in good faith and it cost nearly £300."

His wife, it appears, has a bad back and cannot be expected to climb over seven beds whenever she wishes to go to the lavatory in the night, as she frequently does. Probably many hosts abroad are experiencing this sort of problem at the present time. My solution is to put these people out in a field where I know there are two, possibly three vipers' nests, and keep my fingers crossed.

Wednesday 5th August
The best newspaper in France is called *Ici Paris*. Today, its London correspondent, who writes under the name of James Butterfly, reveals that when Lady Bathurst names Princess Margaret in her divorce action against the Earl, this will not be the first time the illustrious lady has been named in a divorce action:

"For the Queen, the affair is even more delicate than Margaret's earlier imbroglio of the same type ten years ago, when the Swedish actress Britt Ekland, at the time of her divorce from Peter Sellers, invoked the excessive affection of her husband for Margaret in front of the judges. At that epoch, the Sovereign used her prerogatives as Chief of British Justice to forbid the newspapers from printing the name of her sister, and the decision was considered by the Press as an intolerable abuse of power."

I don't know who James Butterfly is, although I suspect him of being a friend. In any case, I would not want to do anyone out of a job in these difficult times, especially someone as nice as Patrick Cosgrave[1] or as enterprising as my old friend Kenneth Rose. But if the editor of *Ici Paris* really wants to know what goes on at Buckingham, he should apply to me.

He would learn of the amazing incident this summer when it seemed that the Queen was going to abdicate out of a passing infatuation for John Wells, the gifted mimic and man-about-town; of Prince Charles's night of passion with Ms Barbara Castle, Wislon's revoltingly ugly Secretary for the Social Services; of an unpleasant book about oral sex found under Prince Edward's pillow. But everybody can relax. Until I receive a large cheque from Paris, my lips are sealed.

Thursday 6th August
Winston S. Churchill Jr., the former Boy Scout and Member for Stretford, reveals the activities of badge-wearing Communists in the BBC's Portuguese Service, but where on earth does he want these people to be?

One of the pleasanter aspects of English life has always been that these Communist badgers are concentrated in various recognisable areas of boredom — the BBC, the House of Commons, Times Newspapers Ltd., and the trade union movement — where sensible people can easily avoid them.

The only result of Churchill's silly behaviour must be to disperse them. Soon they will be knocking at the doors of Gnome House again. This tiresome young man threatens to become as great a nuisance as his loathsome grandfather, the war criminal, mass murderer and persecutor of Wodehouse.

Friday 7th August
A sad day for the prospects of Britain's survival with the news that Tina Onassis has married a Greek. I attribute the failure of British males in this field to the crippling effect of public school education.

This makes many Englishmen painfully *gauche* with members of the opposite sex, and correspondingly slow to take whatever opportunities are available. They expect women to force their way into their bedroom after they have done no more than raise their eyebrows over a glass of whisky — a reasonable enough attitude where native talent is concerned, but foolish when £400 million of Greek shipping is at stake.

Some will argue that by no means all Englishmen have had the misfortune to attend public school. No doubt this is true, but contrary to modern propaganda on the subject I believe that many of those who haven't are more or less impotent, at any rate on six nights of the week. The real shame is that none of our virile Amazonian women was able to interest the young lady in these exciting new philosophies.

Saturday 8th August
Paul Johnson[2]'s column in today's *Daily Telegraph* puts all the blame once again on the unions. Worst of all, he thinks that their greed and stupidity may be beginning to threaten the viability of our armed forces, on which so many people depend.

At last Paul seems to have found his ideological home in the perplexities of modern politics. His principled stand may do him some good when we come to consider our choice for National Leader, although I am not sure he has quite the steadiness of my cousin Bernard Dru, for instance.

In any case, I am not convinced that his analysis is the correct one. An alternative explanation for the stupidity and wetness of our age might be that such a high proportion of the English middle class spends its time in a dozy haze, pouring tranquillizer and euphoriant drugs into its mouth and scarcely noticing how the workers have stopped working and the country is falling to pieces.

Sunday 9th August   *Languedoc, France*
My wife and I are planning a little celebration early next year at Bognor Regis, the Sussex resort over which Russian and American astronauts staged their disgraceful scenes last month[3].

The date is the fortieth anniversary of King George V's death, on January 20, 1936. *The Times* mendaciously reported next day that his last words had been "How is the Empire?" but people in Bognor know better.

---

1. A journalist. As a joke, Waugh has changed his name from Cosgrove to Cosgrave.

2. Former editor of New Statesman, ousted by Crossman (q.v.). Born 2 July 1928, noted for occasional nervous breakdowns.

3. As part of the American policy of 'detente', astronauts from America and the Soviet Union had met in space and shaken hands.

Some time earlier the King had gone to Bognor to recuperate after an illness; henceforth it was called Bognor Regis. Shortly before the King died, a sycophantic courtier said he was looking so much better he should soon be well enough for another visit to Bognor, to which the old brute replied "Bugger Bognor" and expired.

"Bugger Bognor" will be the theme of our celebration, whose purpose is to put the town to fire and the sword in expiation for the shame brought on us all by those revolting astronauts. *Eye* readers are invited with their friends, bringing bottles of petrol, bicycle chains etc.

Monday 17th August
Today is my official birthday[1], celebrated with fireworks and dancing on three village squares throughout the Languedoc. As England prepares to be engulfed by a catastrophe of unimaginable proportions, let us take stock of the year that has passed.

On the positive side, I have done rather well in my chosen profession. I have been appointed Granada's Journalist of the Year, and have some hope of winning the coveted IPC Crusading Journalist award for my campaign against the ordination of women in the Church of England. I have been told that the Queen of Holland much enjoyed an article of mine about Dr George Steiner in *Books & Bookmen*. I have met some delightful young persons and somewhat improved my knowledge of Ugandan affairs. I have also, after much intriguing, managed to secure an entry in *Who's Who*. I have met William Davis and think I may have been kissed on the cheek by Jan Morris, although I am not absolutely sure it was she.

On the less positive side, I have met no response in my approach to the Nobel Committee; I am still stuck with the CBE I was awarded in 1973; nobody has yet thought me important enough to cite as a co-respondent in a divorce suit.

Greetings have been received from the heads of most civilised nations and many savage tribes, but nothing from my cousin, Bernard Dru. I hope he is all right.

Tuesday 18th August
For the Queen Mother's birthday I usually choose something from my own cornucopia of unwanted gifts. This year I am sending her a monkey skin, thus ingratiating myself still further with the ruling house of Sondeburg-Glucksburg-Schleswig-Holstein, to which she is such a gracious adjunct.

Wednesday 19th August
News from England filters through slowly. In one glorious day we learn that "General" Gowon[2] has been deposed, Robin Day[3] mugged, Wedgwood Benn's mother robbed of all her silver and Lady Magnesia cited by the pseud Harold Pinter's wife, who looks to be a most dreadful woman. Serves them all bloody well right except poor Magnesia, who is surely more sinned against than sinning.

As for Benn's mother, half the problems of our poor country can be laid at her door. Perhaps she never read her Spock and forgot to sterilise little Wedgie's nappies with Milton. There can be no pity for such women.

Friday 21st August
One solid result has emerged from all the whimpering and cringing of western politicians at Helsinki[4]. West Germany has bought 125,000 German-speaking Poles from the Polish authorities, for a total of £416 million, representing an average price of £3,328 per German speaker.

Perhaps we should all learn German. Apparently the price for "political prisoners" from East Germany is even higher. These sales are a major source of foreign currency for the East Germans, and suggest a way for Britain to survive after our Marxist Revolution.

Unfortunately, the disastrous fool Denis Healey has already driven out most of London's American residents by a vicious discriminatory tax against them. If we are to have anything to sell to the American government after the Revolution, we must lure them back immediately.

Various schemes occur to me. The most obvious is to revive Swinging London by turning it into the Sex Capital of the world, with Kenneth Tynan taking his trousers off outside Buckingham Palace three times a day. On the other hand, this might not have the desired effect nowadays.

Saturday 22nd August
I was at school with Harry Evans in Manchester, where we were both sent after failing our eleven plus. We used to call him "Poshie" Evans then because his father was the only one in the school with a motor car.

When we learned that he had been given five 'O' Levels on top of all his other advantages, we naturally thought he was destined for great things. Now, of course, when so many of us from St Mary's Central School are doing rather well for ourselves, it is slightly pathetic to see him still stuck as editor of

1. Waugh was, in fact, born on November 17th, 1939.
2. Military dictator of Nigeria.
3. A television 'personality'.
4. The European Security Conference, a sham event between America and the Soviet Union, had just closed in Helsinki.

a crummy old newspaper like the *Sunday Times* as it gets more and more boring and illiterate, its Books and Arts pages the laughing stock of the civilised world.

Poor old "Poshie". Just another case of early promise never quite fulfilled.

Thursday 27th August   *Languedoc, France*
One of the dangers of living such a large part of the year in France is that one may lose touch with what young people in England are thinking. For this reason I have taken to telephoning Princess Anne, finest embodiment of the Young Idea, at her ridiculous little house in Camberley.

By the total silence at the other end of the line I judge the telephone is always answered by her speechless husband, Captain Phillips. I try whistling to encourage him to talk, although friends tell me that when you do this to dogs it only makes them pee.

If the result of all my friendly approaches is that her husband has more or less permanently wet knickers, I can understand why the Princess describes them as "nuisance calls". But if she just objects to being telephoned, I think she is being rather hoity-toity[1].

Friday 28th August
More thoughts about dogs. Everybody in my French home has become desperately worried by the problems of re-cycling the 66 tons of dogshit dropped on London pavements every day. I suppose people get these worries at the end of their holidays.

In any case, it is time to return to poor, embattled England and prepare for the Glorious Counter-Revolution. Middle class homes would be well advised to stockpile a little dogshit for use as a biological weapon in the civil war.

At present I am searching the French countryside for any little doggie with a funny look in its eye[2]. Even your average British "worker", crawling with germs as he is, will probably think twice before risking a spot of rabies.

Saturday 29th August
In private conversation over the past few months I have made no secret of my belief that the man to lead Britain out of her present difficulties is my cousin, Bernard Dru. The time has plainly come to start a great popular movement behind him.

He is young — 24 or 25, I think — and good-looking in an old-fashioned sort of way.

He is sober, modest and clean. In preparation for his awesome responsibilities he has secured a Degree at Oxford University and is fluent in the French and German languages, having visited these countries on more than one occasion.

At present he is farming quietly in the West Country, treating workers and poor relations alike with a firmness which might prove a model for British industry. Where money matters are concerned, his conduct is marked by a prudence and sense of cautious responsibility which would do credit to any nation.

If modesty prevents this admirable young man from putting his own name forward, there is no reason why it should inhibit the rest of us. Britain has desperate need of a leader at this terrible moment, and I have no doubt in my own mind that Bernard Dru is the best candidate.

Sunday 30th August
Back in England. In moments of despondency I often think what it must be to be poor. If I were poor, I don't think I would sit around waiting for the government to do something about it. I think I would go and hang myself.

Monday 31st August
To Scotland, where I have missed the opening of the grouse season by nearly four weeks and find there are practically no birds left. I had thought that with Parliament sitting so long the birds would be practically untouched.

But the days are past when moors were trodden by fat *nouveaux riches* Conservative MPs in tweeds. Now they are left to Japanese, who come with eight-barrelled automatic shotguns and never miss, or to Arabs who are even worse, with their hawks and flashing scimitars and horrible oaths.

An old keeper tells me he had great difficulty preventing one Japanese from eating the nests after he had slaughtered all the grouse inside. At any rate, that's what I think he said, although to tell the truth I can hardly understand a word the man utters. My first day on the moors I bag a brace of motorbike manufacturers from Hamamatsu and a dealer in electronic components from Toyama.

Tuesday 1st September
Figures published by the Office of Population Censuses and Surveys confirms what I had already noticed, that practically no women

---

1. There had been many reports in the press about 'nuisance' telephone calls received by Princess Anne.
2. There was a rabies scare in France.

in the 20-29 age group are having babies any more. Soon old age pensioners will comprise 95% of the population.

The OPCS appears to attribute it to declining fertility in women, but this strikes me as untrue as well as insulting to women. The real reason, I suspect, is an epidemic of impotence among young males.

This is partly because from their tenderest years they are now barraged with what used to be thought of as sexual stimuli, so that when they reach maturity virtually nothing can stimulate them. It is also due to feminist propaganda which has succeeded in creating far more powerful feelings of guilt and sin than religion ever managed to do.

In New York, I am told, the epidemic has spread to males of all ages, but here at least it is confined to those in their teens and twenties. No doubt that is why we 35-year-olds are so much in demand among the young. Nothing else can explain the extraordinary letters I receive, many from young married women I have never met. But when one thinks of those empty cradles and hungry old age pensioners, one can only do one's best.

Wednesday 2nd September
September 10th will always be remembered as Cyril Connolly's birthday in the West Country although this year, alas, there is little to celebrate[1]. In the evening, I call the tenants, farm workers and domestic servants together for a quiet half-hour, reading to them from his various essays on Ezra Pound[2].

In their simple, unaffected way, I think they are as moved as anyone by these thoughts from the man who was once described by Alisdair Clayre as the Greatest Living Englishman.

But O, O for the touch of a vanished hand and the sound of a voice that is still. Clayre's description is now more tragically inept than ever, but I think it is important that posterity should remember Cyril, as we remember him who knew him best, one of the great English Comic Characters of the century.

I have decided to write a book about him in competition with the official biography, which I fear may neglect this vital area. Anyone with first-hand reminiscences is invited to send them to me on a postcard, or good second-hand material for that matter, or even an amusing anecdote about anyone which might be made relevant by changing the names involved and attatching it to this amazingly gifted book reviewer.

Monday 7th September
A pilgrimage to East Somerset to interview Anthony Powell, the man who has been chosen to win this year's Queen's Award for Knitting. As I walk up the drive with my heavy suitcase (I never go anywhere without my Proust, my Boccacio's *Decameron*, *The Diaries of Anais Nin*, Milne's *House at Pooh Corner*, Liddell & Scott's Lexicon and the *Oxford Companion to Music*) I feel I have entered the world of Powell's knitting.

Toni greets me courteously. He shows me a delphinium in his garden, saying it is a dahlia and hinting that he has read Linnaeus's *Philosophia Botanica* and *Species Plantarum*. He asks me if I am by any chance related to a Bron Waugh who he used to know — with whom, indeed, on one occasion, he shared a lavatory — in the halcyon autumn of 1933. When I reply that I am the same person I cannot tell from the thoughtful look he gives me whether, as Madame Leibnitz wrote about tea with the Spinozas, this was a very good answer or a very bad one.

At luncheon we discuss the morality or otherwise of taking sugar in one's coffee. He hints that he has read William Harvey's *Dissertation Upon The Movement Of The Heart And Blood* (1628) to which I reply with a light, self-deprecating laugh that my only knowledge of such matters comes from a hazy memory of reading Galen's *Systems* in Arabic at the age of five.

Later, when Toni hints that he has read Euclid's *Elements*, I balance a lump of sugar on my nose and sing Pythagoras's Theorem in Greek, amusingly set to the tune of Lilliburlero by Ronald Knox[3]. It is pleasant to spend an afternoon in such pre-eminently civilised company.

Tuesday 8th September
In seven weeks abroad I never saw the *Sunday Times* and so missed Alan Brien's moving Defence of Lesbianism which appeared on July 26: "Many radical feminists argue that the ultimate freedom for women must be found in lesbianism," he warbles, and goes on to pooh-pooh suggestions that excessive lesbian activities can result in colitis and other unseemly ailments.

Poor Alan, nobody has better claim to the title of Radical Feminist than he. Probably it is something to do with his wealthy, over-protected childhood that he now finds himself racked night and day in this terrible anguish of clitoris-envy. I think it is time he stopped cringeing and made up his mind: either to have everything cut off (including his repulsive beard); or to pull his shoulders

---

1. For Connolly's death, see 13th December 1974.

2. Earlier, Waugh announced that he had dismissed all the servants and given his tenants notice to quit. These, presumably, are the survivors.

3. R.A. Knox 1888-1957. Essayist and translator of the Bible. See Life by Waugh (1959).

back and try to carry himself like a Man. Whichever he chooses, I promise not to laugh at him.

Wednesday 16th September
Re-reading my French diary, I wonder whether I may not have struck an alarmist note. Expecting to find a Civil War on my return, I feel rather silly now with my sack of dog-mess and kennels of rabid dogs.

It is easy to forget how slowly everything happens in England. Instead of rampaging drunkenly through the streets in bloodthirsty gangs, the lower classes seem almost entirely to have disappeared and there is not a "worker" in sight, although I must admit that the best man at a wedding I attended on Saturday spoke rather oddly.

Thursday 17th September
There has been enormous response to my suggestion in *Private Eye* that the best person to lead the country out of its present troubles is almost certainly my cousin, Bernard Dru. Letters and telegrams of support continue to pour in from school-children, old-age pensioners, retired clergymen, houswives' associations and ex-servicemen living overseas.

Obviously I can't approach him with my suggestion until everything has been arranged, and I think the best thing at this stage would be to set up a regional network of Bernard Dru Centres, which I would inspect from time to time.

These Centres will be staffed night and day by a network of beautiful young female secretaries who have volunteered their services to the Movement. Obviously, I would not wish these secretaries to wear their skirts any shorter than comfort or fashion dictates, although something a little more go-ahead than Girl Guide uniforms may be called for.

On the other hand, I have always found nurses' uniforms quite exceptionally attractive in their simplicity and virginal allure. Obviously, there are many problems to iron out.

Friday 18th September
An exciting piece of news reaches me from Zarephath, New Jersey, where *The Herald of Freedom* is published. It is one of America's leading newspapers.

This issue reveals that Kissinger, architect of the Helsinki fiasco, is in fact a Soviet agent, having been recruited into the KGB while stationed in Germany during World War II. *Henry Kissinger, Soviet Agent*, a new book by Frank A. Capell, spells it all out:

"It would not have been possible for Henry Kissinger to have promoted the interests of the Communists over all his years in power had the CIA made available the information supplied years earlier concerning his recruitment under the code-name of Bor into ODRA, a secret KGB unit formed during World War II. This information was published 13 years ago. . . As Head of National Security amd the Secret Forty Committee, in fact head of all our intelligence services, Kissinger undoubtedly has taken the steps necessary to prevent the documentation concerning his KGB recruitment from being supplied to Congressional committees."

Which might make all the European statesmen who rushed to Helsinki at his bidding look rather silly, except that I imagine most of them are Soviet agents too. Certainly, I have never attempted to disguise my belief that Harold Wislon is one, recruited in Moscow and London in 1956/8, although I have no evidence to support this apart from intuition. It is only the traditional Russian obsession with secrecy about such matters which prevents all the statesmen of Europe from embracing one another as brothers and weeping on each other's shoulders.

Saturday 19th September
Reading through the final version of my father's *Diaries*, admirably edited by Michael Davie for publication next year, I have the ticklish duty of suppressing whatever may cause undeserved pain.

There was a curious episode in his last years when he agreed to be interviewed by a journalist called Julian Jebb[1] out of affection for the journalist's grandfather, Hilaire Belloc. The young man (as he then was) turned up while my father was in bed at the Hyde Park Hotel.

Talking about the incident afterwards my father spoke of his grave embarrassment at suddenly being confronted by what he described as a "funny little pansy". This strikes me as a particularly unkind way to describe Julian, who is slightly plump, and I was relieved to discover no mention of the incident in the *Diaries*. It might have hurt Julian's feelings and would certainly have upset his grandfather, had he been alive.

Sunday 20th September
From the feverish gleam in the cook's eye I guess that she has been reading the *Observer* again. A search reveals this filthy newspaper under her mattress. I confiscate it and lock her in her room for the rest of the day.

---

1. Jebb is a bachelor.

It is good to see that novels are no longer being reviewed by the idiotic Lorna Sage, but her place has been taken by Anthony Thwaite who is if anything even sillier and duller. He does not even have the excuse of being a woman and having to cope with the curse etc. I resolve to write to Astor about this.

Then I see on the front page a photograph of my late Father, luridly captioned: "Violent!" "Snobbish!", "Frequently drunk!". I write immediately to Astor, warning him that unless he desists from this campaign of vilification I shall send my younger brother[1] round to see him. That should put a little wind up his anguished knickers.

Monday 28th September
To Birmingham Town Hall, where I am guest of honour at a centenary dinner for the firm which makes HP Sauce. Harold Wilson is here, despite firm instructions from me that he should not be invited.

The sauce itself, a horrible brown gluey substance which tastes of metal polish and curry powder, is very much on display, although nobody eats any. It was often to be seen on the tables of the poorer classes during the Depression of the 1930s, and a few people still pretend to feel sentimental about it.

Its chief claim to fame nowadays is that it inspired *Private Eye*'s famous HP Sauce column of inside political analysis[2]. This ran for nearly three years until we realised that nobody was reading it through general lack of interest in politics. Another reason for dropping it as a regular feature was that money-crazed MPs took to suing for libel every time they were mentioned.

Wislon himself threatened me with a writ over some amusing allegations I once made in HP Sauce about his personal financing. When I mention this to him in Birmingham he falls on his knees and starts licking my ankles, so I sprinkle a few drops of the revolting liquid on his head and decide to forgive him.

Tuesday 29th September
A slightly puzzled letter from David Astor pointing out that I myself had sold him most of the material used in his campaign of vilification against my late Father. Oh dear. How embarrassing.

Wednesday 30th September
To Bristol, for a meeting of the Association for Research into Restricted Growth. This is in fact more of a social occasion than anything else, when people of four feet and under like myself can gather together and discuss the various insults we have received throughout the year.

My life's ambition is to politicise the Association and turn it into a meaningful tool for the advancement of Dwarf Power. My dream is of a national uprising under Lord Snowdon, when we shall join forces with the Black Dwarves of the Welsh mining valleys and the Poison Dwarves of Clydebank to massacre the giants who have oppressed us for so long, just as the tiny Hutu people rose up and slaughtered the overweening Tutsis in distant Rwanda.

There are more of us wee folk than people realise, but we do not show ourselves much for fear of ridicule, preferring to spend our time quietly in cupboards, suitcases and little holes in the ground while we await the call.

Thursday 1st October
While in Bristol, I hear of some research being carried out at the Southmead Hospital into the practice of granny-battering. Dr G.R. Burston has isolated this exciting new leisure activity and believes that the social services should take a hand in it.

I suppose he is right. At present the sport is limited to those privileged persons who have grannies left to batter, which is obviously unfair. There must be an enormous pool of old age pensioners on the welfare who have no grandchildren, and these could be mobilised.

On the other hand, I am not sure that I approve of this new sport. It strikes me as cruel and possibly dangerous. Dr Burston and his colleagues should take an interest in some healthy outdoor activity like Morris-dancing which is great fun and not nearly as ridiculous as people make it sound.

Friday 2nd October
A letter from Bevis Hillier, the learned and entertaining editor of *Connoisseur*, asking my help over an exhibition at the Victoria and Albert to commemorate the 25th anniversary of the Festival of Britain next year.

Bevis hopes that the Queen Mother will be able to open his exhibition. She, of course, would be the perfect choice, but in the event of her being unable to come he wonders· whether my cousin, Bernard Dru, might not oblige.

---

1. Septimus Waugh, the Carpenter, b. 1950.

2. This column was written by Waugh from February 1970 until October 1972.

I can only describe this as an inspired suggestion. Bernard, who was born on 29th December 1951, is plainly a Festival of Britain Baby, finest and most enduring product of that carnival year when the whole nation gave itself up to merrymaking and laughter with never a thought for the morrow.

Saturday 3rd October
Oh the ghastliness of bright young women journalists! All this week I have been brooding about someone called Anne Karpf who wrote in the *Sunday Times* that she spent Sunday morning in the bath shaving her pubic hair before composing the usual catalogue of stale half-witted opinions about life.

I hesitate to mention Ms Karpff's disgusting habit in case it starts one of those interminable correspondences in *Private Eye* like the great debate which followed Cyril Connolly's disclosure that he had never masturbated at 18½. Phartt thinks it makes women look lovelier, but I think it makes them look ridiculous. Even if Phartt wants to make herself look ridiculous in this way, and draw attention to it, I wish she could find some more original method, like having her ears cut off or growing a moustache.

Sunday 4th October
The Pope's action in canonising an American woman — Elizabeth Bayley Seton — can only be interpreted as another provocation aimed at the Church's few remaining believers.

Typically, this squalid event was tied in with International Women's Year, hitherto seen as a conspiracy among a handful of militant lesbians to bore us all on the subjects of abortion and rape. I have never understood why these dreadful women should all choose to be pro one and anti the other, but they must be entitled to their opinions without having the Pope barge in to steal the show.

But we should not repine. Any time now, we will see the emergence of our first anti-pope of the 20th century — the first, indeed, since the death of Felix V in 1449. I often think that Bath would be a pleasant town to set up as the new Avignon. Before long, we shall see dancing in the streets again.

Monday 5th October
At Blackpool for the Labour Party Conference. In the morning, I take poor, twitching Wedgwood Benn aside to ask him why he keeps predicting the imminent collapse of capitalism. For my off-the-record briefing we go into a sort of broom cupboard under the auditorium of the Winter Gardens, and he explains everything in a calm voice with only the occasional roll of his terrible eyes to show that his emotions as well as his intellect are engaged.

He says that nobody is going to invest in British industry any more because the unions will successfully demand ruinous over-manning on all new plants. In the unlikely event of new investment showing a profit everybody knows it will be confiscated in the interests of social justice. Soon, not even the Government will be able to help as nobody is going to lend it money when people realise that they have spent all the proceeds from North Sea oil for the next 50 years keeping the workers happy these last few months.

When I ask him why he is so thrilled by this scenario, he gives me a pitying look, as if my stupidity is probably the result of deprivation in childhood. "Then we can start killing people," he explains, stabbing at the air with his ballpoint pen.

Oh dear. Where did Caroline Benn go wrong?

Wednesday 7th October
To a public meeting of the Revolutionary Workers' Party in the ballroom of Park House Hotel, Blackpool. Vanessa Redgrave is there, spouting her usual tosh about how wonderful the working classes are and how we must all allow ourselves to be ruled by these ludicrous people immediately.

The most depressing thing about Ms Redgrave is not that she will ever have the slightest influence on the political scene. It is the dreadful certainty that she is growing into one of the great showbiz legends of our time.

Like Caruso, Houdini, Eddie Cantor, St Bernadette of Lourdes, we may be sure that films are going to be made about her before she is stiff in her coffin, claiming that she was a peerless beauty, an actress of genius who defied convention and shocked an entire nation by riding rough-shod over everything it held most sacred.

Yet what I see is a hideous, squinny-eyed fanatic mouthing tired old slogans which even her bird-brain should be able to identify as a load of nasty rubbish, and being cheered by an adulatory gathering of mental deficients. It makes you think.

Thursday 8th October
In all the ugliness and spite of the Blackpool conference I suddenly spy the beautiful and gifted Tina Brown. I had not seen her since Oxford days when we attended the same dancing class and now, among the dim, resentful faces of Labour Party delegates she reminds me of the time I met the Queen on a State visit to Aberfan after the disaster and wept on her shoulder to see a human face at last.

She tells me she is doing 'One Woman's Week' for the *Sunday Times*. This is Alan Brien's slightly-soiled slot on the back page, now filled by a bewildering succession of lesbians, negroes and Jewish ladies who wish to describe how they shave their pubic hair.

It is a sad commentary on our times that a woman of such surpassing wit and talent can only find these seedy little holes in the corner of British journalism to occupy. But she looks lovelier, more radiant and more fulfilled than ever, and there's the real horror of it.

Friday 16th October
Back to Blackpool for the Tories. The atmosphere is silent and grim with an unspoken awareness of the great counter-revolutionary movement grouping itself behind my cousin Bernard Dru in the West Country. Never have the Tories felt so ignored.

I spend the morning handing out stickers ("Our Leader: Bernard Dru") and lapel buttons ("I'm for Bernard Dru") to delegates. Knowing how few of them have ever read P.G. Wodehouse, I sidle up to anyone who refuses my offer and hiss in his ear: "We know your guilty secret".

My greatest success so far has been with Michael Heseltine, described as the 'epitome of classic English chic' in today's *Express*. He swoons on the ground and can only be revived by an application of Dior's *Eau Sauvage*[1] behind his ears and the loosening of his underpants.

Sunday 18th October
The Roman Catholic archbishoprics of Westminster and Liverpool are both up for grabs, and it is no surprise to find one of my main rivals — Bishop Worlock of Portsmouth — mouthing and posturing on television this evening.

He is speaking in favour of the repulsive new travesty of the Mass and hints that his one year as Rural Dean in the East End of London gives him special insight into this.

Watching him, it is hard to decide if he is more of a villain or more of a fool to provoke at least half the Catholic intelligentsia so gratuitously. If he is appointed to either archdiocese, I think I shall join the Eucharist Catholic Church of New York, whose bishop, the Most Rev. Robert M. Clement, has just launched "the world's first gay religious publication" called *Via*.

Clement has also opened the first "gay" church on West 14th Street. Ceremonies included a Pontifical High Mass, at which Bishop Clement was assisted by the Right Rev. John Noble D.D., his Vicar General, and "lover of many years". Festivities began with a buffet supper and quiet dancing and then swung into "disco" dancing as the hour neared midnight. Photographs of Bishop Clement and Father Leo, his Chancellor, are supplied.

Not being much inclined to sodomy these days, I don't suppose I shall really find a spiritual home there, but at least I shall be away from the temptation to commit even more gross and unspeakable sins against Bishop Derek Worlock whenever I see his unctuous face around.

---

1. For a fuller description of Heseltine's cosmetic routine, see earlier.

Thursday 22nd October

My friend Brian Roberts, editor of the *Sunday Telegraph*, tells me that his newspaper has overtaken the *Observer*'s circulation for the first time since it was launched in 1961. He has richly deserved this prize for some time, if only on the strength of the *Sunday Telegraph*'s novel reviews. Novel reviews in the *Observer* are a national disgrace.

I hope that when the *Observer* staff come to choose their new editor, they bear in mind the sad fate of the *Scottish Daily News* which, when taken over by its workers, managed to reduce an initial circulation of 325,000 to something under 100,000 in five months — possibly a record in newspaper history.

When one looks at the new proletarianised *Sunday Times*, the story is much the same. We supposed, for a time, that the lower classes liked reading all this illiterate drivel about hairdressers, but the readership slumped last year and it has already lost 105,000 readers in the first six months of this year. This means losing them at over seven times the percentage rate of the *Sunday Telegraph*.

My colleagues on the *Observer* would be well advised to appoint a sensible editor from the unglamorous middle classes. The silly fashion for working class whizz-kids like Lord Ryder has landed this country in quite enough trouble already[1].

Friday 23rd October

Although I have read Dr Coggan's message to the nation four times and even tried singing it in my bath, I still don't quite see what he wants me to do in the crisis ahead:

"What I am asserting is that unless we lift our whole national debate about our condition today up to a higher level, we shall not even be asking the right questions, let alone finding the right answers."

In other words, he has no idea either, and just wants to make a noise and draw attention to himself like everybody else. Silly old fart.

This is just the moment when the nation would be turning to William Rees-Mogg as its natural Leader, if only he had not disgraced himself by his recent contemptible behaviour in suing Lord Gnome! Why can't Lord Thomson pay his editors enough money so that they don't have to supplement their incomes by raiding the coffers of their more successful rivals in this ignominious way? Where Rees-Mogg is concerned, it is enough to break one's heart:

> *We that had loved him so, followed him,*
> *honoured him,*
> *Lived in his mild and magnificent eye,*
> *Learned his great language, caught his*
> *clear accents,*
> *Made him our pattern to live and to die!*

Now the Curse of Lord Gnome has descended and we must look somewhere else for the Leader we crave. All eyes inevitably focus on an unassuming manor house near Minehead in Somerset, where a certain young cousin of mine, whose name I'm not prepared to reveal at this stage, is busying himself with his farm animals in preparation for the nation's Call[2].

---

1. They eventually chose Donald Gilchrist Trelford, of middle class but restricted growth. See 2 Jan. 1976.
2. It is hard to suppose this refers to anyone except his cousin Bernard Dru (q.v.).

Saturday 24th October

In my *Daily Mirror*, which grows more disgusting every day, there is a huge grinning photograph of Denise Varley, the 25-year-old hairdresser who sent her former lover to prison for 15 months when he assured her that he was unmarried in order to have intercourse with her.

I never knew this was against the law, but if it is, I hope that the same penalties apply to women. Many is the time I have met a female rather late in the evening who has solemnly assured me she is a Catholic virgin of 19. Only next morning do I discover, waking up with a headache, that she is some raddled old divorcee of 55, as often as not a freethinker of Jewish or Non-Conformist origins.

Sunday 25th October

Going into Westminster Cathedral for a lunchtime sandwich and snooze, I am disturbed to see six women carrying placards in front of the altar. They are chained together like suffragettes, and have come from the National Abortion Campaign conference at Imperial College to demonstrate their belief in a Woman's Right to Choose.

It might have been a welcome diversion if the women were not all so ugly and so desperately serious. As it is, I find myself quite put off my cheese sandwich. There is a murderous boredom in their fish-like eyes which makes me doubt whether they can have had many opportunities to indulge this bizarre preference.

Unlike suffragettes, they lack the courage to chain themselves to the altar rail. If only they dared, we could leave them there for ever as a terrible warning of what happens o women who lose their sense of humour.

Monday 26th October

As I muse on the fate of passengers blockaded on the car ferry *Eagle* by striking pickets, I think I may have one practical suggestion to make for the crisis ahead: we should all carry poisoned sweets with us wherever we go.

Attempts to overpower these people might be dangerous, but I have never met a British "worker" able to resist the offer of a free sweet. The same goes for policemen — there is really very little to choose between them.

I don't know what refinement of this plan Dr Coggan is suggesting when he says "the right approach to the nation's problems is *from both ends*", and I don't really like the sound of it, but perhaps he will make himself plainer next time round.

Tuesday 27th October

I am intrigued to learn that Karl Miller has written a book at last. He is the 44-year-old *literatus* whose appointment as Lord Northcliffe Professor of Modern English Literature caused such mirth last year; more recently he has been appointed Assistant Editor of Ian Hamilton's pathetic *New Review* — a post better suited to his outlook and talents. Duckworth are publishing his book at the unsubsidised price of £14.

He has chosen as his subject a study of my great-great-great-grandfather, Henry Cockburn, the great Scottish Whig. Cockburn strikes me as deserving rather better than these belated attentions from an ambitious young academic on the make.

The reason for his choice, it appears, is that Miller was brought up in the Perthshire coal-mining village of Gilmerton, in the shadow of my great-great-great-grandfather's castle at Bonaly. Cockburn always dismissed the inhabitants of Gilmerton as "black scoundrels", and Miller replies 130 years later with a load of pseudish rubbish to suggest that Cockburn suffered from an Oedipus complex.

Books & Bookmen have kindly sent me a copy of this preposterous book to review. When I have finished studying it, I shall consult with my cousin Claud about whether we should call the young puppy out and give him a thrashing.

Tuesday 3rd November
Lunch with a senior Civil Servant whom I shall call Sir John Hunt[1]. After a few reminiscences about our boyhood at Downside together which are of no interest to the general reader, I ask him what he thinks of the general situation.

He tells me there can be no question but that Wilson is mad. He thinks it is terror of Lady Forkbender which has driven him that way. On one occasion recently, at tea with President Sadat of Egypt, he put strawberry jam in his milk and burst into tears when this was pointed out. Healey is a flabby incompetent who has sold out and has trouble with his wind.

I show him some poems, letters and notes he sent me when I was in the Classical Remove and he was in the Lower Sixth, but the real purpose of giving him lunch is to make sure I get on the new Civil Service Central List of candidates for public office.

It is not that I really want to be Chairman of the Electricity Board, but all of us who are excluded from this List of the Great and Good must feel discriminated against to a certain extent. After a certain amount of humming and hawing he agrees to do what he can when I point out that I am under 40 and live in the Regions. He is terrified I will mention him in my *Diary* and begs me to call him Sir Burke Trend[2]. I must try and remember to do this for the published version.

Wednesday 4th November
The Feast of St Guy Fawkes, soldier and martyr, is marked by the usual display of naked funk from MPs. Perhaps their hysterical cowardice in the face of a christmas cracker or tuppenny sparkler is no more than another example of what has become our chief national characteristic. But I prefer to think they are beginning to realise how the spirit of St Guy Fawkes is sweeping the land. After the Glorious Counter-Revolution, when Wilson, Healey, Crosland and Foot are swinging from lamp-posts in Parliament Square, and Benn is gibbering to the moon from a padded cell in Rampton Hospital, I hope that St Guy Fawkes will be recognised as the new patron saint of England.

In fact, far fewer people have been killed by fireworks in the whole of British history than have been killed by politicians and would-be politicians in the last few months. If the IRA had any sense of humour they would use this great national festival to blow up the House of Commons with all its horrible overpaid occupants inside.
The present policy of trying to blow up MPs one by one strikes me as wasteful and doomed to failure, as well as being dangerous to the general public.

1. Sir John Benedict Hunt, b. 1919. Educ. Downside. Secretary of the Cabinet 1973 — . Noted for curious reaction to Crossman Diaries (q.v.)

2. Lord Trend (Life Peer 1974). A rival Civil Servant, now Rector, Lincoln College, Oxford. b. 1914, noted for curious name.

Thursday 12th November
All 25 members of *Private Eye*'s editorial staff
are former Presidents of the Oxford Union
and so are most of the 73 barristers who call
every week to read the magazine for alleged
libel, but I can't bring myself to support
Harold Macmillan's £750,000 appeal for the
Union launched today.

When one looks at the list of its former
officers — Hailsham, Heath, Thorpe, Jenkins,
Foot, Benn, Crosland and Norman Anthony
Francis St John Stevas — one sees that they
are all in their different ways profoundly
unhappy men.

Even looking around my colleagues I can't
help feeling that without this millstone
around our necks, we might have been able
to find more gainful and socially desirable
occupations elsewhere, whether in cancer
research or showing Arab gentlemen around
London.

Sunday 15th November
Among the many absurdities of the new
Roman Catholic "people's meal" which has
replaced the old Mass is a stage direction for
everybody present at a given moment to
give his next door neighbour the Kiss of
Peace.

Obviously, this was thought up by some
repressed old pervert in the Congregation of
Rites as a means of getting people into
church, and it has produced nothing but
embarrassment. The Stage Directions do not
specify how far one can go, and it has become
common for fighting to break out all over
church at this point, with screams, noises of
tearing clothes and knickers flying in the air.
This is especially the case in places like
Taunton where sexual passions run high.

Now a ruling has come, from the Archbishop of Southwark, Mgr Cyril Cowderoy
(he is not to be confused with the Anglican
Bishop known as Moscow Mervyn) in an *ad
clerum* to the clergy: no person in the congregation is bound to give or accept the Kiss
of Peace, and it must not include physical
contact.

Swingers will condemn the venerable
Archbishop, but I can assure them it is no
joke for sensitive young men like myself
who have what I suppose can only be called
a certain physical attractiveness to the
opposite sex when we suddenly find ourselves
held in a bear-hug by some toothless old bag
of an Irish meths drinker who smells of fried
cabbage and vomit and burst sewers.
There are those who feel that this is just
what religion is all about, but I can't help
feeling it detracts from the community
atmosphere.

Friday 20th November
We who supported General Franco[1] in the
Glorious Revolution of July 17, 1936 and
fought shoulder-to-shoulder throughout the
Civil War, often against wailing hordes of
potheen-crazed Connollys, the peat still
sticking to their wild Irish hair — we, that
small band of survivors, should pay no
attention to rumours of the Caudillo's ill-
health or death.

For as long as I can remember there have
been these rumours about Uncle Frankie, as
we used to call him when as children he let
us paddle in the fountains of his El Prado
palace. I can't seriously believe he has shot
his last quail or garotted his last would-be
politician, and if those clever doctors can
keep so much as a big toe of his alive it will
lead Spain through many more decades of
stability and moderate affluence.

His successor, Juan Carlos, has a ratlike
and furtive air about him and is not to be
trusted. He once took 20,000 *pesetas* from
me at backgammon by altering the rules, at
a time of my life when I could ill afford it.

Saturday 21st November
In Paris for the Rambouillet Conference, I
rush to buy my copy of *Ici Paris*, the best
newspaper in Europe, to find out what is
really happening in England. The main headline on the front page is promising:
L'AMOUR ADULTÈRE DE PRINCE
CHARLES.

Can the secret be out which I thought was
known only to myself and to a handful of
social-climbing millionaires in Berkshire? As
I hastily turn to page 56 for the full story,
I see it is a smokescreen. *Ici Paris*'s London
correspondent, the great James Butterfly, is
pouring cold water on a story which has
already appeared in the German weekly,
Sieben Tage, linking the name of Prince
Charles with ex-Queen Anne Marie of Greece.

This report, Mr Butterfly reveals, has in-
furiated the English. He goes on to attribute
the "odious calumny" to the fact that they
are childhood friends and have been meeting
in secret only so that Charles can console her
in exile. Theirs is a brother-and-sister
relationship, he opines.

So poor Anne Marie is left in Neasden with
her ghastly ape of a husband and crazy
mother-in-law. I think this is a shame and a
national scandal. Wake up, John Wells.

Sunday 22nd November
Paris today celebrates the Feast of St Hubert,
when all the huntsmen from miles around
crowd into the Church of St Eustache to
blow their French horns throughout Mass.

1. Franco d. 1975 after 36 years as military dictator of Spain.

Wandering through the cafes and restaurants of Les Halles after Church and savouring the foodstalls and throngs of attractive women (who are also amazingly inexpensive, the way prices are going nowadays) I reflect that France is an island of civilisation and sanity in the dismal sea of stupidity and proletarian values. Then, like a gasp of bad breath, I come across today's *Sunday Times,* fresh from England.

One Man's Week is written by Craig Raine, a bright and amiable Oxford don I met a few months ago in circumstances of great frustration. He has chosen to reminisce about his childhood:

"Mother brings in my father's Yorkshire puddings — baked in loaf tins, they come about a foot square, two of them, like spring interior mattresses, well over the edge of the plate. He salts them and the table cloth, anoints them with mint sauce and gravy and cuts them in half. Each huge, wobbling chunk is pronged into his mouth like someone backing a lorry."

Ugh! As a boy, I am sorry to say I sometimes ate mice and slow-worms — not out of hunger so much as a mixture of curiosity and greed. My father once claimed to have eaten a hedgehog, but it would never occur to me that these were the most interesting and memorable things we had done.

I suppose Craig felt this was expected of him: a half-witted father who enjoyed eating this sort of filth in this sort of way is his passport to the thrilling world of Colour Supplement executives with flat accents and open-plan houses who spend their evenings in dark glasses, tapping their feet to the hi-fi.

In the present mad rush to suck up to the working classes, we must be prepared to say they are cleverer, handsomer, wiser, more sensitive in an intuitive sort of way, better at sexual intercourse and more honest than the rest of us — even (excuse me while I snigger) harder working. But I wish to God we did not have to pretend there is anything droll or endearing about the things they eat or the way they eat them.

Monday 23rd November
Back in Somerset after addressing the Franco-British Junior Chamber of Commerce on the subject of the English libel laws over lunch in the Rue Castiglione, I devote the rest of the afternoon to counting my Krugerrands.

This takes me well into the evening, and I never get the figures to agree. Perhaps there is something strange in the English air.

Tuesday 24th November
I hope we will not let ourselves be stampeded by grief at William Hardcastle[1]'s death into supporting any idiotic suggestion for a Hardcastle Memorial Fund. People are either going to remember him or, as is the fate of most journalists, they are not, and no amount of money will make any difference now.

There is a craze in Fleet Street for these fatuous gestures. Far better let the hacks devote a few minutes before the bars open every day to looking eternity in the eye than stage these mawkish exhibitions of drunken sentimentality every time one of them drops off his perch.

Saturday 5th December
To Manchester where I am interviewed for the job of Token Male on the government's new £2.2 million per year Equal Opportunities Commission. The interview is conducted by Ms Netty Lockwood, a spinster, who is chairman of the Commission and Msldy Elspeth Howe, a female, who is vice-chairperson.

It may seem silly to be changing jobs at my age, but the appointment carries a salary of £28,000 p.a. with inflation-proofed pension, plus use of a private train (with drawing room, dining room and colour television) for personal travelling and two years on full pay if I should happen to have a baby.

Ms Lockwood's conversation is all about the extraordinary powers which have devolved on her. She can inspect and investigate any school she fancies, and make enforceable rulings if she thinks that sexual inequality is occurring. "I think the Commission will need to use its powers," she says.

Another power is to call school medical inspections at any hour of the day or night, at which all boys must show that their penises have not grown above the recommended size (Dept. of Health 'Blue' Guide *TS/1004/6114-4/0003*) cutting them down where necessary. These parades are compulsory for all male children except first-born sons of trade union members whose union is affiliated to the TUC.

"In time we hope to be able to cut these things off altogether," says Msldy Howe, 46. "Medical opinion is coming round to the view that they are unnecessary and in some circumstances, harmful. Both Ms Lockwood and I have managed perfectly well all these years without them," she adds to loud applause and the clinking of a hundred tea-cups.

---

1. Hardcastle was one of about eight sacked editors of the Daily Mail around at this time.

Sunday 6th December

The season of Christmas Books has arrived with critics' choices for the best book of the year. These serve as a useful guide to which literary pages are in the hands of the timid, the clapped-out and the pseudish.

I must ask readers to take my word for it as somebody who has read them all that quite easily the best novel published this year was Malcolm Bradbury's *The History Man* (Secker & Warburg, £3.10). The worst novel by a respectable author was Saul Bellow's *Humboldt's Gift*. The most pseudish book of the year was Dr George Steiner's *After Babel*, 500 pages of commonplace drivel rendered in gibberish. The book most likely to appeal to insecure punks who don't read much but like to be thought well-read was Anthony Powell's *Hearing Secret Harmonies*.

Of the two Critics' Choices out so far, *The Times* has four writers who name *The History Man* as best book of the year; four who choose *Hearing Secret Harmonies*; two who choose *Humboldt's Gift*; and one who chooses Steiner. The *Sunday Times* has three who choose *Secret Harmonies*; one who chooses Steiner and none who chooses Malcolm Bradbury's *The History Man*.

Conclusion: The *Sunday Times* book page is entirely and exclusively manned by punks, pseuds, and insecure twits; *The Times* is largely under their control, but has a few bright spots. Now use this scale to judge other book pages as their Christmas lists appear.

Monday 14th December

"Vulgar, crude and dirty", are the words used by Marje Proops the *Daily Mirror*'s magnificent old Duchess of Holborn Circus to describe a new pamphlet issued by the Family Planning Association, called *Getting It On*. This purports to teach less gifted members of the under-privileged socio-economic groupings how to put on a male contraceptive.

"The pamphlet is written in a style they will understand," says a spokesman for the Family Planning Association. I very much doubt it. In my experience it is almost impossible to communicate anything to these people by means of the written word. But if by any chance the pamphlet succeeds, a much more horrible situation may arise.

When I telephoned the Family Planning Association headquarters in a state of some agitation, a cool young lady in the Press Office agrees that there are no instructions given for taking these things off again. She does not seem to think it part of her job as Press Officer to make any suggestions, either.

This failure on the part of the FPA to provide clear instructions strikes me as a grave abdication of responsibility. One dreads to think what the consequences will be for all the bemused young men who have followed their instructions so far. I am happy to report that Gnome House is rushing out a second pamphlet, *Taking It Off Again*.

Tuesday 15th December

West Somerset is buzzing with rumours of a most unsavoury description following reports in the *West Somerset Free Press* about an incident which occurred recently on Exmoor. Mr Norman Scott, a 35-year-old writer, of Coombe Marten, North Devon, who claims to have been a great friend of Jeremy Thorpe[1], the Liberal statesman, was found by an AA patrolman weeping beside the body of Rinka, his Great Dane bitch, which had been shot in the head.

Information about this puzzling incident has since been restricted, on Home Office orders, but a man arrested at London Airport on a firearms charge will be appearing before Minehead Magistrates on December 19th, when we may learn more.

My only hope is that sorrow over his friend's dog will not cause Mr Thorpe's premature retirement from public life. Jeremy is not only a very wonderful man in his own right, he is also a gifted impersonator of London celebrities like Lady Dartmouth and Mr Heath. Indeed, in the whole of fashionable London I can only think of John Wells as possibly being his equal in this field and Wells, of course, has other disadvantages.

Thursday 17th December

Normally I read lists of new Life Peers with a wrinkled lip and cold sneer on my good-natured face, but for once Wislon has surprised us all. Of the nine people named today, none is an obvious Soviet agent, none (so far as I know) has paid Wislon large sums of money, and none is a particularly close friend of Lady Forkbender. What can this mean?

Uncle Tom Driberg[2] it is true, has had to wait rather a long time for his honour. Perhaps Wislon feels that a man has to have had his first stroke and be over 70 before he is out of mischief's way, but I think Uncle Tom may surprise us all. In many respects he is very well preserved.

Initially it was upsetting to see a man like Robert Carr[3] honoured who is one of the greatest disasters of modern times, but I suppose it was the only way Mrs Thatcher

---

1. **This incident was later to culminate in a series of elaborate denials from Mr Thorpe, and his eventual resignation.**

2. Tom Driberg. High Churchman and Left Wing Labour MP 1942-74. b. 1905, educ. at Lancing with Waugh's father. Not an uncle. Became Lord Bradwell. m. 1951 Mrs Ena Mary Binfield.

3. Robert Carr. Conservative Home Secretary 1970-74.

could get rid of the brute. Where she really shows sensitivity and imagination is in her award of a Life Peerage to Miss Marianne Faithfull[1].

Ever since I saw her in the film *Girl on a Motorbicycle* I have felt that Marianne should be given something, even if a peerage is more than I had hoped for. She may find the House of Lords rather dull especially with the appalling Robert Carr there, but perhaps I shall introduce her to my old friend Lord Gowrie. He is a graceful Negro art dealer who briefly made a name for himself as adviser on Ugandan affairs to Lord Jellicohen in Grocer's ill-fated administration.

Friday 18th December
For Christmas shopping in London I go by force of habit to Harrods. The toy department is still full of loud-voiced Englishwomen all rich, all claiming to have highly intelligent six-year-olds, and all damned. But I do not see a fellow Englishman anywhere until I chance upon the Women's Underwear Department.

To these unhappy people, Christmas is no more than a pretext for buying female underwear. As I pass, I hear a Major of the Household Brigade ask for some knickers with pussy fur; another man, almost certainly from the Treasury, asks in a hoarse whisper for some crotchless briefs. They all look like rats, they're all going mad, and they're all damned.

To those who ask what I was doing in the Women's Underwear Department, I can only say — no, I am not planning any unseemly celebration for the end of International Women's Year. I had simply lost my way to the Food Halls.

Saturday 19th December
With guilty feelings of pleasure I take a day off urgent affairs of state to work on my book about Cyril Connolly, the controversial book reviewer who died a year ago. A new issue of *Adam*, the international review, is entirely devoted to articles in his praise and should not be missed by students of the subject.

The anthology includes two bitter attacks on myself whose effect is blunted by the fact that neither assailant dares name the person he is assailing. One, describing me as "a vitriolic scribbler whom I am sure nobody takes seriously", and, less happily, as a "sterile reviler" is by Martin Seymour-Smith. He is an ambitious young charlatan whom I exposed at great length in the pages of *Books & Bookmen* some time ago for basing

his claim to literary punditry on the pretence of having read books he has not read in languages he does not even understand.

The other, referring to "the impertinences and ruderies of someone so totally inconsiderable as a recent horsefly in journalism whom [Connolly] should have been able to brush aside or ignore altogether" comes in the course of an excellent piece by T.C. Worlsey. This saddens me, as I believe Cuthbert Worsley to be a good writer and a good man.

He is right of course that if Connolly and his friends had not over-reacted so preposterously to a little gentle ribbing from these quarters over the years, there would have been little incentive to continue. But this over-reaction is an essential part of the comedy, and Mr Worsley should take heart. With industry and good luck, I think my little book may yet turn out to be the Missing Masterpiece which Connolly always promised himself.

Monday 21st December
To Skinners' Hall where I have been invited with other Companions of Literature to celebrate the 150th anniversary of our Royal Society. We are a funny collection, when all is said and done, but everyone is very friendly.

I am in the middle of talking to a deaf old woman about ladybirds when somebody comes up behind me, covers my eyes and asks in a pretty, refined voice: "Guess who?"

You could knock me down with a feather. Among all my acquaintances, the one I least expect to meet at a Lit. Soc. "do" is the Queen of England. When I ask her if she has read any good books lately she puts on her haughty look and says yes, she is quite enjoying Mr Heath's book about sailing.

The deaf old lady I was talking to thinks she said "Gide", and launches into a long harangue about the morals of the French *avant-garde* between the wars, a subject on which she holds vehement opinions. The Queen mentions that she read Georges Duhamel's *Le Notaire du Havre* in the schoolroom, but is too diplomatic to say whether she enjoyed it or not. I still don't know why she bothered to come.

Tuesday 22nd December
Today, General Augusto Pinochet of Chile buys half a page in *The Times* to answer some of the charges levelled against him by scheming international Marxists and unhealthy young Catholic priests of the New Wave. Describing a UN resolution against his country as "false, artificial, slanderous and

---

1. There is a confusion here. Ms Marianne Faithfull was not ennobled.

profoundly unjust", he refers to the "truth that Chile today proclaims in noble solitude"

She will not be proclaiming it alone for long, I feel sure. Now we have left the febrile excitements of International Women's Year behind us, we must look for something to make 1976 equally memorable. I would like to propose an international "General Pinochet is Beautiful Year" exalting the male virtues of leadership, commonsense and thrift with weekly articles in the newspaper by prominent Maleists from every walk of life.

Incidentally, I hear that when my cousin Bernard Dru opened the Conservative Party annual Bring-and-Buy sale in the nearby town of Dulverton recently he made a profound impression on all the retired generals and their wives who inhabit these parts of West Somerset. Things may be looking up!

Wednesday 24th December
How I shall miss International Women's Year! Today *The Times* devotes four columns to an amazing article about St Paul by Olivia Manning; the aged cat-lover[1]. She objects to St Paul's injunction (1 Corinthians XIV, 34-35):

"Let your women keep silence in the churches: for it is not permitted unto them to speak. . . And if they will learn anything, let them ask their husbands at home: for it is a shame for women to speak in church."

Ms Manning thinks this proves St Paul was "almost certainly a suppressed homosexual with a hatred, fear and envy of women". Possibly, but he may just have been nervous in case they said something stupid.

The ban on women talking in church is probably the greatest single attraction of religion nowadays. Almost everywhere else one goes, one hears nothing but women talking. Can't they see what a mistake this is? Once women are ordained, the churches will be completely empty except for a sprinkling of lesbians and people like myself who use them for a snooze in the afternoon.

But then this evening we watch a carol service from King's College Chapel, Cambridge. The choirboys are as pretty as anybody could hope for, but in the cruel glare of colour television their rouge and lipstick becomes horribly obvious. Is this what we are fighting for?

Thursday 25th December
For dinner, we have a goose which has ingeniously had a pheasant put inside it. Inside the pheasant is a duck, inside the duck, a woodcock, and inside the woodcock no doubt a grasshopper, although I do not care to inquire too closely.

I can't help thinking how much Cyril Connolly would have enjoyed this dish. It might have reminded him of the aphorism which made him famous when it appeared in *The Unquiet Grave* (1945): "Imprisoned in every fat man a thin one is wildly struggling to be let out".

In fact, as a correspondent to *Encounter* pointed out last September, Connolly borrowed this idea from his schoolfriend George Orwell who wrote in *Coming Up For Air* (1939): "Has it ever struck you that there is a thin man inside every fat man, just as they say there is a statue inside every block of stone?"

Never mind. The great point about Cyril was how much he enjoyed his food.

Friday 26th December
Still no newspapers, but I find I can understand practically nothing which is said on television nowadays. Today it is full of comedians with incomprehensible accents imitating other comedians I have never heard of. In desperation we turn to *The Magic Flute* sung in Swedish — a very good joke to play on the lower classes for Boxing Day. At least I can recognise a few of the tunes.

---

1. Ms Manning objected to this description on the grounds that she was not aged.

1976

Wilson's resignation marks the end of an era. The country continues to wrestle with the horrors of the Equal Opportunities Act, a measure designed to humiliate British women by their impotent, homosexual menfolk. A few British mercenaries go to Angola, which the Portuguese have abandoned, and are disgraced. The Government continues to do nothing about inflation except make it worse. Harold Wilson is made a Knight of the Garter and reveals his friendly feelings towards a businessman called Mr James Goldsmith. As the Diaries go to press, it seems as if every warning contained in them is about to be fulfilled.

Sunday 2nd January

My New Year's Resolution is not to mention the *Sunday Times* for the next 12 months. With luck, it will have disappeared by then. To help me, I have taken the momentous step of cancelling my order and re-ordering the *Observer*.

This may seem foolish. The only time I saw the *Observer*'s new editor, Donald Trelford, he was in a witness box trying to give evidence against me. Although the judge soon sent him packing, I can't really believe the bugger has long to live. My chief worry is what to do with such sexual passions as may be aroused of a Sunday morning while my poor wife is preparing lunch. Possibly the best answer lies in prayer. To the pure all things are pure, although where the *Observer* is concerned, it puzzles me how anybody can miss the filth.

But anything is better than what has happened to the *Sunday Times*. We must not dwell on it. One possible reason occurred to me while I was reading the New Delhi *Indian Press*, where a sycophantic article by someone called S. Venkat Narayan reveals that fewer than ten *Sunday Times* employees went to Oxford or Cambridge. If true, this explains much.

Another explanation may lie in an article by Professor Hugh Thomas in this week's (sadly diminished) *New Statesman*[1], where he reveals that for writing an obituary on General Franco recently the *Sunday Times* paid him exactly half what the *Sunday Telegraph* had paid him for writing an obituary on Franco ten years ago. But from now on, my eyes are averted.

Monday 10th January

I am driven to distraction by not having the faintest idea what is contained in these stolen Wislon papers which have been bouncing around the underworld and selected police departments for so long[2].

Nobody else in Fleet Street knows and — what is even more alarming — nobody even pretends to know. Joe Haines has not given a single confidential briefing to mislead his drunken toadies, and none of Wislon's enemies has the faintest idea either.

What on earth is happening? I have £500 in used pound notes for anyone who can produce the complete photostats; £15 for a convincing resume of their content. Don't all call at once.

Tuesday 11th January

In my days as a Parliamentary reporter I never quite managed to distinguish between Francis Boyd of the *Grauniad* and Harry Boyne of the *Telegraph*. Both were old, both ugly, both boring, both rather unpleasant, and both incredibly pleased with themselves.

Now I see they have both been knighted for their countless years' service to Lobby "journalism" — at the same time as clever, hard-working Iris Murdoch gets a paltry CBE. It is this sort of thing which makes a farce of the Honours System. I'm glad I turned down Wislon's cowardly offer of a Life Peerage.

Wednesday 12th January

On my way up to London, I find myself terribly depressed by an article in the *Grauniad* about housing the lower classes. It appears that as soon as you put them into a luxurious new block of council flats, they start going to the lavatory in all the halls, corridors and lifts until nobody wants to live there and the flats fall empty.

Soon, we are told, these same people will be moving into the corridors of power with all their filthy habits. And what, one asks, is my cousin Bernard Dru doing about all this?

He has been so quiet that I constantly receive letters — many from young girls — enquiring if he really exists. They may rest assured: BERNARD DRU LIVES!

He is unmarried, very handsome in an old-fashioned way, and has just celebrated his 24th birthday quietly in Somerset. If they wish, they may even discover his address — one of the most closely guarded secrets in Britain — on page 487 of the new *Burke's Peerage* under Carnarvon E., collaterals.

But there are no grounds for panic. We of the Bernard Dru Movement will not rest until we have ensconced our Man of Destiny in Downing Street, even if it means pushing him there all the way from Minehead in a wheelbarrow.

Thursday 20th January

A new crisis of conscience over the Pope's *Declaration On Certain Questions Concerning Sexual Ethics*, which forbids masturbation and extra-marital sex. It puts the responsibility for spreading the news and giving wholesome sexual advice on us journalists, so I suppose I'd better say "Stop it at once!" But a new and more terrifying injunction is that homosexualists "must certainly be treated with understanding".

---

1. Waugh left the New Statesman and returned to write a weekly article in The Spectator on Jan 1 1976.

2. Further batches of these stolen papers continue to occupy public attention as we go to press in summer 1976.

Does this mean we must ask the brutes to
tea and listen to their horrible problems?
Many lesbians are disturbingly violent nowa-
days and might easily bite my fingers off if
I offer them a scone. This time, I think the
Pope has gone too far.

My Spiritual Aeneid took a lurch towards
the Church of England anyway, last week,
with Bishop Montefiore's splendid remarks
on Concorde. Now this saintly man, whose
conversion from the errors of Judaism must
surely rank beside Newcastle's buying Malcolm Macdonald from Luton Town, has been
bitterly attacked by Wislon's henchman in the
Department of Industry, Gruppenfuhrer G.B.
"Kurly" Kauptffman. Just like St Thomas
A Becket.

It only needs the Pope to appoint Derek
Worlock, the slimy "progressive" Bishop of
Portsmouth, to be Archbishop of Westminster[1],
and my conversion will be in the bag.
Then God help the homosexualists, as in my
mitre and surplice I lead the queer-bashing
gangs of Anglicans through all the lanes
and bosky spots of West Somerset, beating
kettle-drums and singing psalms.

Or perhaps I shall embrace the Jewish
religion, which will at least allow me to make
jokes about Jews without receiving 500
abusive letters and being formally banned
from the New York stage. These are difficult
times, and we must all learn to trim our sails
to the prevailing wind.

Friday 21st January

A friend told me recently that he thought
interest in Cyril Connolly, the controversial
book-reviewer, is due to decline. This is particularly sad for me as I am writing a book
about him.

Re-reading the new volume of Connolly's
Amorous Letters To Noel Blakiston (Constable, £5.50) last week I was particularly
struck by the passage in which Connolly
describes how he and his first wife place a
white mouse between two ferrets in a stove-
pipe and watch the ferrets as they "pulled it
practically in two".

At the time I wrote to the director of
Madame Tussauds' in Baker Street, drawing
attention to this passage and suggesting that
"The Connollys and their Pets" might make
a crowd-pulling tableau in the Chamber of
Horrors.

Today I receive his reply: the scene would
be too disgusting for contemporary British
tastes. Oh dear, what *is* happening to this
country of ours?

Saturday 22nd January

I fear I'm beginning to lose my admiration
for the Thoughts of Bernard Levin, although
I shall always love and hero-worship him as
a person. Why has he joined the chorus of
randy London bachelors saying we must not
snigger at sexual equality?

Because, like all of them, he's frightened
he won't get his greens if he doesn't toe the
line. Well, I hope he catches a dose. But perhaps you have to be a married man living in
the country to understand the cruel and unnatural thing which is being done to our
women.

What is there to do but laugh? Bernard
compares us with those who laughed at the
introduction of free teeth, spectacles and wigs
in 1948. Well, I still laugh whenever I see a
member of the working class with any of
these bizarre appendages, although I suspect
I'm about the only person left who does.
If I were to weep every time I saw one, they
would probably lock me up. But the Labour
government's action in 1948 was not nearly
as cruel as these new proposals to equip our
women with free beards and moustaches,
make them work as navvies and beat them
from a tender age.

I have never been certain about the beating of boys, which often strikes me as sadistic
and probably unnecessary, although I suspect
that boys may be born to be beaten, like deer
to be hunted. It is not generally known that
stags frequently go mad if nobody shows
any interest in hunting or stalking them.
But the beating of girls is a vile and despicable
activity, and anybody who supports it should
be treated with contempt.

Sunday 23rd January

My New Year's Resolution to read the *Observer* is severely tested once again when I come
to Lorna Sage's novel reviews. The grinding
silliness of this half-witted woman makes me
feel slightly ill for the rest of the morning.

Perhaps I shall go on week after week
pointing out Ms Sage's imbecilities until she
has a nervous breakdown. Or perhaps I can
manage to last out the twelve months by
shutting my eyes and trying to imagine she
has a beautiful face, like Ms Anne Pfartt,
the Demon Shaver.

Thursday 27th January

A very grand party in the Notting Hill home
of Anthony Howard, editor of the *New
Statesman*, to mark the departure of the
great and good Alan Watkins from his newspaper.

---

1. **Pope Paul avoided this error, appointing Abbot Hume of Ampleforth instead.**

The Prime Minister turns up to honour Alan, so do most of the Cabinet and many Ambassadors. Music is by the Grimethorpe Colliery Band, recently chosen to tour America as Britain's contribution towards the Bicentenary Year of American Independence.

But what a sad occasion this is. I can't see the *New Statesman* ever being quite the same again as its old readers die off one by one or switch their orders to *The Spectator*, where I believe Watkins has gone[1]. It is hardly surprising that when the band finally breaks into "Love's Old Sweet Song", we are all weeping into our tankards of Newcastle Brown. Howard is sobbing convulsively on Gerald Kaupfman's shoulder.

There *will* be another Dawn. Some day, some how we shall inspire the new generation of young people with those ideals, that vision of a better society which sustained us in our youth, and our parents and grandparents before us. One day, workers and intellectuals will march once again towards that certain future. Just for the moment, though, I have decided to leave the *New Statesman* and join *The Spectator*, too. I hope nobody notices.

Friday 28th January
In Cambridge to deliver the Tradescantian Lecture. My subject is the British Press with special emphasis on recent development in the "quality" Sundays, but I fear I rather shock my audience by addressing them in medieval or Church Latin, rather than the classical form they expect and claim to prefer.

I have always found this medieval or 'dog' Latin much the more beautiful language. I expect it is also closer to the spoken form in classical times — if they really constructed their speeches with the main verb at the end of the sentence nobody can have known what they were talking about half the time. This may explain why Cicero was such an unsuccessful politician.

But the moment is approaching when all serious discussion of the press must be held in some learned or dead tongue as a protection against writs.

Saturday 29th January
Still in Cambridge after a riotous evening in a certain Senior Combination Room which had better remain anonymous. I was told of a particularly cruel joke which had been played by the Fellows of King's College.

King's College, which has the finest buildings in Cambridge, has always been notorious for homosexuality. Recently, under pressure to improve its image, the Fellows have agreed to accept a quota of female undergraduates.

I murmured something about this being a sensible and wholesome idea, whereupon the whole Senior Combination Room collapsed. "Wait until you see the girls they have chosen," I was told.

So this morning I am taken on a tour of the King's College talent by an agreeable young don from Peterhouse, whose name I never catch. Slowly, the full implications of the Joke are borne in on me.

Clearly, the girls have been hand-picked. Some are just plain ugly, which one can forgive; others look as if they know they have a nasty smell, but that, again, is an awareness which sometimes visits young persons at a sensitive age. The real fright comes from those who think they are pretty, chosen for the ghastly boredom in their eyes, their grinding humourlessness, the hysteria and blubbering self-importance of their underdeveloped young minds. Oh dear, how those gay young Fellows must have laughed!

Sunday 30th January
Propinats exventis *Observer* in 'sciglione radram peknorno emfugisti taljommen. Eglit sillonica Lorna Sage! Stugschitska lendroi.

Monday 31st January
Mr Heath, of course, is not a homosexual or anything like one, but I think his spectacular failure in politics may be attributable to an unfair suspicion in the public mind that he could be one. Needless to say, this suspicion has no firmer foundation than envy of the healthy, celibate life. Nobody has ever claimed to have had a homosexual relationship with him.

No doubt Jeremy Thorpe is as innocent of this disturbing charge as he is of everything else, but I am afraid the time has come for him to retire from public life for the good of his party. It is part of the price we have to pay for living in a democracy that our noblest statesman can be destroyed by an irresponsible whispering campaign of this sort. Next week I shall be writing about the personal life of Mr Denis Healey[2]

Tuesday 8th February
Down to Stonor Park, near Henley, for the auction sale which marks the tragic break-up of this ancient Catholic home. Bidding fiercely against my co-religionists, I secure a job lot of two old Catholic hot-water bottles and an interesting Catholic chamberpot for £92.

---

1. In fact, Watkins had gone to the Observer, although Waugh never seemed to acknowledge this.
2. Waugh appears to have forgotten this promise.

Might it have been used by Cardinal Newman? An "expert" tells me it was made in the Staffordshire factory of Ramsbottom, Perkins, probably around 1935. This would put it too late, although it might easily have been used by Archbishop Matthew.

In any case, many so-called "experts" nowadays are blinded by atheistic dogma. I shall certainly build a shrine for it in the chapel in Combe Florey, probably in alabaster with delicate gold-leaf points, thus providing employment for a few artisans in these difficult times.

Wednesday 9th February

To Durham University, where I debate a motion about the Press with Mr Nigel Dempster, our greatest living journalist, and Mr John Stonehouse, the well-known businessman and politician.

Poor Stonehouse! I have never before sat so close to anyone who has summoned the Curse of Lord Gnome on his head and he is a pitiful sight to see. Readers will remember how the day after a writ arrived at Gnome House from this misguided man, it was announced that he had been drowned at sea, murdered by the Mafia, pickled in concrete and defected to Russia[1].

His most telling point during the debate is to assure the sweet, idealistic young students of Durham that he has no writs against any British newspaper. Poor man. To think that a promising young Postmaster General is now reduced at the age of 50 to reviewing books for Ian Hamilton's pathetic *New Review*. He has a long haul ahead of him, and we should all try to feel a little compassion.

Sunday 13th February

I would not normally think of going to a party at Larry Adler's sordid home on Primrose Hill, even to celebrate this appalling man's 68th birthday with its happy intimations of mortality. But on this occasion I am told he has just had a vasectomy, and Adler's vasectomy is surely something that all civilised men should celebrate.

So, heavily disguised, I go. The food and the company are as disgusting as one might have expected but at the party I hear a tale to make the blood run cold. It appears that before his whatsits were cut, Adler took a huge specimen where it has been frozen in a sperm bank against the day someone wishes to impregnate herself with it.

So the Hammer Film plot unfolds: somewhere in London are 75-150 million Larry Adlers in a state of suspended animation.

It only needs a freak sun-spot, a little nuclear fallout or a power cut and they will come crawling up the steps of some vault with horrible mouth-organ noises to take over the world. I shall not rest by night or day until I have located the source of this unimaginable threat and destroyed it.

Monday 14th February

I'm sorry to hear that *Encounter* is in trouble. It must be in very serious trouble if its editor applies to me for help.

Its literary pages are bad and its poetry has usually struck me as pure drivel, but there are nearly always two or three original and excellently-written articles in it — the current number, for instance, has an excellent profile of the Dutt-Paukers by Michael Wharton[2] and an interesting study of Christianity's anti-Semitic origins by Hyam Maccoby[3].

Needless to say, it goes against my deepest principles to suggest that any publication should receive government subsidy, and in any case I gather this is not available. The Arts Council's allocation for magazines is in the hands of the gritty Australian Charles Osborne, who has shared nearly all of it between his friend Ian Hamilton for the pathetic *New Review* and his other friend, a conceited old *poseur* and "poet" called Alan Ross[4] who used to employ Osborne on *London Magazine*.

Another beneficiary of Mr Osborne's largesse is a semi-pornographic poetry magazine called *Ambit* (the only worthwhile publication on his list is *Index on Censorship*, receiving a paltry £1,500 against £19,000 for *New Review* and £5,000 for Ross's boring, pseudish *London Magazine*). But I think a solution may be in sight.

There is a growing demand at the present time for pornography to be available on the National Health Service. *New Review*'s occasional incursions into the erotic so far have been too badly written to raise a tickle from the most over-ripe Convent girl, but I do remember wondering whether I should not bring them to the attention of my friend Mary Whitehouse as a curious item of public expenditure.

Now we must plainly agitate for Osborne's list of pets to be transferred to the Health and Social Security vote. This may not help the lower classes with their masturbation problems, but that is not the point. It will leave the Arts Council money free for *Encounter*.

Meanwhile, the magazine is available for an annual subscription of £5.50 from 59 St Martin's Lane, WC2.

---

1. He turned up in Australia and was arrested on 17 charges alleging fraudulent conversion etc. At this time he was on bail awaiting trial.
2. Michael Wharton. Author of the Daily Telegraph's Peter Simple. The Dutt-Paukers are his invention.
3. A Jewish theologian.
4. I think this should read 'conceited, middle-aged poseur and "poet" '. Ross, born in 1922, married Waugh's cousin, Jennifer Fry.

Tuesday 15th February

Pausing to collect my fee for the above advertisement from an American gentleman in Grosvenor Square, I am alarmed to be asked if I would like to go to Angola with the acting rank of Lieutenant Colonel to fight the socialists there. With many weak jokes about the pen being mightier than the sword, I make my excuses and leave.

Wislon's efforts to secure a Russian victory in Angola would indeed be shocking if they were not so foolish. Nobody can seriously suppose that after seven years of Wislon and four of Grocer the English have any fight left in them. If Wislon really wants to help the Russian effort, he should arrange for as many English mercenaries as possible to join the FNLA, complete with National Health spectacles, false teeth and Levin-style utility wigs.

Wednesday 16th February

Rees-Mogg deserves little sympathy after his disgraceful and odious behaviour in suing Lord Gnome for alleged libel last year, but I feel we should all rally round now he's being sued by the Downing Street Press Officers.

It has long been accepted that the underpaid, over-lubricated hacks of Fleet Street will always sue if they see their ridiculous names in print — many of them have been known to issue writs against themselves late at night — but this is a grave new development. If all Fleet Street's hangers-on are going to climb on this gravy-boat — Press Officers, PR advisers, curious little men with red noses who offer to buy one drinks on behalf of the Cheese Council — then there will soon be nothing left for proper journalists who may be in serious need, like Mogg and others I can think of.

I have no idea what Philip Howard, the *Times* journalist concerned, said about the Downing Street press office, but I know Howard to be a journalist of honour, integrity and the highest possible standards of accuracy. I forbear to comment on the reputation of the Downing Street Press Office at this stage, but will happily testify in court if called upon to do so.

During my Wednesday tea at Buckingham Palace, I tell the Queen what I propose to do and she approves. She says she plans to visit Fleet Street next Thursday. I try to talk her out of it, telling her she will see sights such as no human eye should ever see, but she seems quite excited by it. I feel I can't tell her the real reason, which is the effect these visits of hers have on my colleagues.

Thursday 17th February

It is quite untrue, as widely reported in the gutter press, that my visit to Cambridge last week had anything to do with the University's difficulties in finding a new Chancellor.

In fact, as I revealed at the time, I was engaged in a survey of sexual behaviour at King's College. Unfortunately, the results were too nasty to publish.

Friday 18th February

A fleeting, one night visit to Paris on business. I find all the young women here are pining for love of Carlos the Jackal, the plump, pasty-faced gunman. They have photographs of him all over their bedrooms, which is most discouraging.

I may not have shot anyone yet, but I always travel around with a little list of people who might be suitable for assassination one day. I show this to a young French lady of my acquaintance and she laughs in my face when she sees the first name on the list, Mgr Derek Worlock, newly-appointed Roman Catholic Archbishop of Liverpool.

But when I show her a photograph of the man's slimy face, she grows more thoughtful.

Monday 21st February

In the horrible new spirit of the times, I have been asked to write down my monthly budget. I suppose the idea is to encourage people, but I'm afraid it will only make them miserable.

Monthly income

From Lord Gnome	£4.00
Literary prizes & currency transactions	£42.00
From rents	£52.60
Royalties	£10.00
Book reviews	£860.00
From an MP	£32.00
Other blackmail	£650.00
Bribes	£400.00
Fallen from back of lorry	£83.00
Sale of agricultural produce	£422.00
Army pension	£117.00

Monthly expenditure

Food for family of six	£7.60
Drink & Drugs	£332.50
Blackmail payments	£115.00
Bribes	£68.00
Servants' wages	£760.00
do. food	£420.00

Charity & political subs	£1100.00
Gambling	£115.00
Income tax	£12.20

As you can see, this leaves exactly 63p a week to buy clothes, budgerigar seeds, race-horses, false teeth, haberdashery, glass-ware and toiletry articles. You don't know whether to laugh or cry.

Tuesday 22nd February
I suppose young Roddy Llewellyn knows what he is doing gallivanting around the tropical island of Mustique with a foreign lady old enough to be his mother[1].Those of us who watched his grand old father "Colonel" Harry Llewellyn canter to victory in the 1952 show-jumping Olympics at Helsinki on Foxhunter can't help taking a fatherly interest in the lad.

That was the year before the Townsend sensation when Roddy was a toddler of 3½ and the whole nation thrilled to the narrow escape of a daring RAF pilot called Pete Townsend from the clutches of a very similar sort of female[2].

I am sure that Marje Proops would agree with me when I suggest that prolonged association between people of very different age groups seldom comes to much good. But if Roddy is too shy to write to either of us for advice he should go for a quiet word with Group Captain Peter Townsend in the French village near Rambouillet where he has retired and where he is famous for his scarred and hunted look.

Wednesday 23rd February
A curious description of Cyril Connolly's death bed scene appeared in the *TLS* last month:

"From far and wide there arrived in London women of very varied ages, character and appearance who had been loved by and who still loved this difficult and demanding but unique *homme a femmes*. . . perhaps each of his visitors in her way hoped that hers would be the 'fond breast' on which 'the parting soul relies. . . ' "

It appears as part of an embarrassing 'tribute' by Alastair Forbes, the fashionable literary punk and hanger-on. I find his reference to the great man's sex life rather taste-less, but I suppose the moment ought to be captured and preserved by some more competent hand.

Thursday 24th February
The Tate Gallery Bricks horror sensation[3] confirms what I have always suspected, that our irreligious age has decided to use the Arts as a general receptacle and arena for the traditional sport of laughing at village idiots, boobies and simpletons who would normally find a refuge in the Church.

For a glorious moment I thought that Carl Andre might turn out to be a cynic, like the preposterous Sir Norman Reid[4] But no, he is just another of the poor half-wits and social inadequates who are drawn to Pseuds' Corner like dossers to a Salvation Army hostel for warmth, company and free lodging.

1. Llewellyn's name had been linked with that of Princess Margaret.
2. Townsend's name had been similarly linked.
3. The Tate Gallery had bought a pile of bricks from America for £14,000.
4. Reid. Director of the Tate. b. 1915, noted for cautious pseudery.

Friday 3rd March

All day in a Committee Room at the House of Lords listening to the sad case of the Ampthill baby.

If I were Mr Geoffrey Russell I think I would prefer to be thought an honest bastard than the product of some obscure act which falls short of complete intercourse. It adds nothing to the dignity of the peerage to stand up in court and claim to be the winner in a cross-country challenge of 75 million spermatazoa all racing up a woman's legs to see which one ends up a Baron.

Half the Lords are probably bastards anyway. I can think of one, apparently born of white parents, who is inexplicably coal-black. Their Lordships pretend not to notice this discrepancy, and I have certainly never heard anyone asking for a blood-test.

Saturday 4th March

Pope Paul's appointment of Dom Basil Hume, abbot of Ampleforth may yet prove the redeeming act of his ghastly pontificate, just as Grocer Heath's one golden deed in appointing Sir John Betjeman as Poet Laureate should be counted against the otherwise unrelieved squalor of that shameful episode in British history.

Abbot Hume is said to be especially interested in the Church of England through his close friendship with Dr Donald Coggan, the man currently posing as Archbishop of Canterbury in the schismatic hierarchy.

I hope they both join my campaign to have Titus Oates beatified and canonized in time for 1978, when we celebrate the tercentenary of the Popish Plot. This would be a particularly good moment for the abbot to admit that there *was* a Popish Plot and for the Anglican impostor to declare how sorry he is that it failed.

Then St Titus should be made patron saint of all journalists. He is gravely needed at the present time when "responsible" journalists confine themselves to reporting the lies they are fed by other people and never presume — whether from cowardice or lack of imagination — to invent any for themselves.

Sunday 5th March

An abbot who has not been so lucky is poor Dom Wilfrid Passmore, one-time abbot of Downside, whose death at 68 is announced today.

Dom Wilfrid was headmaster of Downside during my time there. I am sorry to say he did not like me very much, nor I him. He beat me savagely throughout three years, sometimes twice a week, and although none of my elaborate schemes to kill him ever came to anything, I took my revenge in various subtle ways.

Looking back, I suspect there may have been a certain magnanimity in the man which I failed to spot at the time and certainly lacked myself.

At his worst, he showed an exuberance and sense of style which is sadly rare among the new breed of clerics. He used to file his teeth, which was an unendearing habit, but I believe he was shabbily treated in his old age. R.I.P.

Monday 8th March

On a visit to Sutton Place, in Surrey, I am taken by my host to one of the cruellest entertainments ever offered by a local authority in this country. The librarians there, not content with destroying the livelihood of writers, now offer the spectacle of a penniless author for ratepayers to laugh at as they take out their books free of charge.

David Benedictus, the 37-year-old Old Etonian, whose first novel about Eton, *The Fourth of June*, was thought quite promising by some people when it appeared in 1962, now receives £600 a year from the Council to sit in the library at Sutton and "encourage" would-be authors in the borough.

Needless to say, this dreadful spectacle has not been universally popular. Complaints about his ragged clothes — a jersey with holes and odd socks — have been taken up by the Chairman of Sutton Council's Environmental Committee, Mrs Marjorie Grimes: "The library is a beautiful new building and Mr Benedictus just lowers the tone of the place," she says.

I think Sutton librarians should be ashamed of themselves. Still, I must admit, I did laugh.

Tuesday 9th March

It was with a heavy heart that I resigned from the Labour Party in November 1974 after a lifetime's service to the Labour Movement.

Needless to say, I was accused of rocking the boat and threatening Labour's chances of survival, but at least I had the sense to bribe the hacks of Fleet Street not to publish photographs of me taken on that emotional evening when my head accidentally got stuck in an ice bucket at Quaglino's[1]

Lord George-Brown is the first politician of either party to wake up to the frightful mess our country is in and the appalling catalogue of errors that has led to this. It might be worthwhile keeping an eye on the gutters of London to see if any other politicians wake up, too, but for the present I'm sending him a copy of the Bernard Dru Manifesto.

---

1. Photographs of Lord George-Brown in an emotional state, lying in a Westminster gutter, had caused a stir in that morning's newspapers.

BRITAIN WAKES UP!

There may be other people than my cousin Bernard Dru capable of leading Britain away from its abyss, but for the life of me I can't think of them now.

Thursday 11th March
Today is Wislon's 60th birthday, so I release a barrel of mild ale to my estate workers, kill 40 rabbits and allow them to sing "Happy Birthday, dear Wislon" in muted, respectful tones.

The old crook hasn't done too badly. Against the destruction of the country's economic prosperity — always over-rated in my opinion — one must count the fact that he has got Britain into the Common Market, something the ludicrous Grocer could never have achieved.

Against the destruction of the State Education system — always of dubious benefit — we must count his knighthood for P.G. Wodehouse, one of the few acts of imaginative kindness which any British government has ever shown to a writer.

I still think Wislon is probably a Soviet agent but I am sure he is an unwilling one, and in any case I've decided not to expose him for the present.

Friday 19th March
Father Corbishley's death at 72 should not be seen as a cause for grief or despair, but as an occasion for thanksgiving and celebration. Beneath his disconcertingly repulsive appearance and awkward manner, Tom always had a genuine desire to please.

Although his opinions were liberal and judiciously progressive, his preaching manner was not such as inspired any exaggerated demonstrations of enthusiasm. The Jesuits used him in a Machiavellian scheme to drive the few remaining worshippers out of Protestant churches, sending him to preach in St Paul's, at Westminster Abbey and in countless humbler Anglican shrines throughout the country.

It is early to say how successful this daring bid for Christian unity will prove, but if ever a Soldier of Christ deserves canonisation in the new spirit of the times, Corbishley is surely the man. Thinking about him in the train this morning, I find that a nasty cold in the head has inexplicably cleared. There can be no medical explanation for this. I offer it as the first miracle through Corbishley's intercession.

Saturday 20th March
Walking to an appointment with my *masseuse* in Soho this afternoon, I see a group of "workmen" on a building site and decide to throw some orange peel at them which I always keep in my overcoat pocket for this purpose.

Today is a memorable day, because for the first time since I adopted this tactic in the class war I actually hit one of them. He chases me into a strip club where I stay for the rest of the afternoon, feeling excited but rather nervous.

Anybody who wishes to take up this amusing idea should be careful not to throw orange peel at black workers. Other blacks tend to take their side, and so do many Englishmen of the middle class who might happen to be passing.

Wednesday 24th March

All day I am approached by a stream of employees, tenants, and old age pensioners from the village asking me who they should vote for in the Prime Ministerial elections tomorrow. I do not have the heart to tell them that they have no vote, and that the issue will be decided by a handful of drunks, crooks and emotional cripples in Westminster.

Instead I warn them that Michael Foot is a vain, silly, weak old fraud who would be intensely irritating as Prime Minister; that Crosland is too conceited and in any case probably doesn't exist; that Healey has no control over his wind; that Smoothiechops[1] is unfortunately a man of working class origins etc. etc. I think it makes them happy.

Thursday 25th March

I find myself thrown into gloom and despair by an announcement from Buckingham Palace:

H.R.H. The Princess Margaret, Countess of Snowdon, and the Earl of Snowdon have mutually agreed to live apart.

Wrong or redundant uses of 'mutual' are a well-known trap, as Fowler points out. In this case, the use is not so much incorrect as otiose. Every agreement between two people is mutual — is it not? — or there would be no agreement. Fowler characterises this as "Betraying lack of the taste or care that should prevent one from saying twice over what it suffices to say once. . . it adds nothing whatever & is the merest tautology."

Worse than this, it is an example of New Proletarian Fine Writing, the English of Peter Lennon and Dave Spart. The English Royal Family, taking its cue from our politicians, has always shunned the world of letters, but at least until now it has had the good manners to make sure its English was respectable. If it can't do better than this, we should send them all straight back to Germany.

At the time of Princess Margaret's wedding I was an undergraduate, and remember many scenes of dignified grief in the Christ Church Junior Common Room as she walked up the aisle with her Welsh dwarf of "artistic" leanings. But we may have felt that after her somewhat chequered past she was lucky to catch anyone, and certainly there was nothing like the shock of humiliation we all suffered when Princess Anne announced that she was going to marry her grinning, speechless stable-lad called Ned Gibbs.

I only hope that by the time the Gibbses break up, Buckingham Palace will have learnt how to construct a decent English sentence once again.

Friday 26th March

In today's post I receive a bundle of letters in photostat, without any indication of their source. Some are affectionate, some merely businesslike, some slightly distasteful. All start: "Dear Bunny", and end, "Love J".

Whoever wrote them presumably owns the copyright, and I would be grateful if he or she could get in touch with me.

Saturday 27th March

In the waiting-room of a massage establishment in Soho I find a copy of *The Sikh Quarterly* for December 1974. There is an excellent editorial on the motorbike helmet question, urging Sikhs who object to the wearing of metal helmets on grounds of religion and morality to join forces with

1. Roy Jenkins, Labour politician, b. 1920. Noted for various speech deformities and taste in claret.

native Englishmen who object to seat-belts:

"The Sikh community is small, and the number of Sikhs who ride motorcycles in this country is even smaller: but the number of people who. . . genuinely experience physical discomfort in wearing a belt, perhaps after an injury or operation, or because they do not have the average shape, size or dimensions catered for by belt manufacturers is very much larger. . . Now is the time for us all to act to preserve personal liberty — a truly precious commodity".

Alas, the British are far too wet and frightened to worry about their precious commodities any more, and we must leave it to our Sikh fellow citizens. Few of them are of average shape, size or dimensions, and I fear they will feel the new indignities keenly.

Sunday 28th March
Jeremy Thorpe's Amazing Denials[1] in today's newspaper are so elaborate and so convincing that for a horrible, empty moment I begin to have doubts. Then the newspaper's sanctimonious half-witted argument — that unless an incident can be proved to have happened, it never happened — restores me to my senses.

It would be a bitter blow if the whole thing proved to be a tissue of lies, but I still think there is room for creative conjecture. After all, I believe Jo Grimond to be an honourable and truthful man. He is someone I have always held in the greatest affection and trust, and nothing is going to convince me to the contrary.

Monday 30th March
Saturday, June 26th marks the centenary of General George Custer's Last Stand against the Indians at Little Big Horn. To celebrate this important anniversary, I am planning a charabanc tour of British Leyland and Chrysler factories in the Midlands, where we will throw orange peel and jeer at "workers"

Dress will be Bernard Dru T-shirts — "Bernard Dru Rules", "Bernard Dru is God" etc. — and gym shoes, also known as *dups.* Coaches leave Trafalgar Square at 7.30 a.m., returning 10 p.m. All-in fare of £19.50 includes cup of tea and free use of toilets on the M1.

Tuesday 31st March
I suppose the resignation of Wislon marks the end of some era or other, but at present we are all worried about the Resignation Honours.

Will Sir George Weidenfeld, the handsome publisher, receive the life peerage he so richly deserves? He has just paid me a large sum of money as advance for my book on Connolly, and plainly needs encouragement, so I am keeping my fingers crossed.

Wednesday 1st April
A year is a long time in journalism and Rees-Mogg is slowly returning to my gallery of heroes after his disgraceful behaviour in suing Lord Gnome for alleged libel last year. Of course he is right to have nothing to do with negotiations for a Press Charter, and his fine principled stand shows his brother editors up for the unprincipled toadies they are.

There is no demand for a Press Charter except from the politicians, and their only motive is to limit existing Press freedoms. After 15 years membership of the National Union of Journalists, I think it is time I began to take an active interest. My first aim will be to "black" all political memoirs, on the grounds that they are not only untruthful and boring but also badly written and bring newspapers into disrepute.

Next I think we might open consultations with other Unions to devise a Government Charter, setting out the terms and conditions under which government may be allowed to continue in this country, if at all.

---

1. Thorpe denied a homosexual relationship with Mr Norman Scott, an out-of-work model.